The Complete Handbook of

Model
Business
Letters

JACK GRIFFIN

Prentice Hall, Paramus, New Jersey 07652

Library of Congress Cataloging-in-Publication Data

Griffin, Jack.
   The complete handbook of model business letters / by Jack Griffin.
     p. cm.
   Includes index.
   ISBN 0-13-769126-2 (C)—ISBN 0-13-769118-1 (P)
    1. Commercial correspondence—Handbooks, manuals, etc. I. Title.
   HF5726.G68   1993   93-25319
   808′.066651—dc20   CIP

Printed in the United States of America

10 9 8 7 6 5 4 3 2   (C)   10 9   (P)

ISBN 0-13-769126-2 (C) ISBN 0-13-769118-1 (P)

PRENTICE HALL
Paramus, NJ 07652

On the World Wide Web at http://www.phdirect.com

Foreword

What's New About *The Complete Handbook of Model Business Letters*?

Someday I'm going to write a book called *The World's Dumbest Predictions*. I'll put into it such gems as the memo that launched production of the Edsel, the marketing report that assured recording company executives that the 8-track was the wave of the future, and the advice of the portfolio manager who told his client to avoid investing in xerographic technology because nothing could ever replace plain old carbon paper. I'd also find the first magazine article of two decades or so ago that told us how the advent of the "electronic office" would forever bring to an end the tyranny of paper documents.

Well, the electronic office is here. Today, even the humblest office has one or more personal computers or word processors, a copier or two, fax machine, and answering machine. Larger offices have voice mail and are electronically networked through e-mail systems.

The result?

Somehow, American business now uses even *more* paper than ever before: 775 billion pages of it per year, enough to make a stack 48,900 miles high.

We copy, and therefore preserve, more documents than ever. The fax machine and overnight couriers have made letters as quick and efficient a means of communication as the telephone. (*Quicker* and *more* efficient: Who hasn't played telephone tag with an answering machine or a labyrinthine voice mail system?) It is true that e-mail—posting personal computer messages on inter- or intra-office "electronic bulletin boards"— requires no paper, but the messages are memos and letters just the same.

The fact is, as we prepare to enter the twenty-first century, the business letter has never been more important. And it has never been more demanding. Because they can deliver the message so quickly, fax, e-mail, and overnight couriers have accustomed the business world to virtually instantaneous communication. Your customers and clients have come to expect an immediate response, and so you must write more letters more rapidly. Electronic media and office copiers make it easy to preserve these letters, so they not only have to be *fast*, they have to be *good*—accurate, clear, effective.

There is more to the new business letter than technology. Until recently, business communication stressed persuasion and authority. A sales letter, for example, had simply to persuade. A collection letter simply demanded payment. But today's business letter employs the more challenging—but far more effective—techniques of negotiation. Its goal is to define and achieve the often elusive "win-win" situation.

Why This Book Is For You

You need letters and memos, lots of them. But you can't rely on the cut-and-dried old standbys—the polite persuaders or the righteous vehicles of demand. You need documents that give your reader the "right feelings," that use real language, directly and clearly, to negotiate results that will achieve your purpose while addressing the needs of your correspondent.

And you need these letters and memos fast. The fax machine is humming, the computer screen glowing, the overnight courier waiting. You don't have time to re-invent the wheel, to start from scratch—especially with the letters everyone finds difficult: asking for a favor, declining a request, terminating an employee, collecting on a delinquent account, apologizing for a mistake, seeking an extension of a deadline, asking for a raise, refusing a request for a raise (without alienating a good employee), expressing sympathy to a business friend who has lost a loved one.

Nor, pressed for time, are you inclined to plow through a treatise on the art of letter writing. *The Complete Handbook of Model Business Letters* does not ask you to do this, although the Introduction "The Electronic Office: Why Letters are More Important than Ever Before," does provide a letter writer's primer and some pointers about letter writing in the electronic age. Instead, *The Complete Handbook of Model Business Letters* provides 735 model letters, ready to use or ready to be customized to your most pressing needs. To the greatest degree possible, the letters are generic (*you* fill in the specifics) yet detailed enough to address the many complex and varied situations of today's business world. They are organized into logical, easily accessible categories that reflect the way most of us conduct business. The letters and memos are clearly labeled and thoroughly indexed so that you never have to waste time hunting for the document you need.

How to Use This Book

Like the ancient Gaul of Julius Caesar, all business is divided into three parts: making sales or obtaining clients and customers; doing business with them; communicating within the company. Accordingly, *The Complete Handbook of Model Business Letters* is divided into

- ✉ Part One: Getting Business
- ✉ Part Two: Doing Business
- ✉ Part Three: Inside Business

The Parts . . . to Guide You Through This Book

In Part One, you will find chapters on "Turning Up Prospects with 'Cold' Letters that Heat Things Up" and "Turning Prospects into Customers with Follow-Ups that Don't Let Go." In the first chapter are model "cold" letters incorporating both the "hard" and "soft" sell approaches. In chapter 2, you will find model letters that are intended to revive inactive customers.

Chapter 3, the first chapter of Part Two, is devoted to communicating with clients and customers, providing information and requesting information and favors, as well as declining to perform requested favors. Chapter

4 presents model correspondence dealing with customer credit and collections and chapter 5 offers productive adjustment letters. Chapter 6 is devoted to letters that will earn and maintain the goodwill of clients and customers.

Next in Part Two are a pair of chapters (7 and 8) treating correspondence with suppliers and vendors, which includes letters designed to secure information and bids clearly, that place orders effectively, that obtain special favors, that secure credit, that make firm, reasonable, and non-alienating complaints, that reject terms, products, or proposals, and that refuse or dispute payment. Also offered are vendor-related apologies and thanks, as well as letters recommending a firm's services or products.

Chapters 9 and 10 contain model letters dealing with "Business Community and Public Community" and "Government and Regulators." These include goodwill letters, responses to complaints, fund-raising letters, "common cause" (or community action) letters, and firm but non-alienating letters declining charitable requests. Letters to government and regulators include cover notes to accompany applications for business licenses, permits, occupational licenses, and sales tax and seller permits as well as model cover letters to accompany applications for U.S. Small Business Administration Loans and for loans from local development agencies.

Part Three—"Inside Business"—is itself divided into three major chapters covering letters and memos "To Employees," "To Colleagues," and "To Supervisors." Employee-related communications cover hiring, evaluation, thanks, apology, recommendation, reprimand, termination, refusing requests—for salary increase, promotion, and others—accepting resignations, and responding to complaints. "The Effective Memo" presents models of communication among colleagues, including news, company policy, and advice and suggestions. Letters and memos addressed to supervisors include employment applications, requests for salary increase, promotion, changes in working conditions, location, or hours, effective complaints and suggestions, graceful and productive letters of resignation, and responses to criticism and reprimands.

Step by Step . . . to What's Best for You

While the emphasis of this book is on the model letters themselves, each major chapter is introduced by a simple, straightforward discussion and outline of the letter structure that is best suited to the category under discussion. For example, the ideal letter rejecting a product or service would:

1. Thank the reader for his/her interest and/or find some common ground for agreement.
2. Enumerate the reasons for rejection or refusal.
3. Clearly state the rejection or refusal.
4. Thank the reader again, offer an honest, helpful alternative (if possible), and (if appropriate) close with best wishes for success.

Here is a letter of rejection written according to this outline:

Dear Mr. Casaubon:

Thank you for giving us the opportunity to consider your manuscript, *Late Etruscan Funeral Customs*, for publication in our illustrated book series. Unfortunately, your work is too specialized for our series, which is intended for a general-interest reading audience. Your book would be better served by a university press, which publishes for the kind of reader who would find your work valuable. I suggest that you review your bibliography of books on Etruscan subjects, make a list of the publishers of those volumes, and offer your manuscript to one of them.

Again, thanks for your interest in Popular Publishers, Inc. I wish you success in placing your work.

Sincerely yours,

By consulting the outlines that begin each major chapter, you can readily "customize" the model letters to suit your particular situation.

Jump Starts . . . to Get You on Your Way

Very often, you do not need an entire ready-to-use model to inspire your own correspondence. For this reason, each major section within a chapter (for example, "Soft Sell Letters" and "Hard Sell Letters" in Chapter 1: Turning Up Prospects with "Cold" Letters that Heat Things Up) includes a selection of opening sentences guaranteed to "jump start" your letters. For instance, condolence letters are always difficult to write and especially hard to begin. The section devoted to such letters includes the following openings:

All of us here at **Name of company** are saddened by the death of your **job title, Name**.

No one is ever ready for death.

Name and I wish to express our heartfelt sympathy to you and your family.

Your **son, daughter, husband, etc.** was impossible not to like.

Words at a time like this offer too little comfort.

I learned only today of your **mother's, father's, wife's, etc.** death.

No one can replace the loss you have suffered, and only one who has experienced such a loss can fully understand what you are going through.

Time, far more than anything I can say now, will console you for the loss of your **husband, wife, mother, etc.**

I have just heard the sad news.

I wish I knew the magic words that could comfort you at a time like this.

Index

The index of this book is designed to make it as easy as possible for you to find the letters you need. Letters are indexed by major category, by subcategory, and by specific topic. For example, you will find letters apologizing to customers for a defective product under *Customer relations, product adjustment letters; Apologies, defective product;* and under *Defective product.*

A Word About Gender

Before I leave this foreword, I offer this word about the personal pronoun. It is no longer acceptable in the world of business to rely on *he* and *him* as a generic pronoun applicable to men as well as women. However, combinations such as *he/she*, *his or hers*, and the like grate on the ear. Therefore, I have used the masculine and feminine pronouns arbitrarily and at random throughout this book. In one sentence I will suggest that you "write him an effective letter," only in the next to advise you to be "sensitive to her feelings about the situation."

Introduction

The Electronic Office: Why Letters Are More Important than Ever Before

The letter has come under attack in the electronic age. Letters—print on paper—some have declared, are anachronisms doomed to extinction in an era of the electronic generation, storage, and retrieval of information.

But look around you—at your office. You probably have some computers, maybe even a whole network. You probably have a fax machine, maybe more than one. You certainly have a telephone—probably several. More than likely, you have an answering machine—perhaps even electronic voice mail. What you also have, in this electronic office of yours, are heaps and heaps of papers. You probably have a computer printer—maybe even a fancy laser job—to produce some of these papers. You probably have a photocopier to duplicate the paper you produce. (Carbon paper was such a mess that you hated to make copies. In fact, you only copied documents that you absolutely had to copy. Copiers are so easy to use that now you copy everything—sometimes two or three times.) In the past, you wrote only the letters you absolutely needed to write. You had to type them out, put them in an envelope, then take the mail down to the post office or, if your business were big enough, to the mail room. Now, the fax machine invites you to send a note as casually as you would make a phone call. Or you might just call one of the expedited courier services, who'll send somebody to your office to pick up whatever you write and deliver it the very next day.

Far from displacing paper, the electronic age has produced an avalanche of it.

This is a fact, although the electronic purist might argue that the paper is really unnecessary. The truly modern office, he'll tell you, consists of networked computers, both within the four walls of the office and reaching out to remote locations. Want to send a letter? Just use electronic mail—e-mail.

Relatively few businesses use e-mail on a large scale, and even those that do still have to communicate with the outside—that is, the paper-driven—world. But, I'll concede that it is possible to write letters without using paper.

So what?

Electronic mail is still *mail.* It still involves the writing of letters—but in the absence of paper. And as e-mail becomes more and more common, the number of business letters people will write, already astronomical, will increase even more.

Traditional Values—The Importance of Well-Written Letters in the Electronic Age

Why does the letter persist—indeed, flourish—in the world of business?

No matter how modern the product, business is by nature conservative. It is based on concepts of value and the exchange of one valuable item for another. Electronic blips, rows of binary digits, the canned sound of the answering machine and voice mail all serve a purpose. So does a paper cup. But you would not offer a valued friend a draft of fine wine from that paper cup. A more precious vessel, a vessel of greater value, is called for when serving a valuable beverage to a valued friend. So in business, when value is being discussed, negotiated, or presented, a more precious vessel than blips, digits, or synthetic speech is called for. In our culture, at least since the days of the pharaohs, that vessel of heightened value has been the letter.

Letters, then, are culturally powerful tools. In business, a powerful tool can generate income, gain customers, produce goodwill, provide gainful employment. As with any tool, the quality of the result depends on the skill with which the tool is used. Misused, a tool can cause injury. Business correspondence, clumsily handled, can cost you money, can retard your advancement, can wreck your career and deep-six the entire enterprise.

The good news is that the opportunities vastly outweigh the liabilities. Contemporary business practices demand more letters than ever—more opportunities for effective, profit-making communication. The bad news is that the technology of modern business tends to pressure us to produce more letters faster. This directly conflicts with the single most important "rule" of business letter writing I want to present here:

Rule #1: Take your time. Wait 24 hours before sending the letter you have just written.

Your only decent shot at objectivity in looking at a letter you have just produced is to get away from it overnight. That's very important, but, quite often, it is impossible. That's where these ready-made model letters can be a tremendous help.

The Other "Rules": A Guide to Business Letter Basics

Aside from the 24-hour rule mentioned above, there are no hard-and-fast, absolute rules for writing good business letters. As I have just observed, the 24-hour rule, important as it is, is often impossible to observe. Nevertheless, there are several guidelines that apply to all business correspondence and that can help ensure effective business communication. For the sake of simplicity, let's call these guidelines "rules."

Rule #2: A business letter is the attempt of one human being to communicate with another.

I have said that business is by nature conservative. The word *conservative* is not to be confused with *stuffy, stilted, starched, dead, embalmed, pompous, robotic,* or any other term that suggests the absence of life. Remember that you are a person—representing a company, yes, but not trying to impersonate that company—writing to another person. Use language that comes naturally to you. Rather than attempt to define here what I mean by that, I invite the reader to skim through the letters in this book. All of them have been written in natural language. Before skipping to these letters, however, please read the next rule.

Rule #3: Know your audience (i.e., your reader).

Yes, be a human being. Even more, be yourself. Don't try to be the Voice of Business. However, give thought to the person who will read what you write. This is actually something we do, more or less unconsciously, every day. We don't speak to our sons or daughters the same way we speak to our supervisors or employees or colleagues or clients. We communicate differently with close friends than we do with mere acquaintances, and we do not address strangers as we do even casual acquaintances. Moreover, if we know that Fred Smith has a special interest in, say, baseball, we might direct the conversation to that subject. Now let's say that we want to sell Fred Smith on an idea. We could tell him that "This is a really good idea," or we could say something like, "You'll hit a homerun with this one." Think about your audience.

Rule #4: Find the right words and use them.

Take the time to think about precisely what you need to communicate. Let's say you want to convey to an associate how you feel about a proposed business deal. You could say: "It makes me feel funny," or "I have some bad feelings about this," or "I don't feel quite right about this thing." The language, to be sure, is English. The words are correctly spelled, and the grammar and syntax are fine. But the communication is not effective. "This deal makes me nervous because Apex Corporation does not have a good track record with most of its joint ventures." Notice that finding the right words does not primarily mean groping for some complex or colorful or exotic adjective. Pay greatest attention to nouns and verbs. Show rather than tell. Use the words that are closest to the objects—the things and the ideas—you need to describe. Connect your letters to the real world by means of object words rather than abstractions. "The wall is white" is not as effective as "The wall is slightly off-white," which is less effective than "The wall is eggshell white."

Rule #5: Be thrifty.

Communicate economically, using the fewest words necessary. However, you need to think carefully about how to define *necessary*. Usually, an effective business letter communicates more than some simple fact or instruction. It can communicate an attitude, feelings, respect, contempt, good humor, confidence, competence, stupidity—in short, everything people convey to one another each and every time they communicate. So while you may simply need to tell a vendor when and where to deliver something—a letter absolutely requiring but a single sentence—your letter will be more effective if you also manage to convey, for example, your pride in your company and your expectation that the vendor will provide service of the highest quality. Be economical, but not stingy in your communication. Don't be afraid to let your personality show through. Having said this, you should note that many business people consider it most desirable to hold a business letter to a single page in length.

Rule #6: Keep it positive.

Well, that's easy if you are thanking somebody for something, praising a colleague, or conveying the good news of a great sales quarter. What if you are complaining that you never received an important order? You could say, "Can't you people do anything right?" And you will be certain to alienate your reader and lower her self-esteem, thereby sharply reducing any motive she may have had for performing well. Alternatively, you might say, "You are always so efficient. What happened this time?" There is still no doubt that you are complaining about a problem, but it is clear that you are addressing the *problem* as the problem, not the *reader* as the problem. If anything, you have bolstered the reader's self-esteem, perhaps sufficiently enough that she will attempt to live up to your opinion of her by actually shipping your order.

Rule #7: Think about the structure of your letter.

Throughout this book, you will find guides to structuring your letters. As a general rule, you might simply attempt always to include in each letter you write the famous Five Ws every journalism student engraves upon his cerebral cortex: Tell WHO, WHAT, WHERE, WHEN, and WHY. Structure is especially important in the Age of Silicon. Your reader knows that word processing technology makes it possible for you to move your thoughts around the page easily. It is expected that you will take the time and effort to organize your thoughts. Give your letter a beginning, middle, and end. Except for special effect, as in direct-mail appeals, adding a postscript ("P.S."), especially in this era of the word processor, is unacceptable in business correspondence.

Rule #8: Be literate.

Misspelling and bad grammar were never acceptable in business correspondence. Today, when many of us work with word processing programs that incorporate "spell checkers" and perhaps even grammar checkers (many of which, be warned, are of dubious value), such errors are even less tolerable.

In addition to these general rules of composition, most effective business correspondence follows certain conventions governing appearance and how to address your reader.

Business letters should be single spaced, with double spaces separating the paragraphs. Most of the letters in this book are in so-called block style, with everything—date, inside address, salutation, body, complimentary close, and signature—aligned "flush left," that is, aligned against the left margin. It is also quite acceptable to use a modified block form, in which the date, complimentary close, and signature are aligned with a center margin, while the inside address and body text are flush left. Indented style resembles the modified block form, except that each paragraph in the body text is indented.

If at all possible, address your letter to a person, not a company. Before you give up and write to a job title ("Dear Manager") or "To whom it may concern," try telephoning ahead to determine to whom you should address the letter. One sure way to alienate your reader is to address her as "Dear Sir" or "Gentlemen."

Visually, there is a distinct advantage to making your first paragraph a short one. It invites your reader to come into the letter rather than challenging him to plow through a mass of verbiage.

If your letter includes lists, set off the items in the lists with bullets (especially effective on a word-processed document), or dashes, or numbers.

You need to exercise judgment in deciding whether to call your reader by her first name. If you address the reader by the last name, always use the appropriate title, if you know it (for example, Dr., Fr., Reverend, Professor, etc.). In the case of a female correspondent, unless you know for certain that she prefers Mrs. or Miss, use Ms.

The way you sign the letter tells your reader how she should address you. Generally, if you've used your reader's first name, sign only your first name. If you wish, sign your first name above your typewritten full name. If you have addressed your reader by his last name, it is usually most appropriate to sign your full name. However, you might use the occasion to communicate your desire to adopt a first-name basis by deliberately signing your first name only—above your full typewritten name.

The "complimentary close" is a time-honored—and, perhaps, a time-worn—convention. It's true, if you examine them too closely, phrases like "Yours truly" and "Sincerely yours" seem pretty silly. Nevertheless, they're expected, and it is not acceptable to end a letter without some complimentary close. The most neutral of the complimentary closes are "Sincerely" and "Sincerely yours." If you wish to express a greater degree of familiarity or warmth, try "Cordially," "Best wishes," or "Best regards." "Yours truly" is still widely used, but "Very truly yours" smacks of an earlier age. Special circumstances sometimes call for special closes: "Respectfully" is good if you are reporting to a supervisor. "Regretfully" or "With regret" is sometimes appropriate in the case, say, of an apology.

Although it is seldom acceptable to include a postscript in business correspondence ("P.S."), you should indicate the presence of an enclosure accompanying a letter by noting "Encl." or even spelling out "Enclosure" (or plural, "Enclosures") below the typewritten name under the signature.

Finally, a general word about appearance. All businesses benefit from attractively designed stationery, which includes the company name, address, telephone number(s), fax number, and so forth. Printed stationery is relatively inexpensive and conveys substance, stability, and professionalism. It is very important that the envelope match the stationery. Using, for example, buff-colored paper with a white envelope conveys a haphazard approach to detail that does not speak well for your business. Of course, the letter itself should be free of smudges, stains, splashes of coffee, droplets of mustard, and the like. It should also be folded correctly—the first time—two neat folds, straight across.

The widespread use of personal computers, word processing programs, sophisticated printers, and a variety of fonts (typefaces) has done much to enliven business correspondence and to raise standards of presentation. Here are some assets and liabilities:

Word processing forever renders obsolete and unacceptable the unsightly use of abrasive erasers and correction fluid.

Fancy computer fonts offer attractive alternatives to plain old Courier or Pica.

Advanced printers, especially laser, LED, and ink jet "non-impact" printers, are capable of producing a beautiful page that resembles work professionally set from type. Page-oriented printers—such as laser printers—allow the use of letterhead and heavier paper stocks. Twenty-four-pound bond works very well in laser printers and makes a most attractive letter.

Now the liabilities of word processing.

Fancy fonts invite excessive window dressing. In general, avoid using more than two fonts in a single letter. Usually, one is sufficient. It is best to avoid eccentric typefaces, especially script faces that imitate handwriting. Best bet: stick to Times Roman (for a traditional look) or Helvetica (for a more contemporary look) or a typeface related to these.

Avoid flimsy "computer paper." This is the kind that works with continuous-feed printers. If you must use this paper, make sure that the printer ribbon is fresh (they tend to fade rather quickly) and that you tear off the perforated strips on the sides. Faded ink and the presence of perforated strips tell your reader that he is the target of some impersonal mass-mailing campaign. At some level of consciousness, your reader will recall all the bad news that comes via computer forms: overdraft notices, IRS audit letters, auto insurance increases, and so on.

So much for rules. The best approach to writing business letters is— always bearing your reader in mind—to develop your own personal style. Working with the letters in this book will help you to do just that.

Contents

PART II: DOING BUSINESS, 61

Chapter Three: Working with Clients and Customers: Information and Favors, 63

Letters Providing Information, 65

Letters Requesting Information, 78

Letters Requesting Favors, 83

Chapter Eight: Working with Suppliers and Vendors: Complaints, Apologies, Thanks, and Recommendations, 221

Letters of Apology, 233

Thank You Letters, 236

Letters of Recommendation—Services or Products, 239

Chapter Nine: Working with the Business Community and the Public, 241

Letters Requesting Favors from Business Associates, 244

Apologies, 296

Reprimands, 299

Refusing Request for a Raise, 309

Turning Down Request for Promotion, 314

Refusing Other Requests, 317

Chapter Thirteen: Communicating with Supervisors and Potential Employers, 349

Requesting a Raise, 357

Requesting a Promotion, 359

Requesting Changes in Working Conditions, Location, Hours, 362

Responding to a Reprimand, 372

PART I

GETTING BUSINESS

Chapter One

Turning Up Prospects with "Cold" Letters that Heat Things Up

Step by Step . . . to What's Best for You

You will find no shortage of books that attempt to reduce the art of sales to this or that formula. It would be nice if things were that simple, but the truth is that successful sales depend on a minimum of four variables no formula can fully control:

1. The personality and perceived character of the seller.

2. The skill of the seller.

3. The desire of the buyer.

And the fourth variable, which no sales "expert" ever acknowledges:

4. The quality (attractiveness, desirability, value) of the product.

There is a time-worn adage in sales: You don't sell the product, you sell yourself. To a degree, this is true. But you cannot ignore the underlying product, and it is far easier to sell a desirable product of high perceived value than it is to sell blatant junk.

All of this said, do we now pack our valises and go home? No. For while the first three variables cannot be controlled fully, they can be influenced and modified. A good sales letter can positively influence the reader's perception of the seller's personality and character—his integrity, if you will. A well-structured sales letter creates a skillful sale. And a letter that manages these first two variables effectively will significantly work to create desire in the buyer.

What is the best outline for a sales letter? Let's begin by observing that the best sales letters are written by people who believe in their product and who successfully convey that belief to an audience of readers/potential customers who they believe have a genuine need for this product. In short, the best sales letters embody and convey passion and integrity.

What if you are stuck with selling something about which you have, at best, lukewarm emotions? All is not lost. You can still communicate effectively. Here is the outline:

1. *Get the reader's attention.* This is usually best accomplished with a short declaration or a rhetorical question (that is, a question to which you know the answer: "Could you use $100 cash right now?").

2. *Develop the reader's interest.* Explain the deal, always stressing that it is an *opportunity* for gain, not just another "opportunity" to part with cash.

3. *Put into words the reader's desire.* You have interested the reader in your proposition. Now let her know that what you offer is not only desirable, but that it is within your reader's power to attain. ("Everyone would like extra cash to buy that little something you've been denying yourself, to take a much-needed vacation, to get that credit card debt off your back. Now you can get the money you need.")

4. *Move the reader to act.* Inertia, the tendency of a body to resist acceleration, is an immutable law of physics *and* psychology. But the key word here is *tendency.* The close of a good sales letter is directed toward overcoming that tendency and ac-

celerating your reader to action. Tell the reader what to do in order to act on his desire *now*. If appropriate, add thrust by means of a special offer or additional incentive.

SOFT SELL LETTERS

Jump Starts . . . to Get You on Your Way

We're not writing to everybody.

You are a successful professional.

It is clear that you know how to make money. But what about investing the money you make?

If you love your children, please read on.

The following letter contains information of special interest to **group**.

As a frequent user of **product/service**, you won't want to pass up the offer I'm about to make.

Wouldn't it be great to enjoy a fine gourmet meal each and every month in the most comfortable setting imaginable—*your home*?

Just a reminder that your **service contract, subscription, etc.** will expire on **date**. I'd like to tell you about a very special renewal offer.

Give me the opportunity of helping you save time and money.

Allow me to share some very good news with you.

I've got some good news for you.

Okay. I've got good news and bad news.

Here's something you want to know about.

Auto Insurance

Dear **Name**:

Are you paying too much for automobile insurance?

Your car costs you plenty—to buy, to run, and to service. Why pay more than you should for insurance?

We'd like to help you cut your insurance costs *now*.

Company is an independent full-service automobile insurance agency dedicated not only to finding you the lowest-priced auto insurance, but the coverage that is tailor-made for you, the coverage that gives you what you want.

Nothing more. Nothing less.

Company has served the **Town** community for thirty-three years. We'd be pleased to add you to our family of satisfied customers—folks who would not *think* of paying more than necessary to insure their cars.

Why not let us help you? Use the enclosed reply card or give us a call at **telephone number** today.

Sincerely yours,

Health Insurance

Dear **Name**:

How much is your family's good health worth?

It's priceless, you say?

Your doctor, hospital, and a legion of health care professionals say otherwise. The hard fact is, these days, your health and that of your family comes with a price tag few of us can afford—unless we have very good health insurance.

And that brings us to another hard fact. Fewer and fewer of us today are satisfied with the kind of health insurance our employers provide. Perhaps you've already faced problems like this with your present insurance:

- High deductible
- Too many forms to fill out
- Takes forever to get reimbursed
- Does not pay in full
- Won't let you visit the doctor of your choice
- Doesn't pay for prescriptions
- Dental coverage is a bad joke

If any of the above applies to you, let's talk. We're **Company**, independent full-service insurance agents dedicated to finding you the best coverage to meet your health insurance needs. We specialize in tailoring plans to fit you, whether you already have some coverage or none at all.

Good health is infinitely precious—and, these days, very costly. We have been helping families like yours in the **Town** community for **number** years. Why not have a talk with us? Please use the enclosed reply card or give us a call at **telephone number** today.

Sincerely yours,

Life Insurance

Dear **Name**:

Find a photo of you and your family. Look at it.

Now imagine yourself out of that picture.

What is going to happen to your family?

You work hard to provide for your family, to see to it that they get the very best. Let us work with you to make certain that your family continues to get the best—even if you are no longer there to provide for them.

For **number** years, **Company**, full-service independent insurance agents, have helped the folks of the **Town** community face life's hardest moments. Let us help you now. Why not have a talk with us? Please use the enclosed reply card or give us a call at **telephone number** today.

Sincerely yours,

Mortgage Insurance

Dear Mr. and Mrs. **Name**:

Bricks, boards, glass, and a lot of loving memories—your home. You cherish it, protect it, paint it, maintain it, insure it against theft, fire, and flood.

Now what happens if, suddenly, you can no longer pay for it? If you die, become disabled—or simply lose your job?

More and more families like yours are supplementing their household insurance portfolios with low-cost mortgage insurance. We offer a wide variety of plans designed to make your mortgage payments when you cannot. Why not let us discuss the options with you?

We're **Company**, full-service independent insurance agents, and we've been helping to protect the homes of the **Town** community for **number** years. Please use the enclosed reply card or give us a call at **telephone number** today.

Sincerely yours,

Consulting Service

Dear **Name**:

Since **year**, **Company** has been helping companies like yours with their ongoing human resources training and development programs. Our primary business is creating, customizing, and conducting fully interactive workshops to help your people

- maximize their service skills

- maximize their sales skills

- maximize their follow-up skills

- maximize their leadership skills

- maximize their project management skills

All of our workshops are live, interactive, and spontaneous. Nothing comes out of a can, and we work with you to tailor the workshop to the specific needs of your business.

Enclosed is a brochure describing our workshops, together with the latest listing of the distinguished and dynamic companies and institutions that use **Company**. Why not call us today at **telephone number**?

No pressure. No nonsense. Just the human resources help you need, when you need it, and how you need it.

Sincerely,

Investment Service

Dear **Name**:

We don't write to everybody. Our letters go exclusively to the leaders of the business and professional community, people who have demonstrated a will to excel and a determination to maximize their assets.

People like you.

People who work hard for their prosperity and who want something more than a place to "put" their money.

Company name Investment Services specializes in creating portfolios for the successful, discriminating investor. We offer a wide range of "packaged" products, carefully graded according to risk versus reward. We will also structure investments exclusively for you.

At **Company**, we don't write to everybody, and we don't believe in "cold calls." If you would like to investigate the special world of **Com-**

pany investing, we invite *you* to call *us*, at **telephone number**. If you like, one of our counselors will set up an appointment—at our place or yours—to discuss your investment needs for the present as well as the future.

Sincerely,

Loans

Dear **Name**:

You can go to a lot of places to get money these days: this bank or that and any number of private lenders. You could also wander into the first doctor's office you happen to find or choose an attorney at random from the Yellow Pages.

But you wouldn't do that, would you? Doctors, lawyers—they have your life in their hands. Choosing them takes careful thought and consideration.

Why treat your loan needs any differently?

A good loan can make a major difference in your life. So can a bad one.

At **Company name** Finance, we offer an array of personalized loan services, customized to your individual needs. Our loan counselors will talk with you—and listen *to* you—before we create a financing package to fit your situation.

Whether you want a home equity loan, an auto loan, enterprise capital, or a line of credit, give us a call at **telephone number** to set up an appointment. We know how important a loan can be.

Sincerely,

Credit Counseling

Dear **Name**:

There's an old way and a new way to manage your finances. The old way we might call "reactive." You wait for a problem to develop, for the bills to pile up, for the monthly expenses to bury you, for the overdue notices to trickle then pour in. And you react—somehow—to try to patch things up.

The new approach is different. Call it "proactive." Instead of waiting for the bad news, you manage your finances to anticipate and avoid problems.

How?

We can show you.

At **Company name** Financial Services, we specialize in helping you make a rapid transition from reactive to proactive financial management.

And just because you're heavily in debt—even behind with some of your bills—don't think it's too late for you. We'll work with you *and* your creditors to consolidate debt and create a payment plan you can live with—one that will preserve or restore your good credit without putting you on bread and water.

Call us at **telephone number** to set up an immediate appointment.

It's up to you. Act now. Or just keep reacting.

Sincerely,

Educational Service

Dear **Name**:

What's the difference between a secretary and an executive administrative assistant?

In this metropolitan area, about **$ amount** a year.

Not to mention a quantum leap in self-esteem and career potential.

It's a quantum leap, but one you can make, provided you have the right training. At the **Company name** School of Business, we've helped four generations of people just like you make that leap to more money for the present and a better future of continued professional growth.

We've enclosed a brochure describing the many programs **Company** offers. Financial assistance is available, and, of course, our hours are tailored to the needs of hard working men and women.

Why not make a phone call now that could change your future forever? Our toll-free number is **telephone number**.

Sincerely yours,

Health Club Membership

Dear **Name**:

There's a reason I've sent this letter to you at your office rather than your home. How many times has the phone rung this morning? How many problems have you handled? How many fires have you put out? How many meetings have you sat through? How many battles have you fought?

How's that knot in your stomach? That ache in your head? And that pain in your neck?

It would be nice to go somewhere and work off all that tension, wouldn't it?

Company name Spa is a health club for professionals. We offer a complete gym, indoor track, two pools, sauna, and steam room. We're geared to offer you a vigorous breakfasttime workout before work, or fast and efficient lunchtime workout at midday, or something more when you have the time at the end of the day.

Just tell us what's best for you.

The enclosed brochure describes our various programs. Pick the one that looks right for you right now, or talk to one of our fitness counselors at **telephone number** today.

In the meantime, just hang in there.

Sincerely yours,

Home Improvement

Dear **Name**:

Everybody's got a contractor horror story to tell you.

The job cost twice what he said it would!

The contractor ruined my kitchen!

He tore the place up and didn't put it back together for six whole months!

It took four times longer than he said it would!

The room looked better before!

He made us want to move!

At **Company name** Construction Company, we've heard the stories, too. And we don't want these nightmares to come true for you.

All of our work is 100 percent guaranteed. This means:

1. We give you a full and accurate estimate.

2. We give you a realistic schedule.

3. We do *all* the work you want done and *only* the work you want done.

4. We strive to give you the best workmanship at the best price possible.

5. We're fully bonded and insured.

6. We put it all in *writing*, for your protection.

Company specializes in interior as well as exterior work, making small repairs or engineering a major remodeling and renovation. Don't risk being a part of a horror story plot. Give us a call at **telephone number**, and tell us what you need.

Sincerely,

Residential Real Estate Offer

Dear **Name**:

Greetings from **Company**, your neighborhood realtor!

If you're like most folks in our community, you like to keep in touch with the local real estate market. That's why we've enclosed our monthly brochure, "Home Highlights," which features some of the best homes for sale in our area.

We invite you to call us if you have any questions about buying or selling a home. Remember, nobody knows **Town or Neighborhood** like **Company**.

Sincerely,

Commercial Real Estate Offer

Dear **Name:**

Company, your neighborhood realtor, is pleased to announce that prime retail space is now available in two highly desirable historic properties located in downtown **Town**.

The 1894 Krestmont Building features 18-foot-high stamped tin ceilings and rich oak wainscoting, both fully restored. Large, charming windows look out onto Elm Street, affording an ample and inviting showcase for your merchandise. Twenty-eight hundred square feet of prime retail space can be yours!

The 1924 Oak Block offers a lovely second-floor shop ideal for a specialty boutique. This 1200-square-foot space features many original fixtures, including lighting and floor-to-ceiling solid oak display cases.

Why not call me, **Name**, at **telephone number** today to arrange a personal showing of either of these fine retail spaces? I'd love to show them to you.

Sincerely,

Vacation Property

Dear Mr. and Mrs. **Name:**

If combing through brochure after brochure, making phone call after phone call, juggling reservations, calculating prices, fighting crowds, and scheduling months in advance doesn't sound like your idea of a vacation, please read this letter.

Relaxing and having fun shouldn't be harder work than the job you do five days a week for most of the year. Getting there shouldn't be as tough as your morning commute. And being there shouldn't be as public as Times Square on New Year's Eve.

You work hard, and you deserve a vacation that's easy, always available to you, relaxing, and so private that *it's all yours and yours alone.*

Imagine owning beautiful lakeside or other wooded property only a few hours' distant but a whole world away from the daily grind. It's like a dream, isn't it?

Well, **Company**, your neighborhood realtor, has been making this dream come true for **number** years. We offer vacation properties ranging from as little as one-third acre to 24 acres, in the woods, on the lake, and even near the beach. Some properties are ready for building, others already include beautiful cottages, some suitable for year-round living, if you prefer.

Vacation property is the best investment imaginable. It is an investment in your health, peace, and enjoyment. It is also an investment in good, solid, highly attractive real estate with proven *resale* and high *rental* value. What other vacation *pays* you back—in cash income?

We have enclosed a full-color brochure highlighting just some of the vacation property opportunities waiting for you.

Why not look it over and give us a call, toll-free, at **telephone number**?

Who knows? It may just be the last vacation brochure you'll ever have to read.

Sincerely,

Magazine Subscription (General Interest)

Dear **Name**:

Junk mail. Don't you hate it? Slick brochures and order forms that waste your valuable time and take up space in your mailbox, garbage can, and, finally, our waste-burdened planet.

The last thing you need is another piece of it.

That's why I'm sending you this single, personal letter instead. No pictures, no slick brochures, no thick envelope, no garbage. Just a letter to tell you about an exceptional opportunity to subscribe to one of the nation's favorite magazines at a very special price.

- *For a limited time, you can receive* **Magazine name** *for only* $ **amount** *per year.*

- *That's **percent amount** off the newsstand price.*
- *And **percent amount** off the regular subscription price.*

I told you that I'm not going to waste your time, take up your space, or clutter our environment with junk mail. Instead of some dumb foldout brochure, why not let me send you a copy of **Magazine name** itself—absolutely free?

Just fill out and mail in the enclosed reply card or call us toll free at **telephone number**.

Wouldn't it be nice to get something useful and entertaining in your mailbox for a change?

Sincerely yours,

Publisher

Magazine Subscription (Special Interest)

Dear **Name**:

Do you share your desk and chair with somebody else? How about your pens, pencils, and computer?

No?

Then why are you sharing the office copy of **Marketing magazine**?

We don't have to tell you how valuable **Marketing magazine** can be to your business. For **number** years, it's set the standard for marketing journalism. And, as you also know, timing and timeliness are everything in marketing. Can you, then, afford to wait for that office copy of **Marketing magazine** to reach your desk?

Use the enclosed card to subscribe today. Secure your own copy of **Marketing magazine**. It's time you stopped waiting.

Sincerely yours,

Book Club Membership (General Interest)

Dear **Name**:

I'd like to invite you to join a club that doesn't charge dues and doesn't hold meetings, but that will introduce you to the most interesting and influential people you'll ever meet: celebrities, thinkers, artists, novelists, poets, journalists, musicians, educators, and leaders in government and industry.

The Book Lovers' Guild selects the best of each season's crop of new books and offers them to you at substantial savings, ranging from 20 to 40 percent off publisher's cover price.

How does it work?

Each month you'll receive a copy of *Guild News*, listing over 75 new books plus a main selection and an alternate.

If you want the featured book, do nothing. You will receive it automatically.

If you decide that you want the alternate selection or any of the other 75 titles—*or no book at all*—just return the card enclosed with your copy of *Guild News*.

All books come to you with a special no-risk guarantee. Return any book within ten days and you will receive a full credit for the purchase price. No questions asked.

To make it easy for you to join we've enclosed a copy of the latest *Guild News* with this letter. Select any three books, fill out the order form, and then pay for only two.

That's right. The third book is our way of welcoming you to the Book Lovers' Guild, easily the most rewarding club you'll ever join.

Sincerely,

Book Club Membership (Special Interest)

Dear **Name**:

As a computer professional, you know the value of timely information. Technologies change dramatically and rapidly. Yesterday's cutting edge is today's standard and tomorrow's outmoded design.

The trade journals help you keep on top of developments, but for an in-depth knowledge of the varied technologies you must command, nothing takes the place of a book.

Unfortunately, finding *all* the books you need *when* you need them can consume more time than you can afford.

That's where Byte Size Computer Book Club can help. *We* find the best and most important books in the field, from the classics to the cutting edge. *We* buy them in quantity at discount prices. *We* offer them to you, delivered, for less than you'd pay at the store.

Byte Size saves you time and money while ensuring that the books you need don't escape your notice.

At Byte Size, there are no automatic shipments and no minimums. Your one-time membership fee of **$ amount** is applied toward your first purchase. Membership entitles you to receive our monthly *Byte Size Bulletin*, which lists the hottest new titles, complete with insightful commentary from our editors and from you, our members.

Send in the enclosed membership form today, call us at **telephone number**, or contact our Internet BBS at **telephone number**. Start enjoying the benefits of membership right away.

Sincerely yours,

Record (CD) Club Membership (Classical)

Dear **Name**:

How do you build a fine classical music library, one you and your family will be proud of?

You find and buy the best recordings of the greatest works performed by the leading artists of the world.

A time-consuming and expensive task? As members of Classics Unlimited have discovered, it need not be. Each and every month, they let our experts offer them an enticing selection of the great recordings of today and yesterday, recordings by such artists as . . .

list

. . . performing works by composers including . . .

list

To help them decide which of the many offerings to select, members receive the monthly *Classics Chronicles*, which brings you news from the worlds of concert and opera, together with stories on the featured recordings of the month.

You'd expect to pay a premium for the magazine and the advice of classical music experts, wouldn't you?

In fact, what you'll get is the world's finest classical CDs at discount prices. All delivered to your doorstep.

And there is absolutely no risk. Return any CD within **number** days, and you will receive a full credit for the purchase price. No questions asked.

Why not use the enclosed reply card to start your membership and receive your first issue of *Classics Chronicles*? If you prefer, call us toll free at **telephone number**, and have your major credit card ready.

Sincerely,

Record (CD) Club Membership (Jazz)

Dear **Name**:

As a serious lover of jazz, you're one of a special breed. You know what you like, and you won't settle for anything else or anything less. Trouble is, your kind of music isn't always easy to get. The chain store in the mall isn't likely to have the classic jazz record or CD you want. And if it's something new from one of the independent labels—well, you might as well be asking for music from Mars.

What do you do if you aren't fortunate enough to live near one of the nation's very few major jazz music stores?

Join other discriminating jazz lovers like you who have discovered the Windy City Jazz Record Club.

Let's be frank. We're in this business for two reasons: To make a living—*and* because, like you, we love the music. We look for the best jazz recordings around, old, new, big labels, and small, domestic and imported, and we make them all available to you.

Here's how it works: Each month members receive *Take Five*, our illustrated magazine, which profiles the month's three featured recordings and three alternates. If you want the featured CDs, do nothing. You will receive them automatically.

If you prefer the alternate selection or any of the other **number** titles listed each month—*or if you decide that you want no recordings at all*—just return the card enclosed with your copy of *Take Five*.

It's not only hassle free, it's risk free. Return any CD within ten days and you will receive a full credit for the purchase price. No questions asked.

To make it easy for you to join we've enclosed a copy of the latest *Take Five* with this letter. Select any three recordings, fill out the order form, and then pay for only two.

Yes. Pay for only two. The third one's on us. It's our way of thanking you for joining the Windy City Jazz Record Club.

We look forward to hearing from you.

Sincerely,

Record (CD) Club Membership (Rock)

Dear **Name**:

It's important to you to get the music you want when you want it. And that includes, of course, all the hottest new albums—the very CDs your local music shop runs out of first. So if you're tired of following the crowds and always getting the latest music after it's *too* late, do the smart thing. Join **Club name** today.

Let us catch the biggest hits for you, as they climb the charts.

We offer the hottest CDs by the biggest artists for a better price than you'll find in any store. Just dip into the enclosed catalog brochure.

Here's how it works.

There are no upfront fees of any kind. Pick any three CDs from the brochure and pay the **Club name** special discount price for two. Get the third for free.

That's right. Get a great discount deal on two CDs. Pay nothing for the third.

It's our way of thanking you for joining **Club name**.

And now that you're in, here's what you'll receive. Each month a copy of **Publication** will be delivered to you. It lists over **number** hot CDs plus the month's three main selections and three alternates.

If you want the featured selections, just sit back and do nothing. You will receive them automatically.

If you decide that you want the alternate selections or any of the other **number** titles, or if you want *no CD at all*, just return the card enclosed with your copy of **Publication**.

And there's more. Each and every CD is backed with a special no-risk guarantee. Return any CD within **number** days and you will receive a full credit for the purchase price. No questions asked.

Isn't it time you started getting the hits before they're history? Take advantage of our introductory buy-2-get-1-free offer and join today.

Sincerely,

HARD SELL LETTERS

Jump Starts . . . to Get You on Your Way

Would you throw away **$ amount**?

You're going to love this letter.

Could you use some extra cash—*now*?

The good news is, this is *not* another bill.

Someone new has come into your neighborhood.

I am president of **Name of company**, and I would like to offer you an opportunity.

I don't want your money.

I know what your biggest problem is, and, more important, I know how to fix it.

You're making more money today than ever before, but you are saving less and less.

Peace of mind—how much is it worth to you?

Sleek, beautiful, desirable. That describes the new **name of product**.

Stop throwing away your hard-earned money!

Now you *can* cut costs while boosting sales.

I am absolutely certain that you are paying too much for **product/service**.

You have been chosen to receive an exclusive offer for **product/service**.

Time is running out.

We are pleased to announce a brand new **product/service**.

You can live without what I am about to offer you. But why should you?

Fast-Approval Loans

Dear **Name**:

Let us treat you to the five most beautiful words in the English language:

THIS IS NOT A BILL

But it does concern money. Money we bet you can use *right* now. Money to pay off credit cards, car loans, college loans, household expenses. Money to buy a car, add a room, buy some furniture, or just take that vacation you've been putting off and off and off . . .

Company has money to lend. We have it now, we have it available, and we want to lend it to you with a minimum of paper work.

Company has a wide variety of plans to suit practically any financial situation. We make home equity loans, auto loans, and personal loans on your signature. We offer no-income verification plans, and if credit has been a problem in the past—let's talk.

So stop waiting and stop worrying. Call us toll free at **telephone number** or stop by at any of our convenient locations:

list

We're here to help.

Sincerely,

Health Club Membership (Limited-Time Offer)

Dear **Name**:

"Just do it" is more than the slogan of a popular brand of running shoe. It's good advice. Especially now.

If you've been thinking about getting in shape, maintaining the shape you have, or just finding a time and place to unwind and have some fun, now is a very good time to stop thinking and start doing.

For a limited time, **Club** is offering special discounts on an array of membership plans:

list

Club offers state of the art facilities, including a Nautilus-equipped gym, indoor track, two pools, sauna, and steam room. We are conveniently located in downtown **Town**. But you must act now. Prices like these will not last long.

We've made it extra easy for you to "just do it." Please use the enclosed postage-paid reply envelope and card to enroll today. Or call us at **telephone number**.

To your health!

Home Improvement Special

Dear **Name**:

House falling down?

Don't worry. So are our prices!

For a limited time only, **Company** is offering a special "Just Like New" tune-up package for your home.

We will

- repair siding
- repair detailing

- renovate roofing material
- "new up" gutters and downspouts
- *and* paint your entire house

for one low package price.

What are you waiting for? Our estimates are always free. We'll be happy to come out, evaluate the job, and give you our special package price.

We're at **telephone number**.

But don't call yet. Why not ask your neighbors about us first? We've been serving the **Town** area for **number** years.

Sincerely,

Auto Repair Promotion

Dear **Name**:

Nobody likes to pay for auto repair, but, like the man says: You can pay me now. Or you can pay me later.

If you pay me later, it will cost you **percent** more.

Because, for a limited time only, **Garage** is offering a **percent** discount on

- major tune ups—**$ amount**
- oil change and chassis lube—**$ amount**
- muffler replacement—**$ amount**
- front-end alignment—**$ amount**
- transmission tune up—**$ amount**
- engine overhauls—**$ amount**

Prices like these just won't last. In fact, they definitely won't last past **date**.

So bring in the family bus now before we have to tow it in and charge you more than you want to pay!

Sincerely,

Residential Real Estate "Last Chance" Offer

Dear **Name**:

We're not a bit surprised.

Name of residential development has filled up fast. In fact, there are only **number** units left, and it's clear: They won't last long.

Especially after **date**, when we are hosting a special open house to show off the last available townhomes at **Name of development**.

Please take a moment now to review the enclosed brochure describing these gracious residences located in **Name of town**'s most prestigious neighborhood. Both inside the development and in the surrounding area, amenities abound.

Why not come out on **date** and see for yourself? Enjoy cake and coffee with us and take a leisurely look at homes that are moving fast.

Sincerely yours,

Commercial Real Estate Special Offer

Dear **Name**:

As you probably have heard, **Store** is going out of business and will vacate their landmark retail outlet at **location** on **date**.

All of us in **Town** are sorry to see them go. But their going affords you an unprecedented opportunity to move your business up and into the spectacular building at **location**. **Store** is offering the remainder of their lease —**number of years**— at the sacrifice price of **$ amount**.

Opportunities like this one are indeed rare, and that is why we are writing to you personally. Can you afford to pass it up?

Let us walk you through the building at **location**. Call today at **telephone number** for an appointment.

We politely suggest that you do not delay.

Sincerely,

Realtor

Vacation Property Limited-Time Offer

Dear **Name**:

Picture yourself in your own private paradise. Sand as white as sugar. Turquoise water meeting azure sky. Balmy temperatures in the 80s. And your house just beyond the beach and over the dune. *Your* house. *Your* place. No crowds, no traffic, nobody's radio blaring in your ear.

Too good to be true?

It can be yours. And, for a limited time only, it can be yours at an amazingly low price.

Realtor is proud to announce **Name of development**, a new beachfront community at **location**.

Only **number** hours from **City**, **Name of development** offers all the amenities of a world-class vacation beach resort, including a fully equipped clubhouse and boathouse, as well as 24-hour security patrols.

How much does all this cost?

A lot less than you'd think.

But there is one catch. The availability of these deluxe properties is strictly limited—and they will not last long.

You have to see it to believe it. Don't be left out. Why not come out this weekend? See **Name of development** for yourself, examine a prospectus, and stake your claim to paradise.

Sincerely yours,

Magazine Subscription Promotion (General Interest)

Dear **Name**:

You could endure the heat of the noonday sun, or brave the chill of the winter storm, fight your way through rush-hour traffic, then stand in line at the checkout counter and pay **$ amount** for your copy of **Magazine**.

Or . . .

You could send in the enclosed reply card today and get **number of copies** of **Magazine** delivered to your doorstep each and every **month, week** for the very special discount price of **$ amount**.

That's **percent amount** off the newsstand price and **percent amount** off our regular subscription price.

So don't hurry out the door, hurry to your car, or hurry to the store. Just hurry up and mail the card. (We'll bill you later.)

Then sit back and relax with one of America's favorite magazines.

Sincerely,

Magazine Subscription Promotion (Special Interest)

Dear **Name**:

As an avid coin collector, you know that three things are absolutely true:

1. Great bargains are few and far between.
2. Great bargains quickly vanish.
3. When you find a great bargain, it's time to act.

Here's a great bargain, and

1. It's rare.
2. It will quickly vanish.

3. It's time to act.

Treasury: The Magazine of Coin Collecting is celebrating its 50th year as the bible of numismatists with a very special offer:

Get **number** issues of *Treasury* for only **$ amount**. That's **percent amount** off the regular subscription price!

What's the catch?

You must act now. The offer expires on **date**. Absolutely and forever— or, at least, until we celebrate our 100th anniversary.

Use the special postage-paid order card enclosed or call us at **telephone number**.

Sincerely,

Book Club Membership (General Interest)

Dear **Name**:

Book clubs come, and book clubs go. We know, because we've seen 'em all. We've been here for **number** years, and we'll be here for years and years to come.

So what's the rush to join our **number** other members?

Well, *we* will be here for a long time, but this special offer won't.

Right now, you can join **Club** by ordering **number** books for **$ amount**—a **percent amount** discount off the publisher's cover price— AND get **number** books absolutely free.

But act now. Because the offer expires on **date**, and orders postmarked after that date will *not* be honored.

We've made it easy.

Look through the enclosed brochure, make your choices, and send in the order/enrollment form. We'll do all the rest.

Special offers come, and *this* special offer will very definitely go—after **date**. Hope to hear from you!

Sincerely,

Book Club Membership (Special Interest)

Dear **Name**:

Take command. Charge now—while our prices are in retreat!

War & Books, the nation's leading military book club, announces its lowest prices in years—not just on "bargain" titles, but on new releases as well as the most sought-after classics, including:

list

These prices are our way of mustering you into the ranks of the most exciting book club you'll ever join. But our recruitment drive won't last forever. After **date** all prices return to their usual club discount levels.

This is no time to be caught AWOL. Take command — and take advantage of this very special, very limited offer.

We've made it easy.

Each month, members of War & Books receive a copy of *The Dispatch*, our up-to-the-minute catalog, which lists over 75 new books plus a main selection and an alternate.

If you want the featured book, stand at ease. Do nothing, and you will receive the selection automatically.

If you decide that you want the alternate selection or any of the other 75 titles—*or no book at all*—just return the card enclosed with your copy of *The Dispatch*.

Every book comes to you with a special no-risk guarantee. Return it within ten days and you will receive full credit for the purchase price. No questions asked.

We've enclosed a copy of the latest *Dispatch* with this letter. Select any three books at our limited-time-only super discounts, fill out the order form, and then pay for only two.

That's right. Not only do you benefit from our special introductory discount, you actually get one book absolutely free.

Your marching orders are clear, and we respectfully suggest that you get the lead out.

Let's hear from you today.

Sincerely,

Record (CD) Club Membership Promotion (Classical)

Dear Member:

Once a year we make available to our members a rich selection of the choicest "cut out" albums from all the leading classical labels. These are fine recordings, often of great historical interest, that, for one reason or another, have been dropped from the record company catalogs. They share two special qualities:

1. They will never be available again. Ever.

2. They are priced—now—far below their original retail cost.

Fair warning to you: Our members know a great deal when they see one. Traditionally, demand for these fine recordings has been intense, and supplies are *absolutely, irreversibly limited.* So we ask that you

1. Order a minimum of five albums.

2. Specify five first choices and five alternates.

3. Order before **date**.

Because of the very special nature of this offer, all sales are final, and we cannot make any refunds or exchanges except in the case of defective recordings or errors on our part.

Don't miss out. Let's hear from you—now.

Sincerely yours,

Record (CD) Club Membership Promotion (Jazz)

Dear **Name**:

As a lover of jazz, you know only too well how quickly some of the best albums come—and go. Lucky for you, just for our members, we have cached a treasure trove of gems that are *out of print and no longer generally available*. These include:

list

Remarkable? You bet.

But face the facts: Before you know it, these titles and the others listed in the enclosed catalog flier will soon disappear from the marketplace.

If that doesn't bother you, do nothing. But if you want to own any of these classic sides, get out your major credit card and get on the phone. Dial **telephone number** and order by number only.

For this very special offer a few very special rules apply:

1. We will accept telephone credit card orders only.

2. Minimum order is three albums.

3. Some albums may no longer be available. Please specify an alternate for each album you order.

4. Sorry, all sales final. No refunds or exchanges, except for defective merchandise or error on our part.

They're going fast.

Sincerely,

Record (CD) Club Membership Promotion (Rock)

Dear **Name**:

Better take this sitting down.

Of course, you've heard of the Top Ten.

If you went out your door and to your local record store right now to buy all the current Top Ten albums, it would set you back about $120.

This is where you should sit down.

We're going to give them to you—FREE.

You don't need glasses. Read it again:

We're going to give you the current Top Ten rock albums absolutely free.

Here's how it works. You use the enclosed reply card to join **Club** today and agree to purchase—all at our special discount prices—ten albums by **date**. When we get the card, you get the Top Ten.

This offer is too hot not to cool down. In fact, it will be dead cold by **date**, and reply cards postmarked after that date will *not* be honored.

So, it's time to get up now. Fill out the card, walk to the mailbox, and get ready for some great listening.

Sincerely,

Chapter Two

Turning Prospects into Customers with Follow-ups that Don't Let Go

Step by Step . . . to What's Best for You

Prospecting for new customers is, of course, a vital first step in getting fresh business. But just as raw minerals, once found, require processing in order to bring profit, your prospects often require additional communication to persuade them to become customers. Letters to facilitate this "refining" process fall into three functional categories. Some help the potential customer focus his needs. Others make the prospect feel less like a customer (one who parts with money in exchange for goods or services) and more like a participant in a win-win situation (an active negotiator who has swung a profitable deal). A third category of follow-up letters is addressed to your firm's second-greatest source of business: currently inactive customers. That's not just a euphemism for "former customers." Banish that self-defeating phrase from your vocabulary. As matter is neither created nor destroyed, but merely transformed, so customers are neither current nor former customers, but currently *active* customers or currently *inactive* customers. Both are potential sources of revenue. (What, by the way, is your firm's number-one source of new business? *Currently* active customers. New customers come in at third place.)

As with "cold" letters, the success of follow-ups depends on the writer's skill and personality, as well as on the merchandise itself. The added element in the follow-up is the relationship between your company and the customer. This may be very slight, defined only by the fact that you have written her once before. Or it may be of genuine substance, as in the case of a currently inactive customer. In either case, your letter should build on whatever relationship exists, using essentially the same structural outline as the "cold" letter.

1. *Get the reader's attention.* But be aware that, this time, you aren't coming at your reader "out of the blue." You've written before, or you've done business before. You have the basis of a relationship, which you would like to strengthen by offering your reader something of interest or value: an opportunity.

2. *Develop your reader's interest.* This section should be detailed, but interesting reading. To a greater degree than in the "cold" letter, you are furnishing information, not just persuasive rhetoric. You must supply the reader with the information he needs to make his decision.

3. End the informational section by reinforcing all of your reader's good feelings about the decision you want him to make. Increase his level of desire.

4. Conclude the letter by inviting action and making it as easy as possible for the reader to act. Reiterate any special offer made in the "cold" letter. You may even introduce a new incentive at this point to coax your reader over the hump.

LETTERS THAT FOCUS ON CUSTOMER'S NEEDS

Jump Starts . . . to Get You on Your Way

Thank you for giving us the opportunity to talk to you about **merchandise/service**.

Thanks for responding to our recent letter about how we can help you with your **merchandise/service** needs.

Naturally, I'm disappointed that you have chosen not to act on our **merchandise/service** offer, and I can appreciate your concerns. But before I pack up my bag and leave . . .

I enjoyed talking to you the other day about **merchandise/service**.

I am delighted to tell you more about the **merchandise/service Name of company** offers.

Yes, **Name,** you are right. **Merchandise/service** is expensive. But have you considered the costs of *not* making such a purchase?

I am delighted to enclose your application materials for **subscription service**.

Auto Insurance

Dear **Name**:

Thank you for giving **Agency** the opportunity to talk to you about our auto insurance offerings. I hope that you have found some time to consider the **number** options I presented, and I encourage you to call if you have any further questions.

As I mentioned, each of the options balances cost versus coverage in a different way:

- **Option 1: $ amount** liability protection, with **$ amount** comprehensive coverage and a deductible of **$ amount** for **$ amount** per year.

- **Option 2: $ amount** liability protection, with **$ amount** comprehensive coverage and a deductible of **$ amount** for **$ amount** per year.

- **etc.**

All **number** options fall within the specifications we discussed, so the final choice among them is yours. Do take the time to consider the choices carefully, but let me remind you that I can guarantee these premiums only through **date**.

I look forward to hearing from you soon.

Sincerely yours,

Health Insurance

Dear **Name:**

Thanks for allowing me to come into your home to discuss the health insurance options available from **Name of agency**. I couldn't agree with you more: Health insurance is expensive nowadays. But, I think you'll agree with me that getting sick *without adequate insurance* is far more costly.

Hospitals in this area charge **$ amount** per day. A simple appendectomy costs at least **$ amount**, and major cardiac surgery runs anywhere from **$ amount** to **$ amount**. You're charged **$ amount** for each aspirin you receive!

It's scary, to say the least.

The purpose of insurance is to preserve your assets and protect your family *in case* catastrophe strikes. But it pays off even in the good times by providing peace of mind. And that's hard to put a price tag on.

Why don't you give me a call if you have any additional questions, or if you would like me to review the options with you once again.

I look forward to hearing from you.

Sincerely,

Life Insurance

Dear **Name**:

Thank you for responding to our recent letter about buying the life insurance that's best for you.

Our consultants have examined your questionnaire very carefully and have developed the enclosed plans for you. We appreciate that you want to provide for your family's security as fully and as quickly as possible, so please take time now to look the plans over.

One of our consultants will telephone you within a few days to review the plans with you, or, if you like, you may call us at **telephone number** sooner.

We are very pleased with the opportunity to serve you and help you achieve the peace of mind that comes with knowing your family is well protected.

Sincerely yours,

Mortgage Insurance

Dear **Name**:

Of course I'm disappointed that you have chosen not to act on our mortgage insurance offer, but I can certainly appreciate your not wanting to be overburdened by premiums.

I'm also a person who takes *no* as *no*.

But, before I go away and leave you alone, let me ask you to consider how mortgage insurance actually enhances—stretches—your general insurance portfolio by economically addressing one specialized need. This is not over-insurance, but *strategic* insurance.

Perhaps I did not make that sufficiently clear in my original presentation, and I would not want to leave you without having done so now.

Should you decide that you would like to discuss mortgage insurance further—now or later— please do give me a call. In any case, it was a pleasure speaking with you.

Sincerely,

Consulting Service

Dear **Name**:

Thanks for giving us such careful consideration. I understand and appreciate your reasons for not wanting to implement the full program we have to offer. However, I don't want to sign off without being certain that I made it sufficiently clear that we offer a broad spectrum of services, precisely so that you are not compelled to take all or nothing.

I discussed with you our editorial, design, production, and fulfillment package. Perhaps you would rather use your in-house editorial and design personnel and let us handle production and fulfillment. We are willing to give you exactly what you want and no more than you want.

If this modified package appeals to you, why not give me a call at **telephone number** to discuss prices and schedule.

Sincerely yours,

Investment Service

Dear **Name**:

It was a great delight talking with you on **day**. My partners and I have carefully reviewed our notes from the conversation, and we have put together an investment portfolio that we are confident will meet your needs.

Please review the enclosed proposal, and call me at the office at **telephone number** or at home at **telephone number** if you have any questions.

I must ask that you make your decision regarding the substance of the portfolio by **date**, which is the latest we can guarantee availability of the offerings listed in the proposed portfolio.

I look forward to hearing from you.

Sincerely yours,

Credit Counseling

Dear **Name**:

Yes, **Name**, you're right. Credit counseling *does* take a lot of work on your part. You have to review your current expenses carefully, and be sure to list all of your creditors, along with the amounts you owe each. You need to sit down and figure out a rough budget for such essentials as mortgage, utilities, food, clothing, and so on.

Believe me, I can understand your reluctance to undertake the task. It's no fun, and, I'm afraid, there are no shortcuts. Before we can begin to help you, you must complete this first step.

But please consider a moment. Why is it so hard? Because, perhaps for the first time in a long time, *you* are taking control of your finances. *You* are untangling something that's been knotted up for quite a while. Sure, it's hard. But the benefit, ultimately, is control, a healthier financial picture, a much cleaner credit situation, and, above all, peace of mind.

So, before you give up on the project, take another look at the forms we sent. Reread our "Notes on Organizing Your Records," and bite the bullet. Meet us half way, and we can then work with you and your credit to brighten up your financial picture.

I do look forward to hearing from you.

Sincerely,

Educational Service

Dear **Name**:

We are delighted to enclose your preliminary enrollment materials. This questionnaire is *not* a test, but by completing it carefully, you will help us to create a program that's just right for you.

At **School or Training facility**, your needs come first. That's why we want you to tell us as much about yourself as possible.

If you have any questions about the enclosed materials, please call **Name** at **telephone number**. She will be happy to assist you. Remember, the semester starts on **date**. To allow us sufficient time to evaluate and act on the questionnaire, please be sure to return it no later than **date**.

We look forward to hearing from you.

Sincerely,

Home Improvement

Dear **Name**:

We *have* been busy. Response to the special "Just Like New" home tune-up package we advertised last month has exceeded even our expectations.

That's good news for us.

Now here's some good news for you. We're extending the offer for another month. That's right, through **date** you can still order the whole tune-up package at a very special price.

We will

- repair siding
- repair detailing
- renovate roofing material
- "new up" gutters and downspouts
- *and* paint your entire house

for one low package price.

As before, it costs you nothing to get our estimate. Give us a call at **telephone number** while there's still time.

Sincerely,

WIN-WIN LETTERS

Jump Starts . . . to Get You on Your Way

I am looking for some very special people to enjoy the benefits of a very special offer.

Let us help you.

I am about to offer you a partnership with one of this nation's biggest **type of company** firms.

If you discovered that you were losing **$ amount** each and every month, you'd be pretty upset, wouldn't you?

You good friend and neighbor, **Name,** suggested we contact you about the **type of service** we can offer you.

Here is everything you've asked for.

We want you back—and we'll make it worth your while.

Personal-Service Insurance Agent

Dear **Name**:

I am looking for *particular* people. I don't mean I'm looking for this or that particular person. What I mean is that I am looking for *particular* people—men and women who are very *particular* about what they want, what they purchase, and with whom they choose to work.

You see, I am a particular person myself. I choose my clients carefully, because I plan to work hard for them in order to create a long-term and mutually rewarding relationship. That's the way I choose to do business. And that's what sets me apart from the hundreds of other insurance agents you might choose to secure your assets, protect your property, and provide for your family.

I do not simply *find* you a policy.

I talk with you—and I work with you, to create a policy with you that's meant specifically for you and no one else. Insurance should fit you; you shouldn't have to fit whatever insurance happens to be available. And insurance matters should not interfere with your life. Good protection is invisible—until you need it.

If you're as particular as I think you are, let's talk. I'm at **telephone number**, and I'm eager to work with you.

Sincerely,

A Mortgage Broker (Who Works for You)

Dear **Name**:

Don't bother *applying* for a mortgage.

Shop for one instead.

Better yet, let us do the shopping for you.

Most money lenders like you to think that, because they hold all the money, they also hold all the cards. They want you to come to them and "apply" for a loan.

But, think about it. Without your business, *they're out of business*. Let us find you the best folks to do business with. We won't just connect you with the money, we'll connect you with the terms that are right for you. We'll find you the kind of loan you'll be most comfortable with.

It's easy. Come in and talk with one of our mortgage counselors. Together, we'll decide just what kind of a loan is best for you. Then leave the rest to us. We know who is out there, and we can put together the funds you need from a wide variety of secure sources.

Mortgage money is a product, not a gift. We'll find you the best product at the best price. Why not put us to the test? Call **telephone number** today for an appointment with one of our mortgage counselors, and take real charge of this extremely important aspect of your financial life.

Sincerely,

Personal Tutor Tailored to Your Needs

Dear **Name**:

Thanks for inquiring about **Tutoring service**.

Let me begin with a piece of advice: Whatever you do, don't go back to school!

Let me come to *you* instead—with a series of unique learning programs.

Why unique? Because each one is tailored specifically and exclusively to your needs. The first lesson is one you teach *me*. You tell me what you want and what you need, and I will create a program of study just for you. From basic literacy to computer literacy, from basic office skills to advanced communication strategies, together we will create a program uniquely suited to your needs and goals.

I invite you to read the enclosed brochure and to give me a call at **telephone number** to arrange that first lesson.

Sincerely yours,

Let Us Be Your Personal Auto Mechanics

Dear **Name**:

If you paid your mechanic something each and every month, you'd probably shoot your car, and put it out of its misery.

We've got a plan for you.

- First: Pay us **$ amount** each month.
- Second: Hold your fire!

For that **$ amount** you get a team of expert mechanics *on call* 24 hours a day, 7 days a week. That's right, for **$ amount** you get your own personal team of auto mechanics.

Think that's an interesting deal? It gets better. We'll deduct the cost of one month's fee from one repair or towing bill per year.

Our prices on parts and labor are highly competitive, and all work is fully guaranteed. Isn't it worth **$ amount** for the convenience and peace of mind that comes with having your own personal team of expert mechanics on call, for you, all the time?

Telephone us at **telephone number** or drop by the garage at **address** today.

Sincerely,

Home Improvement: We Listen to You

Dear **Name**:

Your neighbor, **Name**, suggested that we contact you about the home improvement services we offer. The brochure we've enclosed lists the kind of work we do. To be honest with you, it's about what you might expect: room additions, siding work, roofing installation and repair, deck design, and construction.

There is one product we offer that's hard to find nowadays: Our full and undivided attention.

Before we set pencil to paper or put hammer to nail, we talk with you, and we listen to you. We want to learn as much about your taste, your plans, your goals—everything you want your home to be.

Most builders think a foundation is made of stone or concrete. We believe a foundation is made of your dreams and your imagination.

Your neighbor, **Name**, knows. We built his **item**. Why don't you talk to him about us, then give us a call.

We'd be proud to listen to you.

Sincerely,

Extending Magazine Subscription

Dear **Name**:

Please don't leave us!

Your subscription to **Magazine** will expire—gulp!—with the **date** issue.

We don't want to fade out of your life.

So we've come up with a deal we think you'll find too good to pass up.

Renew your subscription before **date** and get a

- **percent amount** discount on a 12-month renewal

or

- **percent amount** discount on a 24-month renewal

or a whopping

- **percent amount** discount on a 36-month renewal

At these prices, you can't afford *not* to let us a stick around a while longer.

Please use the enclosed reply card to renew today. We'll bill you later.

Sincerely,

Special Offer Continued

Dear **Name**:

You asked for it, and we want to give it to you.

Response to our special offer on **Name of product/service** has been overwhelming. You folks love the deal, and, to tell the truth, our boss loves the cash!

So **Name of company** is extending this very special offer for another **time period**, until **date**. That means there's still time for you to take advantage of very substantial savings on list

Why not drop in and see us today. We're at **address**, and we'd love to see you.

(Especially our boss!)

Yours truly,

Try Our Other Investment Services

Dear **Name**:

You've probably been expecting this:

> Thanks for investing with **Name of company**. Now that you're one of our family of happy investors, we'd like to interest you in . . .

Well, the fact is that we *would* like to interest you in making more investments with us. But, after **number** years in the business, we've learned an important lesson. It's a mistake to *sell* clients on investments.

It's a much better idea to *offer* clients additional *opportunities* to invest.

We don't want to come to you as salespeople. We want to come to you as what we are: your investment partners. We don't want to make money *from* you. We want to make money *with* you.

The selling relationship, we've learned, is a short-term one. But partnerships can go on and on. We're investors, and we know that a long-term investment beats a short-term investment every time.

So why not examine the enclosed brochure, which outlines the additional investment opportunities we currently have to offer you. Then give us a call at **telephone number**. We'll be happy to fill in the details, provide updates, and answer any questions.

Sincerely yours,

LETTERS REVIVING INACTIVE CUSTOMERS

Jump Starts . . . to Get You on Your Way

I hear that you are not planning to renew your **subscription, insurance policy, etc.** I am very sorry to hear that, but I do have a few suggestions that might persuade you to reconsider.

I received your letter today requesting that we terminate your **subscription, insurance policy, etc.** We will, of course, follow your instructions. But there is still time to consider a few other options.

We haven't heard from you in such a long time!

I hope that you enjoyed working with me as much as I did with you last year.

We miss you! We love you! Please, come back to us!

The property **or other merchandise** we discussed last **month, week, etc.** is still available. In fact, it is available at a considerable savings to you.

It has been some time since we last spoke, so I thought the moment had come to touch base with you.

I make it my business to write a personal letter to anyone who does not renew his or her subscription to **Magazine**.

We hate to see you lose the advantages of **merchandise/service**.

Do you know that a whole year **or other period** has come and gone since you placed your last order?

Time is running out.

Auto Insurance

Dear **Name**:

Name of agent tells me that you are not planning to renew your auto policy with us. I am very sorry to hear that.

I'm not going to pester you with a phone call, but I would like to invite you to give me a call at **telephone number**. I'd like to hear why you've decided to move your coverage to another agent, and, most of all, I'd like to hear from you what I might be able to do to persuade you to change your mind.

I hope to hear from you.

Sincerely,

Health Insurance

Dear **Name**:

I learned today that you have decided not to renew your policy with us.

There are many reasons why people discontinue health coverage: cost, dissatisfaction with service or claim handling, or perhaps you have found coverage elsewhere.

I will not pester you with a phone call, but I do want to make certain that you are fully aware of just how flexible we can be in tailoring the coverage to the customer. If you are unhappy with your present plan, why don't you give us an opportunity to make you happy? Before you finalize your decision to leave us, why not give me a call at **telephone number**? Let me know why you are leaving and what I might be able to do that would change your mind.

I look forward to hearing from you.

Sincerely,

Life Insurance

Dear **Name**:

I am very sorry to hear that you have decided not to renew your term life policy with us. We've done business with you for **number** years, and, frankly, it was a shock to learn that you are going to leave us.

I don't want to bother you with a phone call, but I do want to make certain that you are fully aware of the full range of life insurance options we offer. I feel confident that we can come up with a plan that will be the equal or the better of any plan anywhere else.

I'm hoping that you'll give me a chance to prove that statement.

Before you take your business elsewhere, won't you call me at **telephone number**?

I hope to hear from you.

Sincerely yours,

Mortgage Insurance

Dear **Name**:

I received your letter requesting that we terminate your mortgage insurance policy effective on **date**.

Of course, we will follow your instructions.

But while there's still time, I wonder if we shouldn't have a conversation first. Mortgage insurance is a prudent component of your insurance portfolio that provides security for your family's future and peace of mind for you here and now. I suggest that we discuss your decision in the context of your entire insurance portfolio. Perhaps there is an alternative to your dropping the coverage?

Why not give me a call at **telephone number**? If I don't hear from you by **date**, I'll call you to confirm that you do, indeed, wish to discontinue the coverage. But I do hope to hear from you before then.

Sincerely,

Consulting Service

Dear **Name**:

Thought it was a good time to touch base with you.

When we worked on **name of project** with you last year, you mentioned **another project**, which you anticipated getting under way by **date**.

Perhaps you can update me on the status of the project, and, if it is a *go*, we would welcome the opportunity to bid on it. It was indeed a pleasure working on **name of project**.

Please call (at **telephone number**) or write.

Sincerely yours,

Investment Service

Dear **Name**:

This letter confirms that we have closed your account **number** per your request. A closing statement and check in the amount of **$ amount** are enclosed.

It has been our pleasure to serve you, and we hope that you will continue to consider us for your investment needs.

Unless we hear from you to the contrary, we will continue to send you our monthly newsletter advising you of the investment opportunities we offer.

Sincerely yours,

Loans

Dear **Name**:

Congratulations on having recently retired your loan with us. It has been a distinct pleasure serving you.

As you know, a loan is useful not only when you're short of cash, but as a cash-flow management tool. We invite you to call us at **telephone number** or drop by to discuss additional lending opportunities you may wish to take advantage of.

Sincerely yours,

Educational Service

Dear **Name**:

We hope that you found last year's **name of course** both personally and professionally rewarding.

School offers a wide range of related courses designed to build on and enrich last year's experience. These include:

list

We would be pleased to discuss any of these courses with you. Like **name of course taken**, they are an investment in your personal and professional future.

Sincerely,

Health Club Membership

Dear **Name**:

It's been a whole year, and we miss you. We'd like you to come back. And we're willing to make it worth your while.

A lot of companies offer their salespeople bonuses for bringing back wayward customers. We've decided instead to give the bonuses to the customers themselves.

Here's how it works: Come back to **Club**, pay for a 52-week membership, and we'll give you an additional 12 weeks as a free bonus.

It's a deal that's hard to beat. So why not give an old friend a call at **telephone number**. We'd love to see you again.

Sincerely,

Home Improvement

Dear **Name**:

I was driving by your house the other day, and, I have to admit, I pulled over to admire the siding work I had done last year. It really does look great, if I do say so myself.

I hope you are pleased with it.

When I finished the job last year, you mentioned that you were thinking of putting in all new railing work on the front porch. When I drove by, I saw that you had not done this yet, and I thought it was a good time to ask you if you had given the job any further thought.

It would be a pleasure to work for you again, and I certainly would welcome the opportunity to bid on the job.

If you decide to move ahead on it, please give me a call at **telephone number**, and I'll come right out.

Sincerely yours,

Residential Real Estate Offer

Dear **Name**:

I thought you'd want to know that the property at **address**, which you looked at **number** weeks ago is still on the market and is being offered at a considerable reduction.

Also, since you last looked with us, **number** other properties, all of which fit the criteria we discussed, have become available. I'm enclosing descriptions of all of them.

If you are still interested in **address** or would like me to show you the other properties, please give me a call at **telephone number**.

I'd be happy to hear from you.

Sincerely,

Commercial Real Estate Offer

Dear **Name**:

It's been **period of time** since we last spoke, so I thought it high time to write and find out if you are still looking for space in **locality**.

If you are still looking, I urge you to give me a call at **telephone number**. Several new properties have become available in the area—a much more inviting selection than when you first came to see us.

I hope to hear from you.

Sincerely,

Vacation Property (Rental)

Dear **Name**:

We miss you. It's been **period of time** since you booked a vacation rental through us, and we've been wondering why.

Even more, we're wondering what would persuade you to come back to us. Maybe this, for starters:

FOR A LIMITED TIME ONLY . . .

we are offering **number** weeks rental at any of the following sites:

list

for the very special price of **$ amount**.

Does that get you thinking?

Why not give us a call at **telephone number** for details and availability. But hurry. At these prices, the deals won't last long.

Sincerely,

Magazine Subscription (General Interest)

Dear **Name**:

I make it a point to write to anyone who does not renew his or her subscription to **Magazine**.

To put it bluntly, I'd like to know why you have chosen not to renew.

Please do me a favor by filling out the enclosed postage-paid card. By knowing what went into your decision, perhaps we can make changes in **Magazine** that will bring you back to us.

I appreciate your attention.

Sincerely yours,

Magazine Subscription (Special Interest)

Dear **Name**:

We'd hate to see you lose your professional edge. But, quite frankly, that's just what you are risking by not renewing your subscription to **Magazine**.

In the coming months and years, **Magazine** promises to bring its readers more expert advice and insider perspectives on the business of **type of business**.

Why risk missing out?

In this business, you need the edge we can provide.

Won't you take a moment to reconsider your decision? Use the enclosed postage-paid quick-renewal card today.

Sincerely yours,

Book Club Membership (General Interest)

Dear **Name**:

It's been a long time since we've heard from you! In fact, club rules say that, unless you order three titles by **date**, we'll have to discontinue your present membership.

We'd hate to see you go, so we've decided to make it easy for you to stay.

Choose this month's three automatic selections, three alternates, or three other titles AND PAY FOR ONLY TWO of them.

Not only will you be taking advantage of a great book lover's bargain, you'll also ensure that your membership in **Club** is uninterrupted.

Remember, if you want this month's three main selections—**Titles**—simply do nothing. All three will be sent to you automatically, and we will bill you for only two. If you would rather receive the alternate selections or some other titles, please fill out the enclosed order form and mail it today. Order three and pay for two.

Need a better offer?

How about: Order six and pay for four! Or: Order nine and pay for six! This month only, we will give you—free—one of *every* three books you order.

Sincerely yours,

Book Club Membership (Special Interest)

Dear **Name**:

We'd hate to see you lose your edge.

In business, the most valuable commodity is information. You read the papers, you watch TV, you subscribe to the major business magazines and probably a lot of specialized newsletters.

That's not enough.

Today's business person needs the kind of up-to-date and in-depth information only books can supply. Whether it's the latest survey of spreadsheet software, the hottest on option strategies for today's volatile stock market, or the most advanced thought on management style, books give you what you need.

You could spend hours looking for the titles you want in this bookstore, then that, and then the next one. But if information is the most valuable commodity in business, time—*your time*—runs a very close second.

Why waste it?

But you know all this. That's why you joined **Club** in the first place. We save you time by selecting the best and most important business books for you and delivering them to your desk. Just as important, **Club** almost always gets the latest titles *before* they become generally available in the bookstores.

We give you the edge. Why give that up now?

Send in the enclosed reply card to reactivate your membership in **Club**, and we'll make you a very special offer. Take this month's three main selections—or choose the alternates, or order any other three books from the enclosed catalog—and you'll pay for only two.

That's right: Get 3. Pay for 2. But you must renew your membership by **date** to qualify for this special offer.

Sincerely,

Record Club Membership Promotion (Classical)

Dear **Name**:

Bribe is such an ugly word. But if that's what it takes to bring you back to **Club**, we're not bashful.

If you reactivate your membership by ordering any three recordings from this month's announcement, we will give you two tickets to your choice of the following concerts—*for the price of a single ticket*. Choose from:

list

A bribe?

There *is* an important difference: A bribe is meant to get you to do something you don't want to do. We are offering you an opportunity to continue to enjoy the pleasure of great music in your home—and to get the added benefit of a concert of your favorite music at a very special price.

Take a look at this month's release announcement enclosed with this letter. Order three recordings, and take advantage of an exceptional offer.

Sincerely,

Record Club Membership Promotion (Jazz)

Dear **Name:**

When you joined **Club**, we made you a promise: We will never pressure you into making a purchase.

But we don't want to see your membership in **Club** lapse without making absolutely certain that you are aware that you are about to leave us.

The sad fact is that, unless you order at least two albums this month, we will have to assume that you are no longer interested in **Club**, and you will no longer receive **Catalog** each month. You will no longer have a direct line to the hottest new albums, the hard-to-find private independent labels, and the rarest old releases.

If you're sure you no longer want the benefits of club membership, just send in the enclosed card with "send nothing" checked off.

But if you would like to continue your membership, either do nothing—and this month's main selection will be shipped automatically—or specify this month's alternate, or order any other recordings you wish.

It's your call.

Sincerely yours,

Record Club Promotion Membership (Rock)

Dear **Name**:

Do you know that it's been a whole year since you left **Club**? We hope you've been listening to a lot of great music during this time.

We sure have—hits like:

list

And we've usually enjoyed them weeks before retail shoppers found them in the local CD store.

If you've missed us during this year—missed the excitement of great recordings delivered to your door each month, the latest and the hottest—why not come back?

It's easy to join again. And there's even a special bonus. Order five CDs today and get three—yes, *three*—for free. That's a total of eight big albums of your choice.

Take time to look through the enclosed catalog now and see what you've been missing.

Yours,

Hairstylist Offer

Dear **Name**:

It's time for our autumn update. A lot's been happening here at **Shop**.

We would like to welcome **Name 1** to our staff of professional stylists. We're delighted to have her with us. **Name 2** deserves congratulations for having won a two-week seminar at **Name** Hair Cutting Academy. And I've just returned from a **Name** University seminar on hair-coloring techniques. I'd like to share what I've learned with you.

It's been quite a while since we've seen you at **Shop**. Let's get reacquainted.

Bring this letter with you to **Shop** no later than **date**, and you'll receive an **amount** discount on the cost of your next cut or hair color service.

Hope to see you.

Best regards,

PART II

DOING BUSINESS

Chapter Three

Working with Clients and Customers: Information and Favors

Step by Step . . . to What's Best for You

The letters in this section provide information, request information, seek favors, and decline favors. In all cases, clarity and economy of expression are most important. That is, you don't want your reader to mull over your language, to think about the words, but simply to find out what he needs to know, to tell you what you need to know, to act as you want him to act, or to accept with understanding that you cannot do what he asks of you. Like an automobile, then, these letters are meant, first and foremost, to get you and your reader from point A to point B. Yet we both know that this avowed purpose of the automobile is not, in fact, the only function it serves. The car we drive can be a source of pride, of good feelings—or, for that matter, of negative feelings. Cars are vehicles of transport as well as vehicles of emotion. The same holds true for the ostensibly utilitarian, no-nonsense letters in this chapter. Informational letters and requests provide a valuable opportunity for projecting your feelings about yourself, your business, and, most important, about your reader/client/associate.

Letters Providing Information

Here is the basic form of a letter providing information:

1. State the subject. If you are responding to a request for information, say so, repeating or summarizing the original request.

2. Provide the information. If appropriate, use a phrase such as "I have the information right here" or "It's no problem," which conveys a high level of professionalism and good management.

3. Close either by thanking the reader for his interest in doing business with you or, whenever appropriate, by offering your cooperation.

Letters Requesting Information

Here is an outline for letters requesting information:

1. State what you need and why. If the request is for information required to do something for the reader—for example, to fill an order or process a credit application—begin by thanking the reader for his order, application, etc., then introduce your request with, "In order to process your order, we need to know . . . "

2. If necessary, define more precisely what you need. "All I need are the records from 1989 to 1993—nothing before then."

3. Thank the reader for his cooperation and, where appropriate, for his business.

Letters Requesting Favors

For many people, requesting favors is a difficult and unpleasant task. You can make it easier by thinking of your request not as an attempt to get something for nothing, but as providing your reader an opportunity to help you. Most people enjoy helping others. Your request can provide an opportunity for your reader to feel good about herself.

1. Introduce your request by providing a basis or reason for it. "We've enjoyed such a long and profitable relationship that I feel quite comfortable asking you for a favor."

2. Define the favor precisely.

3. Explain how the favor will benefit you—how your reader can be of great help.

4. Express your gratitude—but be careful not to thank the reader in advance. This would imply that you take her compliance for granted.

Letters Declining Requests for Favors

When you must decline a request for a favor, do so clearly but gently, always providing a reason for your being unable to meet the request.

1. Refer to the request.

2. Express regret that you cannot satisfy the request.

3. Explain why you cannot.

4. Express your wish that your declining the request will not cause inconvenience.

5. Thank your reader for her understanding in this matter.

LETTERS PROVIDING INFORMATION

Jump Starts . . . to Get You on Your Way

Ordering from us is simple.

To place an order, please follow these simple instructions.

The enclosed catalog tells you everything there is to know about our line of **merchandise**.

Our new catalog is finally out, and we're delighted to enclose a copy just for you.

The information you requested is enclosed.

I'm delighted to send you the information you requested on **date**.

Please note the following corrections to our **date** price list.

Thanks for your order of **date**. To expedite processing of your order, we need to have the following information from you:

Our goal at **Name of company** is to give you the best service possible. To help us achieve our goal, we ask that you provide us with some important information by completing the attached questionnaire.

What have we done wrong? And, please, what have we done right? We would be grateful to hear from you. Please complete and return the question form enclosed.

Thanks for sending the information we requested on **date**. However, I am still unclear on a few points. Perhaps you can fill me in on the following:

It has been such an enjoyable experience working with you that it actually gives me pleasure to ask you for a favor.

Can you help me out?

I need your assistance.

I'd like some advice.

You can be a big help to us.

I received and reviewed your letter of **date** requesting **favor**. I wish that I could oblige you, but . . .

I wish that I could accommodate your request for **favor/service**, but, regrettably, I cannot.

Ordering Instructions

Dear **Name**:

To order any of our **type of product** products, call us toll free at **telephone number** and have the following information ready:

- The item number, if you know it

- Or the model number

- The quantity of each item you are ordering

- A major credit card

- Your shipping and billing addresses

Please be prepared to specify the method of shipment you prefer:

- U.S. Postal Service

- United Parcel Service

- Federal Express

If you have any further questions concerning how to order from **Name of company**, please call us at **telephone number**. We'll be glad to help.

Sincerely,

Dear Customer:

It's easy to order from **Name of company**!

Call us at our toll-free number, **telephone number**, or mail or fax the enclosed reply card.

Please be ready to specify:

1. The name and model number of the item

2. The catalog number of the item, if you know it

3. The quantity of each item you are ordering

Then let us know how you'd like to pay:

1. By major credit card

2. By personal check or money order
   (Sorry. We cannot ship C.O.D.)

Finally, please give us

1. Your shipping and billing addresses
2. A daytime telephone number

That's all there is to it. Orders are shipped, if possible, on the day we receive them. We ship via the U.S. Postal Service unless you specify another carrier.

Thanks for your business.

Sincerely,

Name of company

Cover Letters—New Catalog

Dear **Name:**

We're handing you a whole new line!

The enclosed catalog tells you everything you need to know about our new **Name** Series, the finest **product type** products you can buy.

We've been listening to you!

The **items** you'll find in the pages of the new catalog are, in large part, the products of your suggestions and comments.

And we've listened to you about something else, too. We've lowered our prices, which are now among the **very lowest** anywhere.

About all that stayed the same is our commitment to service, customer support, and high quality.

We're proud of our new catalog, and we believe you'll find it very rewarding—and very exciting—reading.

Sincerely,

Dear **Name of company** Customer:

It's finally here—our **year** catalog. And we're pleased to send it to you.

We're proud of everything we offer, but we're especially excited about our line of **merchandise**, which you'll find on pages **numbers**.

We're including old favorites this year, such as **list**, as well as many terrific new items you've told us you want, including **list**.

So sit back, relax, and enjoy your **year** catalog from **Name of company**.

Good reading,

Cover Letters—New Price List

Dear **Name**:

I'm pleased to send you the updated price list you requested. As you can see, we have held the line on prices this year—and held it more consistently than our competitors.

Please give me a call at **telephone number** when you are ready to order or if you have any questions.

Sincerely,

Dear **Name**:

As you requested, we've rushed you our **year** price list. The bad news is that, because of the rising cost of raw materials, we've had to raise our prices on some items.

The good news is that we haven't raised our prices by much—and we believe we're still the folks to call on for the very best deals available.

Please give me a call at **telephone number** when you are ready to order or if you have any questions.

Sincerely,

Price Corrections

Dear **Name**:

Please note that the price for **item and item number** was misprinted in our **season** catalog.

The correct price for **item and item number** is **$ amount**.

We regret any inconvenience the misprint may have caused you.

Sincerely,

Dear **Name**:

Just a note to confirm our telephone conversation this morning in which I corrected the price quotations I gave you on **date**. The following are the correct prices:

Item and item number $ amount

Item and item number $ amount

Item and item number $ amount

I'm sorry I didn't have my facts straight!

Best Regards,

Dear **Name**:

We made a mistake.

The prices quoted for **item(s) and item number(s)** on **date** were incorrect. The following are the correct prices:

Item and item number $ amount

Item and item number $ amount

Item and item number $ amount

I am very sorry for this error, and I hope it did not cause you any inconvenience.

Sincerely,

Dear **Name**:

I'm afraid we had a miscommunication.

The prices I quoted you for **items** were based on a quantity of **number**, which is what I had understood you wished to order. At a quantity of **number**, which I now understand is what you would like, the per-item price is **$ amount**.

Sorry for the mix-up.

Sincerely,

Price Adjustment—Change in an Order

Dear **Name**:

I am very pleased that you have decided to increase your order for **items and item number** from **quantity 1** to **quantity 2**. This change will allow us to give you a unit price of **$ amount** for a total cost of **$ amount**.

As you requested, I have put the order through at the adjusted cost.

Sincerely,

Dear **Name**:

You don't have to apologize for changing your order—especially when you buy more from us!

As you requested, we are modifying your order of **date** as follows:

item   quantity

item   quantity

item   quantity

item   quantity

This brings the total cost of your revised order to **$ amount**.
It is always a pleasure to serve you.

Sincerely,

Dear **Name**:

This confirms the **date** change in your order of **date**.
Instead of

item   quantity $ amount

item   quantity $ amount

item   quantity $ amount

item   quantity $ amount

You are now ordering

item   quantity $ amount

item   quantity $ amount

item   quantity $ amount

item   quantity $ amount

Please note that, because of the reduced quantities, we have adjusted
the unit prices of each item.
Your order, as revised, will be shipped on **date**.

Sincerely yours,

Shipping Procedure

Dear **Name**:

We will ship your order, **number**, from our warehouse in **location** via **carrier** on **date**, to arrive at your warehouse in **location** between **date** and **date**.

As you specified, we are shipping the order in **quantity** cartons poly-wrapped on pallets.

Sincerely,

Dear **Name**:

Your order will be shipped in **number** parts as follows:

- **Item**
- **Item**
- **Item**
- **Item**

from our warehouse in **location** on **date**;

- **Item**
- **Item**
- **Item**

from our warehouse in **location** on **date**;

- **Item**
- **Item**
- **Item**

from our warehouse in **location** on **date**; and

- Item
- Item
- Item
- Item
- Item
- Item
- Item

from our warehouse in **location** on **date**.

As you specified, all shipments will be made to your warehouse at **location** via **carrier**.

Please give me a call at **telephone number** if you have any questions.

Sincerely,

Cover Letters—Description of Services

Dear **Name**:

The most thorough way for me to respond to your questions about the range of services we offer is to invite you to read the brochure I've enclosed. It tells the whole story, complete with options and prices.

I would be delighted to discuss our services with you, and you can reach me, Monday through Friday from **time** to **time**, at **telephone number**.

Sincerely,

Dear **Name**:

Many thanks for your inquiry about the services we offer. **Name of company** has prepared an informative brochure, which I have enclosed, describing our operation in detail.

In addition to the standard services described in the brochure, we pride ourselves on the personalized custom options we tailor to each individual customer. I invite you to look over the brochure, then give me a call at **telephone number** so that we can discuss your needs.

Sincerely yours,

Meeting Schedule

Dear **Name**:

I am delighted that you will be able to attend the series of meetings planned for **Month 00-00**. Here is the schedule:

Meeting title/topic   date   time   location

Meeting title/topic   date   time   location

Meeting title/topic   date   time   location

Meeting title/topic   date   time   location

Meeting title/topic   date   time   location

Meeting title/topic   date   time   location

Please give me a call at **telephone number** if you have any questions.

Sincerely,

Dear **Name**:

I am very pleased that you will be able to attend the annual meeting of **Organization**, which will be held on **Month 00-00** at **location**. I have enclosed a program, which gives you the full schedule of events. Those I've underscored should be of special interest to you.

I look forward to seeing you!

Sincerely yours,

Dear **Name**:

It's that exciting time again—when we get together to share our thoughts and ideas concerning the direction of our industry. Enclosed you'll find a complete program of events scheduled for our upcoming meeting from **date** to **date** in **location**.

Your insights at past meetings have been stimulating and very helpful. I look forward to talking with you at this year's gathering.

Best regards,

Address Change

Dear Friend:

We've always said that **Name of firm** is a company on the move. Now maybe you'll believe us!

As of **date**, our new address will be:

address information

Our telephone numbers will remain the same:

> Customer Service: **telephone number**
> Shipping: **telephone number**
> Billing: **telephone number**

Why don't you drop by and see our new, state-of-the-art facility? We can offer you a doughnut and a cup of coffee, just like at the old place—but, this time, *fresh!*

Sincerely,

Dear Customer:

Name of firm is moving.

As of **date**, our new address will be:

address information

Our telephone numbers will remain the same:

Customer Service: **telephone number**
Shipping: **telephone number-**
Billing: **telephone number**

Sincerely,

Change in Business Hours

Dear Friend:

We're going to be keeping later hours here at **Name of company**.

Beginning **date**, we'll be open from **time** to **time**, Monday through Friday, and **time** to **time** on Saturday.

We hope our extended hours will make doing business with us more convenient than ever.

Sincerely,

Dear Customer:

From **date** to **date**, **Name of company** will operate on a reduced summer schedule:

> Monday–Thursday   **time** to **time**
> Friday   **time** to **time**
> Saturday and Sunday   closed

Sincerely,

LETTERS REQUESTING INFORMATION

Jump Starts . . . to Get You on Your Way

We won't rest until you are happy. Please help us relax by answering a few questions.

At **Name of company** our goal is to give you maximum service at minimum cost. To help us achieve that goal, we're asking you to complete the brief questionnaire enclosed and return it to us in the postage-paid envelope.

What have we done *to* you? What have we done *for* you? What would you *like* us to do?

Help us serve you better.

Let's do it better next time. Here's how you can help.

Thanks for responding so promptly to my request for information on **product, service, topic, etc.**

Thanks for your order, number **number** dated **date**. We have your standing shipping instructions in our files, but because it has been some time since your last order, I thought it best to confirm your instructions before proceeding with the delivery.

Cover Letters to Accompany Customer Survey

Dear Valued Customer:

At **Name of company** our goal is to give you the maximum of service at the minimum of cost. To help us achieve that goal, we're asking you to complete the brief questionnaire enclosed and return it to us in the postage-paid envelope.

We don't have any prizes or premiums to offer you in exchange for a few minutes of your time, but we do promise to think very carefully about what you tell us and use it to give you the great products and service you deserve.

With thanks for your consideration,

Dear **Name of company** Customer:

Where have we gone wrong?

And where have we gone right?

Please help us out with some answers by taking a moment of your time to fill out the enclosed Customer Response Card.

Your suggestions enable us to provide you with the very best products and services possible.

Thanks for your time and attention,

Dear Customer:

Our pledge to you is to produce products of the highest quality that meet your needs. You can help us keep this pledge by telling us what you think and feel about your **name of product**. We've prepared a brief questionnaire for you to complete.

Please, tell us how we're doing—and what we could be doing better.

We thank you.

Sincerely,

Requests for Additional Information

Dear **Name**:

Thanks for responding so promptly to my request for information on **product, service, topic, etc.**

The information is helpful, but not quite complete. Perhaps you can fill me in on the following points:

list

I appreciate your expediting the information.

Sincerely,

Dear **Name**:

Thanks for sending your brochure on **product line**. It's very informative, but I still have a few specific questions, which I need answered before I can decide whether your product is right for me. Please give me information on the following items:

list

I am eager to make my purchasing decision, so I would appreciate your expediting the information.

Sincerely,

Shipping Instructions

Dear **Name**:

Many thanks for your order, number **number** dated **date**.

Please note that your order did not specify the following necessary shipping instructions:

> **date**
> **destination**

> **carrier**
>
> **number of shipments desired**
>
> **etc.**

Please call me at **telephone number** with instructions or, if you prefer, fax them to me at **fax number**.

We're ready to ship as soon as we have this information.

Sincerely yours,

Dear **Name**:

Thanks for your order, number **number** dated **date**. We have your standing shipping instructions in our files, but because it has been some time since your last order, I thought it best to confirm your instructions before proceeding with the delivery. We have you down for delivery to the rear loading dock at **address** via **carrier** on any weekday except **day**. You accept no deliveries between **time** and **time** o'clock.

If this information is still valid, you need not respond. If you have other instructions, please call me at **telephone number** before **date**, which is our scheduled ship date.

Sincerely yours,

Bid Procedure

Dear **Name**:

We will be pleased to bid on your project **name/number**. Your RFP did not specify the following information, which we need in order to prepare a bid that will be most useful to you:

> **Number of copies?**
>
> **Copies to whom?**
>
> **Costs to include delivery, etc.?**

Narrative proposal required?
Etc.

Please mail or fax the instructions. Our fax number is **fax number**.

Sincerely yours,

Dear **Name**:

We are delighted to bid on your very exciting project **name/number**. Experience has taught us that many firms prefer to receive proposals prepared in a specific format. If you have such a preference, please supply a style sheet by **date**. In the absence of this, we will prepare the proposal in accordance with generally accepted industry standards.

Thank you for giving us the opportunity to present our services to you.

Sincerely yours,

Meeting Schedule

Dear **Name**:

I am very eager to attend the **name** conference. Thanks for asking me. Please mail or fax me a complete schedule of the meeting, with subjects, times, and places.

Sincerely yours,

Dear **Name**:

I very much want to attend the meetings you told me about. Before I can give you a definite *yes*, however, I need to look at the meeting schedule. Please mail or fax me a complete schedule of the meeting, with subjects, times, and places. As soon as I've taken a look at the schedule—and checked my own calendar—I'll give you a call.

Sincerely yours,

LETTERS REQUESTING FAVORS

Jump Starts . . . to Get You on Your Way

We have had such an enjoyable and rewarding working experience together that it actually gives me pleasure to ask you for a favor.

I could use your help.

I have a small request.

I could use about three more days to prepare the figures for our meeting. Can we push the meeting day back from **day** to **day**?

The best-laid plans of mice and men—should be better laid!

You can save my—skin.

I have a substantial favor to ask of you.

Here's a rare opportunity to help another person.

Requests for Recommendation

Dear **Name**:

We have had such an enjoyable and rewarding working experience together that it actually gives me pleasure to ask you for a favor.

Would you be kind enough to write a brief letter of recommendation to **name and address**?

We have bid on the following project for his company: **describe project**. It would be very helpful if, in addition to whatever else you feel moved to comment on, you could make the following points about your experience with us:

List points to make.

Of course, any other general and kind words would be appreciated as well.

Name is working on a tight schedule, so I would greatly appreciate your sending out the letter by **date**. Please call me if you have any questions.

With gratitude and thanks,

Dear **Name**:

Can you help me?

We're being considered by **Name of company** as a contractor for **describe project**. Since our firms worked successfully on such a project recently, and since I believe that you know **Name** at **Name of company**, it seemed to me that you are the ideal reference.

I'd like to ask you either to call or write **Name** to tell her about our experience working together. It would be very helpful if you could make the following points:

list

The telephone number at **Name of company** is **telephone number** and the address is **address**.

This contract means a great deal to us, and I would be very grateful for any kind words you could pass along. Please call me at **telephone number** if you have any questions.

With thanks,

Dear **Name**:

I've taken a liberty with you, sir [madam]!

Name of **Name of company** is considering our firm to do **describe project** for him. In the course of our conversation, I mentioned you as one of our "satisfied clients" and suggested that he give you a call to discuss the work we did for you.

We've worked so successfully together that I did not hesitate to give him your name.

I don't know if he will follow up and actually call you, but, if he does, any kind words on our behalf will be greatly appreciated. You might want to include the following points:

list

Do give me a call at **telephone number** if you have any questions.

Sincerely,

Confine Calls to Certain Hours

Dear Client:

You can help us to serve you better. We are a small office with limited personnel resources. So that we can give you the attention you deserve, we ask that you confine non-emergency telephone calls to the hours of **time** and **time, day** through **day**.

Your cooperation is greatly appreciated.

Sincerely,

Dear Valued Customer:

At **Name of company** we always want to give you our best—which means our 100 percent undivided attention when you need assistance or information.

To ensure that we can give you this level of service, please confine non-emergency customer service telephone calls to the hours of **time** and **time**. That's when we can be sure to give you the attention you deserve.

Sincerely,

Request for a Meeting

Dear **Name**:

I've enjoyed talking with you by telephone and exchanging written correspondence. However, I believe that the issues involved in **name of project** are sufficiently complex to warrant a meeting in person.

I can make myself available, either here or at your offices, any time between **date** and **date**. Please give me a call so that we can set the meeting up.

I look forward to it.

Sincerely yours,

Dear **Name**:

In this age of instant communication—phone and fax and conference calls—it's easy to fool yourself into thinking that you're giving your customer personal service.

Well, I believe that "personal" means *in-person,* and I'd be grateful for the opportunity to communicate with you the old-fashioned, low-tech way: face to face, over a good lunch.

I'll be in your area from **date** to **date**, and I would like to set something up with you as soon as I arrive. So you may expect to hear from me on **date**.

I hope we can meet at last.

Sincerely,

Change of Meeting Location

Dear **Name**:

This is a quick note to ask that we change venues for our **date** meeting. Instead of getting together at **location**, I suggest **location**. The meeting space is larger, and it is located around the corner from a very nice place for lunch. I'd like to take you there.

If this change in plans is okay with you—or if it is not—please give me a call at **telephone number**.

Best regards,

Dear **Name**:

My secretary has just reminded me that on **date**, the day we scheduled for our meeting, my offices will be full of painters. We're redecorating.

Rather than choke on paint fumes and trip over dropcloths, I suggest that we move the meeting to your offices. Why not give me a call to let me know if this is agreeable to you?

Best regards,

Change of Meeting Time

FAX

To: **Name**

From: **Name**

I could use about three more days to prepare the figures for our meeting. Can we push the meeting day back from **day** to **day**?

Please fax or give me a call with your response.

Best,

Dear **Name**:

The best-laid plans of mice and men—should be better laid!

Name has just pointed out to me something I should have been aware of. I've scheduled our **date** meeting on the same day as **another event**. I don't want to make anyone choose between two important events, so I suggest we reschedule our meeting.

Would **date** be good for you? Or **date**?

Please write or call with your preference.

Sincerely,

Extension of Deadline

Dear **Name**:

I thought it was a good time to give you a progress report on **name of project**. We have completed the first two phases of the project, but we are finding that the research for phase 3 is consuming more time than we had anticipated. We know that you do not want us to cut corners at this crucial stage, so we ask that you extend the deadline for completion of the entire project from **original date** to **proposed date**.

I am confident that the results—and the resulting peace of mind—justify the extra time we are asking for.

Please give me a call to confirm or to discuss this proposed adjustment to the completion schedule.

Sincerely yours,

Dear **Name**:

I enclose the completed research reports for the first two stages of **name of project**. The final stage, still in preparation, is consuming more time than we had anticipated because of the following problems:

list

Fortunately, none of these difficulties is insurmountable, and the project is moving along. But it would be unrealistic to promise completion of the final stage by the date we originally anticipated, **date**. We ask, therefore, that you allow us to adjust the schedule for delivery of the complete report no later than **date**.

We've all invested considerable time, energy, and other resources in the project. Let's not risk it all by cutting corners now.

Please call to discuss our proposed revision of the schedule or to confirm your acceptance of it.

Sincerely,

Accelerate Payment

Dear **Name**:

I have a substantial favor to ask of you.

As you know, we set up the payment schedule for **name of project** as follows:

> **date** payment amount
>
> **date** payment amount
>
> **date** payment amount

Our suppliers are now demanding full payment with each order we make. I'm sure you can appreciate that this is putting a great strain on our cash flow—worse, it is a strain we had not anticipated.

You can help us.

If you could rearrange your payment schedule to us as follows, it would make life around here much, much easier—and, ultimately, allow us to serve you more effectively:

> **date** payment amount
>
> **date** payment amount

date   payment amount

Please call me at telephone number so that we can discuss this proposal.

Sincerely yours,

Dear **Name**:

Here's an offer I hope you won't refuse. It's a golden opportunity—to help us out.

The schedule of payments to which we agreed for **name of project** specifies payment due dates by the **date** of each quarter **month, etc.** Unfortunately, certain of our key suppliers and subcontractors are proving inflexible in their payment schedules. I don't want to jeopardize the timely completion of your project by shopping around for new sources of supply. What I propose, therefore, is a revision of our agreement. I ask that you make your payments no later than **revised date** of each quarter **month**. In return, I can offer a **percent amount** discount off the entire contract. I know that won't make you rich, but I hope it will make it easier for you to accept this proposal.

Please give me a call at **telephone number** as soon as possible. If the revised payment schedule is agreeable to you, I'll send you a letter of agreement right away.

Sincerely,

Change in Delivery Schedule

TO: **Name**

FROM: **Name**

RE: Delivery schedule for **name of project**

Our client has asked for some changes in completion dates for this project. Accordingly, we would like you to revise your delivery schedule to us as follows:

list revisions

We appreciate your flexibility and cooperation. Please call me at **telephone number** if you have any questions.

TO: **Name**

FROM: **Name**

RE: Delivery schedule for **name of project**

Our client has asked us to advance the completion date for this project. To do this, we need to take delivery on our order no later than **date**. We realize that it will be a crunch, but can we count on you to ship by then?

Please confirm by phone or fax.

Employment Interview for Friend

Dear **Name**:

You mentioned not long ago that you are always on the lookout for good people in sales **or other position**. An old friend of mine, **Name**, whom I have known and worked with for **number** years, is thinking about leaving his present position as **position** at **Name of company**.

I think that you would both benefit from a conversation. I've taken the liberty of asking **Name** to call you next week, and I hope that you will be able to set up an interview with him. I know that you will enjoy meeting with one another.

Sincerely,

Dear **Name**:

When I get a piece of good news, I'm eager to pass it on to a friend.

Name, a longtime associate of mine, has been **title** at **Name of company** for some **years** now. He's let me know that it's time for a change, and it occurs to me that you would be perfect for one another.

May I suggest to him that he give you a call?

Please let me know.

Best regards,

Employment Interview for a Relative

Dear **Name**:

When I started out in this field, I *swore* I would never do this.

I'm about to ask you to interview my nephew **or other relative** for a job.

Stop groaning. There is a pleasant surprise in this situation.

To begin with, family loyalty aside, I would not send you someone I didn't think would make a great employee for you. The fact is, **Name** is a bright, eager young man, who is just about to graduate from **University** with a major in **subject** and **grade-point average**. He has spent three summers interning at **Name of company**, and they will furnish any references you need. Finally, you just can't help liking **Name**.

So, in this case it wasn't very difficult for me to break my pledge. I've taken the liberty of telling **Name** to give you a call next week. I hope that you'll be willing to set up an interview with him. You'll both enjoy the meeting.

Best regards,

Dear **Name**:

It's true, we can't choose our family, and I'm sure we all have relatives we wish would—well—sort of disappear.

But sometimes we get lucky. That's the case with my nephew, **Name**. I couldn't have picked a finer young man.

He is just about to graduate from **University** with a degree in **subject area** and a grade-point average up in the stratosphere. He has already gained a good deal of practical experience by working summers at **Name of company**, and I am confident that you would both benefit by a meeting.

Would you be willing to set something up? **Name** can be reached at **telephone number**.

I know that you would enjoy talking with one another.

Sincerely,

LETTERS DECLINING REQUESTS FOR FAVORS

Jump Starts . . . to Get You on Your Way

I received your request for **favor**. Unfortunately, I am unable to comply with your request because . . .

I am sorry you will be unavailable for the meeting. Much as I would like to accommodate your schedule, I cannot ask **number** other participants to shift their schedules at the last minute.

I wish that I could accommodate your request for early delivery of **product**, but I'm afraid I cannot.

We pride ourselves on going that extra mile for our customers, but there are some things even we find impossible.

Thank you for your recent inquiry about the availability of **name of product** in a modified form.

I wish I could be of more help concerning your request for **favor**.

Cannot Change Meeting Location

Dear **Name**:

I received your note asking for a change in the site of our scheduled meeting.

Unfortunately, with space in this city at a premium, we had to make the arrangements for the meeting well in advance and secure them with a cash guarantee. At that, we were able to do this only after coordinating plans with **number** participants, who have now all agreed to the meeting site.

For these reasons, I'm sorry to say that we cannot accommodate your request for a change of location. I trust that you will understand our position and that this does not cause you any great inconvenience. If there is anything else we can do to make things easier for you, please call me at **telephone number**.

Sincerely yours,

Dear **Name**:

We received your request asking that we change the site of our scheduled meeting from **site** to **site**.

While you make some very good points, at this late date it is, unfortunately, impossible to move the meeting. You can appreciate the difficulty of coordinating the schedules and travel arrangements of some **number** participants. A change at this time would be an unfair hardship on the majority of our members.

I invite you to join our convention site selection committee for next year's meeting, so that we might have the benefit of your insight and advice before site decisions are made.

Sincerely yours,

Cannot Change Meeting Time

Dear **Name**:

Thanks for your note requesting a change in the time of our scheduled meeting.

I wish that I could accommodate your request, but, unfortunately, the other participants in the meeting—all **number** of them—have agreed on the time and have arranged their schedules accordingly. I can't ask them all to make revisions at this late date.

I am confident that you will understand the position I'm in, and I hope that you can reschedule any conflicting event so that you can attend the meeting. I look forward to seeing you.

Sincerely,

Dear **Name**:

I was sorry to hear that you may not be able to attend our upcoming meeting because of a scheduling conflict. I am also sorry to say that I cannot accommodate your request to change the meeting date. While it is my policy to be flexible, we are talking about coordinating the schedules of **number** participants, all of whom have by now made their plans accordingly. It would be unfair—not to say impractical—for me to ask them to alter their plans at this late date.

If it is at all possible, might I suggest that you juggle your schedule—or perhaps send a trusted deputy to the meeting?

Sincerely yours,

Cannot Make Early Delivery

Dear **Name**:

I wish that I could accommodate your request for early delivery of **product**, but I'm afraid I cannot.

As soon as you asked me to push the delivery date up from **original date** to **requested date**, I called our suppliers. Two were able to make the accelerated schedule, but two, unfortunately, were not—not for love or (it turns out) money. As you know, if *we* can't get what we need earlier, we can't deliver to *you* earlier.

Do be assured that we will shave off whatever time we can, and with expedited shipping we should be able to save at least **number** days. But that is about the best we can do.

Please call me at **telephone number** if you have any other ideas or suggestions.

Sincerely,

Dear **Name**:

We appreciate opportunities to give our customers special service. However, I am unable to expedite shipment of your order (number **number**) for delivery before **date**.

This is our busiest season, and, to make matters more difficult, we have been left temporarily short-handed due to the illness of a number of our employees. We are working on an overtime schedule as it is, and we will do everything possible to shave some time off your shipping date—but I do not want to make you promises I cannot keep.

I will call as soon as I can give you a firm revised date. I appreciate your understanding in this matter.

Sincerely,

Cannot Alter Payment Schedule

Dear **Name**:

Thank you for your recent inquiry about modifying the payment schedule on your account (number **number**). Unfortunately, we are not in a position to oblige you at this time, since the prices we agreed upon were based on the payment schedule currently in force.

We appreciate your understanding in this matter.

Sincerely,

Dear **Name**:

I have received and reviewed your proposal for an altered schedule of payments on your account (number **number**). We at **Name of company** take pride in working to accommodate our customers' needs. However, my records show that we have twice before modified this payment schedule at your request. To make a further modification would cause us unfair financial hardship, and, therefore, I cannot agree to the proposal.

Please continue to render payment in accordance with the schedule currently in force.

Sincerely yours,

Cannot Modify Product

Dear **Name**:

Thank you for your recent inquiry about the availability of **name of product** in a modified form.

Cost conditions will not permit us to make the modifications you requested on an order of fewer than **number** units. We suggest two alternatives: You could reconsider the quantity of your order. An order of **number** or more units would justify the expense we incur in making the modifications you request. Or might consider **number** other products we offer, **list**, which incorporate most of the features encompassed by the modifications you requested.

Why not give me a call at **telephone number** to discuss these options?

Sincerely,

Dear **Name**:

Your inquiry about the availability of **name of product** in a modified form was sent to me for response.

Unfortunately, the cost of making the modifications you request would be prohibitive—for you as well as for us. In reviewing what you are asking for, however, I have come to the conclusion that another model we offer, **name and model number**, should suit your purposes very well and at a most reasonable price. I am enclosing a brochure on **name and model number**, which I invite you to examine. Please give me a call at **telephone number** if you would like to discuss the item. I would also be happy to arrange for a demonstration.

Sincerely yours,

Cannot Fill Order for Odd Lot

Dear Customer:

Thank you for your recent order.

Please note that the minimum order is **number** units. We are unable to fill orders for odd lots below this minimum.

Please advise us as to whether we should ship and bill for **number** units or cancel your order.

You may reply by telephone at **telephone number** or by fax at **fax number**.

Sincerely,

Dear **Name**:

Your order of **date** for **quantity and item(s)** was referred to me for review because it is well below our required minimum order.

Unfortunately, we cannot fill an order for an odd lot of this size. The smallest regular order we can fill is **quantity and item(s)**. Would you like me to modify your order accordingly?

Please reply by telephone or fax at the numbers listed above.

Sincerely yours,

Cannot Provide Special Service

Dear **Name**:

I received your request for **special service**. Unfortunately, we are unable to offer the service you have requested. I can suggest **number** alternatives:

1. alternative

2. alternative

3. alternative

I hope that one of these other services will meet your needs. Please call me to discuss them or if you have any questions.

Sincerely,

Cannot Provide Service Requested

Dear **Name**:

In reply to your request for a bid on **name of service requested**, I'm sorry to report that our firm no longer offers that service.

We do offer the following alternatives, which I would be happy to discuss with you:

1. alternative

2. alternative

3. alternative

You can call me directly at **telephone number**.

Sincerely,

Dear **Name**:

No company likes to turn down business, but I'm afraid we have to. **Name of company** no longer offers **name of service requested**. I can suggest the following alternatives:

list

If none of these suits you, I suggest that you contact **Name** at **Name of company**. That firm may still offer what you request.

I do hope that we can be of service on another occasion—and soon!

Sincerely yours,

Chapter Four

Working with Clients and Customers: Credit and Collections

Step by Step . . . to What's Best for You

In this section you will find letters to help you provide—and to decline—credit to firms and individuals. You will also find an extensive series of collection letters.

Letters acting positively on a customer's credit application are good news and, therefore, fun to write. Take the opportunity to welcome your customer warmly. When you need to write a letter providing less credit than requested, accent the positive and, if at all possible, offer the possibility of an increase at some later, but definite, date or when some set of defined conditions is met.

Of course, rejecting applications is harder. The object is to reject the application without losing the customer. It is, naturally, difficult to accent the positive in these cases, but there are varying degrees of rejection. If possible, offer the hope of reconsideration at some later, but definite time or when some set of conditions is met. If there is no hope, try to strike a tone of firm apology. The rejection, after all, is not your fault, but you want to turn down the credit application without rejecting the customer. Make it clear that you look forward to serving the customer on a cash-with-order basis.

Many volumes have been written on the art of collections and on collection letters. The letters offered here all have one thing in common: Their object is not to threaten or to present a righteous demand. Instead, they are aimed at creating the conditions, the mindset, that will enable the customer to pay you. You may harbor the angry belief that the deadbeat to whom you have just mailed a fourth past due notice does not want to pay you. Here is surprising news: Almost always, even the deadest deadbeat very much *wants* to settle his account—assuming, of course, he does not dispute the amount due and is satisfied with the service or merchandise he has received. I am not saying that the delinquent account wants to part with money. It is not so much that he wants to *pay* you as that he does not want to *owe* you. Looked at from this perspective, the most effective collection letters have as their object the creation of a "win-win" situation: You get your money, and your reader has lifted from his shoulders the cruel burden of debt.

Letters Providing Credit

The letter responding to a credit application should include:

1. Thanks for the application.

2. Acknowledgment of the value of credit with your firm ("our distin-guished family of credit customers").

3. Assurance of efficient and careful processing of the application. If possible, tell the customer how long the process is likely to take.

4. Request additional information, if needed.

5. Close with thanks.

If you reach a positive conclusion, send your new credit customer a letter of welcome. If it is necessary to impose special conditions or allow less credit than requested, state this clearly and explain fully.

1. Welcome the customer.

2. State terms, either confirming all that the customer had requested or setting limits.

3. Thank the customer and mention that you are looking forward to doing business with her.

Letters Denying Credit

Letters rejecting applications should not begin with an apology, but with thanks.

1. Thank the customer for his application.

2. State the rejection.

3. If possible and appropriate, offer hope for reconsideration at a definite time or when certain definite conditions are met.

4. Make it clear that your customer is valuable to you and that you look forward to doing business with him. Assure him of great service (i.e., that he will not be treated like a "second-class citizen").

5. Close with thanks for his understanding.

The most effective collection letters are thought of as a series, beginning with a gentle and friendly reminder (often tinged with humor) and escalating in firmness of tone until credit and legal action are introduced as options. Avoid vague threats. Each action you propose should be well within the confines of accepted business practice. The general form of the individual collection letter is as follows:

1. Reminder: Your bill—state relevant dates and amounts—is overdue.

2. We understand that payments are overlooked from time to time.

3. To continue to provide the high level of service our customers deserve, we need to receive payment on time.

4. Please pay.

5. Thanks for your cooperation.

LETTERS PROVIDING CREDIT (FIRMS)

Jump Starts . . . to Get You on Your Way

Thank you for applying for a line of credit with **Name of company**.

I am delighted to respond to your application for credit with us.

In order for us to complete the processing of your recent credit application, we ask that you furnish the following additional information:

I am delighted to extend to you a credit line of **$ amount** subject to the following terms:

Welcome to our distinguished family of credit customers!

We are pleased to respond to your application for credit with **Name of company** by extending to you a credit line of **$ amount**, subject to the following special terms:

I am pleased to respond to your application for credit. At this time, we are prepared to extend an initial line of credit in the amount of **$ amount**.

Thank you for your application for credit with **Name of company**. Unfortunately, we are unable to accommodate you at this time because of **state reasons**.

Thanks for Application

Dear **Name**:

Thank you for applying to **Name of company** for inclusion in our distinguished family of credit customers. Please be assured that your application will be processed as quickly as careful consideration permits.

We expect to have reached a decision by **date**, and we will notify you by telephone at that time.

Thanks again for your interest in **Name of company**.

Sincerely yours,

Dear **Name**:

We have received your application for credit with **Name of company**. Please bear with us while we review the application so that we may serve you most effectively. The process usually takes about **time period**.

We appreciate your application and your interest in **Name of company**.

Sincerely yours,

Stating Policies

Dear **Name**:

Thank you for your recent inquiry about our retail trade credit and discount policy.

We offer extended terms according to the following schedule:

> 120 days at 1.5 percent
> 180 days at 3.0 percent
> 240 days at 5.0 percent
> 365 days at 8.0 percent

You are billed every 30 days, and this offer is applicable to purchases of $150 or more.

Shipments to stores receive a 46 percent discount. Prepay the first 60 days' charges and freight is free.

We have enclosed a credit application. Please call us at **telephone number** if you have any questions.

Sincerely yours,

Dear **Name**:

I am pleased to enclose our detailed schedule of our trade and discount policies. You will find that they are, if anything, considerably more liberal than industry standard.

Please look over the schedule at your leisure, and give me a call if you have any questions.

For your convenience, I have enclosed a credit application form.

Thanks for your interest in **Name of company**.

Sincerely,

Requesting Financial Information

Dear **Name**:

Many thanks for applying for a line of credit with **Name of company**. Please send us a complete copy of your most recent financial statement, together with **number** of credit references, preferably from firms with which you have maintained a line of credit for at least six months.

Please be assured that any information you send us will be kept in the strictest confidence. Once we have reviewed the requested documents, we will make every effort to expedite your application. Please call me at **telephone number** if you have any questions.

Sincerely yours,

Dear **Name**:

I am pleased to respond to your recent application for a line of credit with us. In order to act on your application I need a complete copy of your most recent financial statement and **number** of current credit references. Of course, all information we receive will be kept in the strictest confidence.

You will hear from me within **number** days after I have received the information requested. In the meantime, if you have any questions, please don't hesitate to call me at **telephone number**.

Sincerely yours,

Follow-up Requests for Financial Information

Dear **Name**:

On **date** we were pleased to receive your application for a line of credit with us, and we responded to it at that time by requesting your most recent financial statements. We are eager to process your application, but we have not yet received the financial information we requested.

Just as soon as we have received and reviewed your most recent financial statement, we will expedite your application. If you have any questions, please call us at **telephone number**.

Sincerely yours,

Financial Information Inadequate

Dear **Name**:

Thank you for responding so promptly to our request for the financial information we need to process your application for a line of credit with us at **Name of company**.

Please note that, while we requested financial statements for **periods**, you have furnished statements covering only **periods**. Please send us statements for **periods**, so that we can act on your application as quickly as possible.

If you have any questions, please call me at **telephone number**.

Sincerely yours,

Dear **Name**:

Thanks very much for your order dated **date** for **quantity** of our **merchandise**. We appreciate the business, especially from a brand-new customer. The **merchandise** will be shipped on **date**.

You indicated that you intend to order from us on a regular basis. I'm sure, then, that you will find it convenient to set up a line of credit. Let me ask a favor of you before we fill your next order. Please take a few moments now to send us a copy of your latest financial statement. We'll take a look at it and tell you what kind of credit line we can set up at this time.

I'd appreciate your mailing the statement today. Once again, thank you for your order.

Sincerely,

Honoring the Application

Dear **Name**:

I am delighted to respond to your application for credit by extending to you a **$ amount** line **subject** to the following terms: **state terms**.

If you have any questions regarding the amount, the terms, or anything else, don't hesitate to call me at **telephone number**.

I thank you for your business and look forward to your next order—indeed, to order after order!

Sincerely yours,

Dear **Name**:

Welcome to our family of credit customers!

We have completed our review of your application for a credit line with **Name of company**, and we are pleased to extend to you a credit line of **$ amount** on the following terms: **state terms**.

We trust that this will make doing business with us convenient and pleasurable, and we look forward to a long and mutually rewarding relationship.

If you have any questions concerning your new line of credit, please call me at **telephone number**.

Sincerely yours,

Honoring an Application—Conditionally

Dear **Name**:

Welcome to our family of credit customers!

We have completed our review of your application for a credit line with **Name of company**, and we are pleased to extend to you a credit line of **$ amount** on the following terms—**state terms**—provided that the unpaid balance on your account shall not exceed **$ amount** during the first year **or other period** following your initial order.

If you have any questions concerning your new line of credit, its terms and conditions, please call me at **telephone number**.

Sincerely yours,

Guarantor Required

Dear **Name**:

We have completed our review of your application for credit with us at **Name of company**, and we are pleased to tell you that we believe your company has bright prospects and a solid future. The fact is, however, that you have been in business only **period of time**, which means that we cannot—at this time—extend credit to you unconditionally.

We can, however, extend a line of credit in the amount of **$ amount** now provided that you secure a guarantor on the following conditions: **state conditions**.

We hope that you will find this offer helpful, and if you have any questions concerning it, please call me at **telephone number**.

Sincerely yours,

Business References Required

Dear **Name**:

Thank you for your application for a line of credit with **Name of company**.

I am happy to say that what you've sent us looks very good indeed. The only additional items we require to complete our review of your application are references from **number** firms with which you regularly do business on a credit basis. For each reference, please provide the name of the firm, the name of the person whom we should contact, his or her title, and the length of your association with the firm.

I look forward to hearing from you.

Sincerely yours,

Setting Limits

Dear **Name**:

I am pleased to respond to your application for credit. At this time, we are prepared to extend to you a **$ amount** line subject to **terms**. Your financial statements reveal a healthy and maturing business, which, we believe, has a promising future. However, we must weigh this against the fact that you have been in business less than two years **or other period**. Immediately after **date**, when you have crossed that two-year mark, let's review your updated financials. If you keep doing as well as your current statements indicate, I am confident that we can fatten the line of credit to your satisfaction.

In the meantime, I hope you find our present offer helpful. We appreciate your business and look forward to your next order.

Sincerely,

Dear **Name**:

Thank you for your application for a credit line of **$ amount**. I am pleased to set up for you a line of **lesser $ amount** at this time. I wish that circumstances would permit me to oblige with the full amount you requested, but your recent financial statements indicate that you are presently too heavily obligated for us to add to your burden beyond **$ amount**.

I hope that what we can offer now will be helpful to you, and I urge you to send us your next quarter's **or other period** financial statement, which we can review (together with your payment record, of course), with an eye toward increasing the credit line just as soon as we can.

We are grateful for your continued business, and I invite you to call me at **telephone number** if you have any questions.

Sincerely,

Dear **Name**:

It gives me great pleasure to establish a **$ amount** credit line for you, subject to the following terms: **state terms**.

I trust this will make doing business with us more convenient. After we've had some more experience together, I will be happy to review your financial statements again with an eye toward increasing your line of credit.

I look forward to a long and mutually profitable relationship.

Sincerely,

PROVIDING CREDIT (INDIVIDUALS)

Jump Starts . . . to Get You on Your Way

Thank you for applying for a credit account with **Name of company**. We will process your request as quickly as possible.

We regard customer credit as one of our most important products.

Thank you for your recent inquiry regarding credit with our firm. I have enclosed a brief application form, together with a full description of the terms and policies we offer.

It gives me great pleasure to welcome you as one of our credit customers.

Welcome! I am happy to inform you that your request for a credit account with **Name of company** has been approved, subject to the following terms and conditions:

Thanks for Application

Dear **Name**:

Thank you for applying for a credit account with **Name of company**. Please be assured that we will process your request as quickly as sound business practice permits. As a rule, this takes about **time period**.

We are grateful for your business and your interest in establishing a credit account with us.

Sincerely,

Stating Policies

Dear **Name:**

At **Name of company**, we regard customer credit as one of our most important products. The credit relationship is one of mutual value and trust. Accordingly, we have, over the years, formulated a set of credit policies we believe is fair and conducive to your profit and ours. These policies are summarized in the enclosed brochure that accompanies our credit application form. Please give me a call at **telephone number** if you have any questions concerning our policies.

Sincerely yours,

Requesting Financial Information

Dear **Name:**

Thank you for your recent inquiry regarding the establishment of a credit account with **Name of company**. I have enclosed our brief application form, which asks you to furnish such financial information as the credit accounts you presently hold, where you do your banking, and whom you would like us to contact as personal credit references. If you have any questions concerning the application form, please call me at **telephone number**.

Please be assured that all information you supply is kept in the strictest confidence and that we will do all in our power to expedite your application.

Sincerely yours,

Follow-up Request for Financial Information

Dear **Name:**

This morning I was reviewing some of our recent credit applications and discovered that we have yet to act on yours because some information is missing from the application—specifically, the names of three personal credit references.

We here at **Name of company** are eager to serve you and to offer you the convenience of a credit account. Furnishing the references will enable us to complete our review of your application.

If you have any questions, please call me at **telephone number**.

Sincerely yours,

Financial Information Inadequate

Dear **Name**:

Thank you for your application for a credit account with **Name of company**. In order to complete our review of your application, we need the following additional information: **information required**.

Once we have received this information, be assured that we will complete the processing of your application as quickly as sound business practice permits. Please call me at **telephone number** if you have any questions.

Thank you for your interest in **Name of company**.

Sincerely yours,

Honoring the Application

Dear **Name**:

Welcome!

I am pleased to welcome you to our distinguished family of **Name of company** credit customers. Your account is now officially opened and is on file at the store. You may begin using it immediately.

We trust you will find your account with us to be a great convenience. Certainly, it will be our pleasure to serve you.

If you have any questions about your account—now or in the future— please call me directly at **telephone number**.

Again, welcome.

Sincerely yours,

Honoring the Application—Conditionally

Dear **Name**:

I am pleased to notify you that your request for a credit account with **Name of company** has been approved subject to the following conditions:

list.

The enclosed credit agreement includes the conditions stated above. If the agreement and these conditions are acceptable to you, please sign the agreement form where indicated and return it to me in the addressed envelope enclosed.

If you have any questions concerning the agreement or the conditions, please call me at **telephone number**.

On behalf of all of us at **Name of company**, let me welcome you to our select group of credit customers. We look forward to serving you.

Sincerely yours,

Personal Reference(s) Required

Dear **Name:**

Thank you for your recent application for credit with us. Because you are so new to the community of **Name of community**, we ask that you furnish us with the names, addresses, and telephone numbers of three individuals with whom you have or have had credit dealings or who have known you personally for at least **number** years. We would like to contact these individuals for personal references on your behalf. Once we have done so, we can speedily complete the processing of your application.

Thank you for supplying this information.

Sincerely yours,

Guarantor Required

Dear **Name:**

Thank you for applying for credit with **Name of company**. Because you have moved so recently to our community and have been employed in your present position for less than **number** months, we can accommodate you at this time only on condition that you provide an acceptable guarantor to cosign our credit agreement with you. I have enclosed the necessary form for the guarantor to complete. Please ask him or her to return it to us in the enclosed envelope.

Please call me at **telephone number** if you have any questions.

Sincerely yours,

Setting Limits

Dear **Name:**

On behalf of **Name of company**, I am very pleased to extend to you a revolving credit account with an initial credit limit of **$ amount**. We customarily review our credit accounts every **number** months. Based on your needs and our experience together, we will consider raising your credit limit at that time.

Welcome to the **Name of company** family of credit customers!

Sincerely yours,

LETTERS DENYING CREDIT (FIRMS)

Jump Starts . . . to Get You on Your Way

We are very pleased that you have asked us to set up a line of credit for future orders, and the financial statement you sent us suggests a very promising future. Unfortunately, since you have been in business less than a year **or other period**, we cannot establish a credit line for you at this time.

Thanks for your recent application for a line of credit with **Name of company**.

Your financial statement shows that you are too heavily obligated at present for us to add to your burden of credit debt.

Thank you for your recent application for a line of credit with **Name of company**. I am sorry that we cannot accommodate you at this time.

Thanks for applying for credit with **Name of company**. Your credit record shows a history of repeatedly slow payment, which makes it necessary to postpone action on your request for **time period**.

Thank you for your application for a line of credit with us. I am sorry to say that we have had to make a very difficult decision concerning your application.

In Business for Too Short a Time

Dear **Name**:

Many thanks for your recent order, which will be shipped on **date**.

We are very pleased that you have asked us to set up a line of credit for future orders, and the financial statement you sent us suggests a very promising future. Unfortunately, since you have been in business less than a year **or other period**, we cannot establish a credit line for you at this time.

I strongly urge you to reapply in **number** months, after we have had more experience with one another. Based on your current financials, I am confident that we will be in a position to establish a credit relationship at that time.

For now, please be assured that we will continue to give you great service on a cash-with-order basis.

Sincerely yours,

Too Many Current Obligations

Dear **Name**:

Thanks for your recent application for a line of credit with **Name of company**.

Your financial statement shows that you are too heavily obligated at present for us to add to your burden of credit debt. Therefore, we cannot accommodate you with a line of credit at this time.

I invite you to reapply whenever you feel that your asset-to-debt ratio has improved. We hope that will be soon, since we are eager to enroll you on our roster of credit customers.

In the meantime, please be assured that you will continue to receive great service from us on a cash-with-order basis.

Sincerely yours,

Poor Credit Record—History of Non-Payment

Dear **Name**:

It was gratifying to receive your order of **date** and to find that you are still interested in working with us. As you may recall, the last time you placed an order with us, we had a difficult time collecting payment and even called in a collection agency.

That, however, was **months or years** ago, and we recognize that conditions do change. We cannot, however, continue to extend credit to you on the basis of your original application. We ask that you send us a copy of your most recent financial statement and that you provide three current credit references so that we can evaluate your current credit position.

In the meantime, we would appreciate your payment in full, by check, for the current order. We will ship it promptly on receipt of payment.

Sincerely yours,

Dear **Name**:

Thank you for your recent application for a line of credit with **Name of company**. I am sorry that we cannot accommodate you at this time. Your credit record shows a history of non-payment, and, therefore, your application does not meet our criteria for inclusion among our credit customers.

Please be assured that we are pleased to serve you on a cash-with-order basis.

Sincerely yours,

Poor Credit Record—History of Slow Payment

Dear **Name**:

Thanks for applying for credit with **Name of company**. Your credit record shows a history of repeatedly slow payment, which, we feel, makes it necessary for us to postpone acting on your request for six months **or other time period**. This should give you time to catch up on your open accounts, and we will reevaluate your application at that time.

For now, of course, we are delighted to serve you on a cash-with-order basis.

Sincerely,

Bad Risk—Nature of Business

Dear **Name**:

Many thanks for applying for a line of credit with **Name of company**.

We have reviewed your application and have had to make a very difficult decision. After much discussion, we have concluded that the nature of your business, which is both seasonal and focused exclusively on a single service, places you outside our minimum criteria for inclusion among our credit customers.

While we regret that we cannot accommodate your credit request, we do want to assure you that we are eager to serve you on a cash-with-order basis.

Sincerely yours,

Bad Risk—Current Conditions

Dear **Name**:

Difficult times and difficult decisions, unfortunately, often go with doing business. Often also, the two go together.

The current depression in the market for **type of service/product** makes it inadvisable for us to accommodate your request for a line of credit with **Name of company** at this time.

Bad business conditions rarely endure, and there is every hope for an improvement in them. We invite you to reapply for credit with us in **number** months, at which time we will reassess the business climate in your area.

In the meantime, we trust that you will continue to do business with us on the customary cash-with-order basis.

Sincerely yours,

Bad Risk—Location

Dear **Name**:

Thank you for your application for a line of credit with us. I am sorry to say that we have had to make a very difficult decision concerning your application. The location of your business does not suggest that you will maintain the level of cash flow necessary for us to consider you for inclusion among our credit customers. Therefore, we cannot accommodate you at this time.

We hope, however, that our assessment is overcautious, and we invite you to reapply in **number** months, at which time we will reevaluate your business.

In the meantime, we trust that you will continue to do business with us on the customary cash-with-order basis.

Sincerely yours,

Bad Risk—Volatility of Market

Dear **Name**:

Thank you for your application for a line of credit with us. As I am sure you are aware, your business is involved in a highly volatile market. This, combined with your present level of capitalization, has put your application beyond our customary criteria for credit customers, and, I'm sorry to say, we cannot accommodate you at this time.

At such time as you feel that your capital position has improved and/or that the market has stabilized, we invite you to reapply for credit with us. In the meantime, we trust that you will continue to do business with us on the customary cash-with-order basis.

Sincerely yours,

LETTERS DENYING CREDIT (INDIVIDUALS)

Jump Starts . . . to Get You on Your Way

Thank you for your application for a credit account. However, I am sorry to tell you that we cannot accommodate you at this time.

Many thanks for applying for a credit account with **Name of company**. We would like to oblige you, but we cannot at this time.

Poor Credit Record—History of Non-Payment

Dear **Name**:

Thank you for your application for a credit account.

I am sorry to tell you that we cannot accommodate you at this time. A review of your credit records shows a number of open accounts, including accounts for which collection proceedings have been initiated.

We value your business, and you may rest assured that we will continue to give you our very best service on a cash-with-order basis.

Sincerely yours,

Poor Credit Record—History of Slow Payment

Dear **Name**:

Thank you for your application for a credit account with **Name of company**.

Our review of your credit records shows a history of significantly slow payment on a number of current accounts. This places your application outside of our criteria for inclusion among our credit customers at this time.

We do recognize that times change and situations improve. We invite you to reapply for credit with us after **number** months, when you have had time to catch up on your slow-pay accounts.

In the meantime, we greatly value your business, and you may rest assured that we will continue to give you our very best service on a cash-with-order basis.

Sincerely yours,

Too Many Current Obligations

Dear **Name**:

Thank you for your application for a credit account with **Name of company**. I am sorry to have to tell you that we cannot accommodate you at this time. Your application indicates that, at present, you are heavily obligated, and I do not wish to add another account to that burden.

I invite you to reapply with us when you have paid down some of your outstanding obligations and can more reasonably take on additional debt.

In the meantime, we greatly value your business, and you may rest assured that we will continue to give you our very best service on a cash-with-order basis.

Sincerely yours,

COLLECTION LETTERS—FROM FIRST REMINDER TO WARNING OF LEGAL ACTION

Jump Starts . . . to Get You on Your Way

Have you overlooked our invoice?

Enclosed is a duplicate of our **date** invoice.

Your account balance of **$ amount** is still unpaid.

I thought that you would appreciate a reminder that your account with us has now passed the 30-day mark, which is the limit of our net terms.

We need your help. Your account is now 90 days **or other period** past due.

Just a note to bring to your attention the fact that your account with us is now past due.

I'm not worried. Just send us another order, and we'll ship it out as fast as we always do.

When a terrific customer like you lets a payment go past due, there's always a good reason.

This isn't the first time you've let your account with us pass the 60-day mark.

We all know how easy it is to mislay a bill.

It has been two weeks since we sent you a reminder about your open balance with us.

This is the fourth notice we have sent you concerning the unpaid balance of **$ amount** on your account with us.

Our legal department has advised me to act without delay and begin proceedings to collect the balance due on your account.

I would rather work with you to collect the balance due on your account, than have our lawyers work against you in court.

All-purpose Collection Series (Business)

First Reminder

Dear **Name**:

No doubt you have mislaid our invoice of **date**. We have enclosed another copy. Won't you mail us a check in the enclosed return envelope?

Sincerely,

Second Reminder

Dear **Name**:

Enclosed is another duplicate of our **date** invoice.

Please note that your payment is 15 days beyond our 30-day terms. We therefore anticipate your immediate payment.

Sincerely,

Third Reminder

Dear **Name**:

Your account balance of **$ amount** is still unpaid.

As we have heard nothing from you on this matter, we assume that you do not dispute the bill. Therefore, we ask that you pay the balance immediately.

Sincerely,

Fourth Letter

Dear **Name**:

You now have our monthly statements for **month, month, month** and **month**. We have attempted to reach you by telephone three times, on **date, date,** and **date**.

We have yet to receive a response, let alone a payment.

We value and appreciate your business and ask that you communicate with us on this matter. If you have a problem with the merchandise you received or with your finances, please let us know. We'll do our best to help.

Please let us hear from you so that we can understand the problem and work with you to resolve it. A phone call or letter from you today will help us both.

Sincerely,

Fifth Letter

Dear **Name**:

Our legal department has advised us to act without delay to collect the balance you owe us. We would rather not resort to such measures, but, as we have received no response to our letters or our phone calls, we may have no alternative.

Please send us your payment in full immediately or, at least, a partial payment with a note of explanation and a proposal for future payments. We would greatly prefer to work *with* you to resolve this matter rather than work with our lawyers *against* you.

Your immediate response is required.

Sincerely,

Final Letter

Dear **Name**:

Despite five letters and numerous phone calls regarding your unpaid balance of **$ amount**, we have had no reply from you.

We will delay legal action for another ten days **or other period** in final anticipation of your immediate response.

Sincerely,

New Customer (Business)

First Reminder

Dear **Name**:

I'm pleased to welcome you to our family of discriminating customers. I thought that you would appreciate a reminder that your account with us has now passed the 30-day mark, which is the limit of our net terms.

Won't you please take a few moments today to direct your Accounts Payable desk to send us a check for **$ amount**?

I appreciate your attention to this matter.

Sincerely yours,

Second Reminder

Dear **Name**:

As you do more business with us, you will find that we strive always to live up to our guarantee of prompt, personal service at the lowest possible price. Maintaining our high standards and low prices requires a commitment from us and cooperation from our customers.

Without special arrangements, we cannot afford to carry unpaid accounts beyond our 30-day **or other period** terms. Your account is now past due 60 days **or other period**.

Please help us maintain the service and prices that brought you to us in the first place. Send us a check for **$ amount** today.

If there is any problem with the bill or the merchandise, or if you are experiencing any other difficulties, please call me at **telephone number**. I'd like to help.

Sincerely,

Third Reminder

Dear **Name**:

We need your help.

Your account is now 90 days **or other period** past due. In order to continue delivering to you the high level of service and attention you deserve, it is necessary that we receive your check in the amount of **$ amount** now.

Please mail it in the enclosed return envelope today.

If there is any problem, we would like to help. So please call us at **telephone number** today.

Your cooperation is both absolutely necessary and greatly appreciated.

Sincerely,

Regular Customer—Previously Reliable (Business)

First Reminder

Dear **Name**:

Just a note to bring to your attention the fact that your account with us is now past our 30-day terms.

Won't you please point this out to your Accounts Payable desk and have a check in the amount of **$ amount** sent out today?

We appreciate it.

Sincerely,

Second Reminder

Dear **Name**:

I'm not worried. Just send us another order, and we'll ship it out as fast as we always do. But it does take cash to pay our bills, and I'm writing you (for the second time) to remind you that your account is now 60 days past due.

Please help us out by sending your check for **$ amount** today. If there is any problem at all, why not let us help you? Just give me a call at **telephone number**.

Sincerely

Third Letter

Dear **Name**:

When a valued longtime customer like you lets a payment go past due, there's always a good reason: sickness, a cash flow squeeze, dissatisfaction with goods or services. Now that your account is passing the 90-day **or other time period** mark, isn't it time that you let us in on the reason?

We've worked together for a long time. I am sure there is no problem that we cannot solve together. Please let me hear from you.

Sincerely,

Regular Customer—History of Payment Problems (Business)

First Reminder

Dear **Name**:

It is always our pleasure to serve you, and we thank you kindly for your continued business.

However, as the enclosed statement indicates, your account is now approaching the 30-day mark. May we remind you that all of our charges are payable upon receipt? It would be a great help to us if you would send a check today for the full balance due or, at least, let us know when you will be sending payment.

Sincerely yours,

Second Reminder

Dear **Name**:

This isn't the first time you've let your account with us pass the 60-day mark, and it isn't the first letter we've written you about it.

Don't get us wrong. We appreciate your business, and want to keep doing business with you. But please take note that the low prices we provide you are made possible by careful cash flow management. This means that we simply cannot afford to carry accounts beyond the 30-day net term period.

Please help us maintain our high level of service and our low prices by settling your account today.

If you have any questions or comments, please call me directly at **telephone number**.

Sincerely,

Third Letter

Dear **Name**:

I'm writing a third letter regarding your account, which is now 90 days past due, not because I'm afraid you won't pay—we've worked together long enough for me to know that you always pay your bills—but because we literally cannot afford to do business on these extended terms.

The problem is simple: We sold you **name of product/services** at the best possible price we could offer—*based on 30-day terms*. Had we made our deal based on 60- or 90-day terms, your cost would have been proportionately higher.

It's only fair.

Please help us now by settling your account today.

Sincerely yours,

All-purpose Collection Series (Individual)

First Reminder

Dear **Name**:

If you're like us, you've learned that it's all too easy to misplace an invoice or a bill. We sent you our statement on **date** for payment by **date**. Here's a copy.

Won't you please mail us a check in the return envelope?

Sincerely yours,

Second Reminder

Dear **Name**:

It has been two weeks since we sent you a reminder about your open balance with us. Enclosed is another duplicate of our **date** invoice.

Since payment is now **number** days past due, we anticipate your immediate payment.

A return envelope is provided for your convenience.

Sincerely yours,

Third Reminder

Dear **Name**:

Please take note that your account balance of **$ amount** is still unpaid.

It was due on **date**.

We have heard nothing from you on this matter, so we must assume that you do not dispute the bill and that you are satisfied with the merchandise. We therefore ask you to pay the balance due immediately.

Sincerely yours,

Fourth Letter

Dear **Name**:

This is the fourth notice we have sent you concerning the unpaid balance of **$ amount** on your account with us.

We have telephoned you on **dates**. We have written you on **dates**.

You have not responded.

We value your business and would like to do everything in our power to assist you in settling your account. But, in order for us to help you, you must help us by responding to our communications.

Please call me directly at **telephone number** so that we can discuss your account.

Sincerely yours,

Fifth Letter

Dear **Name**:

When we presented your account to our legal department, we were advised to begin proceedings without delay.

We would rather do no such thing.

We would rather work *with* you to settle your account than employ our lawyers to work *against* you in this matter.

But we absolutely must hear from you. Please send us your payment today or, at least, a partial payment with a note proposing a plan for settling the balance. Or perhaps you would rather give me a call directly at **telephone number**.

Please, take the necessary steps to settle this account now.

Sincerely,

Sixth Letter

Dear **Name**:

You've put us both in a position that will soon leave neither of us much choice.

Within ten days, we are turning over your unpaid account to our attorneys. At that point, our options—yours and ours—become very limited.

There is still time to keep this matter from proceeding so far.

Please give me a call directly at **telephone number**. We can work together on a plan for settling your account.

Sincerely yours,

New Customer (Individual)

First Letter

Dear **Name**:

It is always a pleasure to welcome a new customer. I want to take this opportunity to welcome you—and to direct your attention to our invoice of **date**, payment for which was due on **date**.

We at **Name of company** strive to give you the best service at the very lowest price. This requires our maximum effort, of course, but also your cooperation. We cannot afford to carry accounts beyond the net terms to which we both agreed. Help us to maintain our great service and our competitive pricing by settling your account today.

A return envelope is enclosed.

Sincerely yours,

Second Letter

Dear **Name**:

As we suggested in our previous letter, we at **Name of company** depend and thrive on your cooperation. Paying your account within the **number**-day net period makes it possible for us to keep our standard of service high while saving you and your family hard-earned cash.

Help us keep delivering great service at a great price.

Please put a check for **$ amount** in the return envelope enclosed. Mail it today.

Sincerely yours,

Third Letter

Dear **Name**:

We take pride in delivering great service at a low price. It's a tough job that—quite frankly—you are making tougher.

Your account with us, in the amount of **$ amount**, is now **number** days past due. This is the third time we have informed you of the past-due status of your account, and it is the third time we have explained that our ability to deliver great service at a low price depends on our receiving payment within the net term period to which we agreed when you made your purchase.

Since you have not responded to our first two letters, we can only assume that you neither dispute the bill nor that you have a complaint about the merchandise. We ask, therefore, that you pay the balance due immediately.

Sincerely,

Regular Customer—Previously Reliable (Individual)

First Letter

Dear **Name**:

If you're like me, you get an awful lot of junk in the mail. It has gotten so bad that, sometimes, the important stuff goes right in the trash with the junk. Perhaps, then, you've misplaced our invoice of **date**.

In any case, payment was due on **date**, and I've enclosed a duplicate invoice. I'd appreciate your sending us a check in the return envelope today.

Sincerely yours,

Second Letter

Dear **Name**:

Enclosed is a second duplicate of our **date** invoice. Payment was due on **date**, and your unpaid balance stands at **$ amount**.

Please use the enclosed envelope to mail us a check today.

Sincerely yours,

Third Letter

Dear **Name**:

Frankly, I'm concerned. When a great customer like you is significantly late in settling an account, there is usually a very good and very serious reason: illness, a cash flow problem.

Your account balance of **$ amount** was due on **date**. We have sent you two letters, to which you have not replied. Please use the return envelope enclosed to send us your check today—or at least give me a call at **telephone number** so that we can work together to help you settle this account.

Sincerely yours,

Regular Customer—History of Payment Problems (Individual)

First Letter

Dear **Name**:

Perhaps you have mislaid our invoice of **date**. A payment of **$ amount** was due on **date**, and we have not yet received it.

To save you the trouble of searching for the original invoice, I've enclosed a duplicate. Please send us a check today in the enclosed return envelope.

Sincerely yours,

Second Letter

Dear **Name**:

We pride ourselves on giving you a fair deal: the best service at the lowest price we can possibly afford to extend. What we ask in return is fair deal from our customers. That means payment in full, as agreed, within **number** days.

Your account is now **number** days past due.

Let's be fair. Please send us a check in the enclosed envelope today.

Sincerely yours,

Third Letter

Dear **Name**:

We appreciate your business. We value your business. We need your business.

But we can't keep doing business with you this way.

Your account with us is past due **number** days in the amount of **$ amount**. Please use the return envelope enclosed to mail us a check for the full amount today.

If there is any difficulty or you have any questions, please call me at **telephone number**.

Sincerely yours,

Chapter Five

Working with Clients and Customers: Productive Adjustment Letters

Step by Step . . . to What's Best for You

Too often, business people look on adjustment letters with a kind of dread as exercises in damage control—something you do after the dam has sprung a leak, but before it crumbles into dust. Naturally, nobody likes to make mistakes or be the victim of a mistake. Nobody wants things to go wrong. It is also true that if I buy an Acme Slicer Dicer and it fails to slice and dice, I'm not going to be feeling too good about Acme, Inc., at the moment of failure. And I'll feel a whole lot worse if I ask Acme to make things right and they ignore me.

But that's only half the story. I don't like the fact that my Slicer Dicer didn't work, but, if I communicate with the company and someone in authority replies positively, telling me that Acme will stand behind its product and will do all it can to get me up and running again, I may still have reservations about the Slicer Dicer, but I will feel good about Acme, Inc.

Adjustment letters are not just an exercise in damage control. They are an opportunity to build and strengthen a good relationship with your customer. If the old salesman's adage—You don't sell a product, you sell yourself—has validity, then adjustment letters are a perfect chance to sell yourself, and your company, thereby turning a negative situation into a positive experience.

Letters Responding to Complaints and Claims

The initial response to a complaint must always communicate one thing—a desire and willingness to help the customer or client—and very often must also secure information from the customer before action can be taken.

1. Acknowledge receipt of the complaint or returned product.

2. Express sympathy or concern for the customer.

3. If you can act now, tell the customer what you propose to do and what he must do in order to make the adjustment possible (for example, take the product to the nearest authorized dealer). If you require more information or some other action on the part of the customer, explain it here ("In order to correct this problem as quickly as possible, we need . . . ").

4. Apologize, and thank the customer for his understanding.

Apologies

Perhaps the only thing harder to write than an adjustment letter is the letter of apology. Yet the same principle applies. Nobody likes to be wrong, and, therefore, nobody likes to be put in a position of having to apologize. However, most people actually welcome the opportunity to forgive. If it is true that "To err is human; to forgive, divine," then your apology can confer upon your reader an opportunity to be—for a moment, at least—something of a saint. It feels good.

1. Express concern.

2. Point out that the problem is an exceptional circumstance, that you value quality, and that you make substantial efforts to ensure quality.

3. Apologize for the error, the defect, or the inconvenience.

4. If appropriate, state the action you will take. Or close by assuring the reader that the error will not be repeated.

5. Thank the reader for her understanding and patience.

Letters Rejecting or Disputing Claims

Of course, many customer adjustment claims are invalid or without basis. In these cases, your task is to dispute or reject the claim without alienating the customer. These letters need to express concern for the customer without abrogating your own rights. The key is to explain the reasons for disputing or rejecting the claim without lecturing or admonishing.

1. State the subject of your letter ("I am replying to your letter . . . ").

2. State the rejection or dispute.

3. Give full reasons for the rejection or dispute. Be as detailed and explicit here as possible.

4. If at all possible, offer an alternative in order to preserve (or even generate) goodwill ("While we cannot make a full refund, we can offer you a 10 percent discount on a replacement part").

5. Do *not* apologize, but do express your regret that the customer experienced a problem.

6. Express the hope that the alternative you offer will be of assistance.

LETTERS RESPONDING TO COMPLAINTS AND CLAIMS

Jump Starts . . . to Get You on Your Way

I am responding to your letter of **date,** in which you complain about a problem with **name of product**.

Your letter of **date** was referred to me for immediate action.

I was sorry to hear that you are unhappy with the performance of **name of product**.

Our service department has just received the **name of product** you returned for warranty repair or exchange.

At **Name of company** our job is not done until you are completely satisfied.

Seeking Complete Information—Product Complaint

Dear **Name:**

I am responding to your letter of **date**, in which you complain of a problem with **name of product**.

I am very sorry to learn that you have experienced a difficulty with the product, and I am anxious to work with you to resolve the problem. In order to do so most quickly and effectively, I will need some more information. I ask that you take a moment to answer the following questions. For your convenience, you may jot the answers down right on this letter and return it to me in the enclosed envelope. Or you might want to take this letter to the telephone, call me directly at **telephone number**, and give me the answers over the phone.

- **Question 1**
- **Question 2**
- **Question 3**
- **Question 4**

I greatly appreciate your taking the time to help me help you. Be assured that I will make every effort to resolve your problem without delay and to your complete satisfaction.

Sincerely yours,

Dear **Name**:

Your complaint regarding **name of product** was referred to me for immediate action, and I am anxious to resolve your problem. To do this, I need some additional information regarding the nature of the problem you are experiencing. Please take a moment to answer the following questions. You need not reply in writing. Just take this letter to the phone and call me directly at **telephone number**.

- **Question 1**
- **Question 2**
- **Question 3**
- **Question 4**

Thanks for taking the time to help me assist you, and you may be certain that I will make every effort to get you and your **name of product** up and running.

Sincerely yours,

Seeking Complete Information—Service Complaint

Dear **Name**:

I was distressed to receive your letter of **date**, in which you point out a problem you experienced with **Name**, one of our sales representatives **or other position**. Before I speak at length to **Name**, I would like to have as much information as possible from you regarding the difficulty you experienced. Your comments of the following questions would greatly help me to understand and resolve the situation you have brought to my attention:

- **Question 1**
- **Question 2**
- **Question 3**

- **Question 4**

To save you further time and trouble, you may want to jot down your comments directly on this letter and return it to me in the enclosed envelope. Alternatively, if you wish, you may call me at **telephone number** with your comments.

We at **Name of company** pride ourselves on service. So it particularly distressed me to learn that your experience with us had been less than satisfactory. Please be assured that I will do everything in my power to see that you are completely satisfied.

Sincerely yours,

Dear **Name**:

Your letter of **date** regarding difficulty you experienced in dealing with a member of our technical service staff was referred to me for immediate response.

It is always a matter of great concern to me when—as sometimes happens—a customer is unhappy with the service he receives from us. Service, after all, is what we sell. You can appreciate, therefore, that I am anxious to get to the bottom of the dispute between you and **Name**. Before I speak to **Name**, however, I need clarification from you on the following points in your letter:

list

If you like, you may jot down your responses on the back of this letter and return it to me. Of, if you prefer, you may give me a call at **telephone number** so that we can discuss the matter.

I appreciate your taking the time to help me assist you and to help us make our technical service department the best in the business.

Sincerely yours,

Seeking Clarification—Product Complaint

Dear **Name**:

Our service department has just received the **product name** you returned for warranty repair or exchange. The trouble report you enclosed mentioned that the **part name** repeatedly malfunctioned. Problems with **part name** are very rare indeed, and our service technicians have tested the **product name** and have failed to discover any malfunction in the **part name**. In fact, the entire unit tested up to specifications.

I don't want to return a problem item to you, but I don't want to try to fix one that isn't broken. Since the **product name** won't "cough for the doctor," I ask that you give me a call at **telephone number** so that, before any action is taken, we can discuss the precise nature of the apparent failure and the circumstances under which this occurred.

I appreciate your effort to help us resolve this problem quickly so that you can enjoy using your **product name**.

Sincerely yours,

Dear **Name**:

Name in our customer support department referred your comments about your **name of product** to me for response.

At **Name of company** we take our customers' comments and complaints very seriously. Our job is not finished until you are completely happy with what you've purchased from us. For this reason, I am anxious to investigate your experience with **name of product** as thoroughly as possible. I need to determine

1. If **name of product** is operating per specifications.

2. If you are using **name of product** in the most effective manner.

3. What, if necessary, we can do to improve **name of product**.

In order to make these determinations, I need very complete information. Please take a few moments to fill out the enclosed Trouble Report

Form and return it to me at your earliest convenience. Be assured that I will respond to you further after I have reviewed the Report Form.

I appreciate your effort to help us help you to get the most out of your **name of product**

Sincerely,

Seeking Clarification—Service Complaint

Dear **Name of company:**

I am distressed, and I am confused.

I am distressed because, at **Name of company**, the customer's complete satisfaction has always been our top priority. When we fail to satisfy, we fail in our number one mission. I am anxious to take whatever steps are necessary to secure your satisfaction.

But I am confused, confused about the precise circumstances under which your difficulty occurred.

The only way I see to clear up my confusion—so that I can work with you to make you a satisfied customer—is to have a chat with you about the incident. Rather than disturb you with a phone call, I ask that you call me, using our toll-free number: **telephone number.**

A conversation will help me to help you achieve the satisfaction you deserve.

Sincerely yours,

Dear **Name:**

At **Name of company** our job is not done until you are completely satisfied. Your letter of **date** makes it clear that you are anything but satisfied.

I am very anxious to resolve your problem, to see to it that your experience with us is thoroughly satisfactory, and to be able to say that we have finished our job and finished it well. To do all this, I want to be certain that I fully understand the details of the problems you experienced. I ask, therefore, that you give me a call at your convenience to go over the incident. You may reach me on my direct line, **telephone number,** or, if you prefer, we can meet in my office over coffee. In either case, please give me a call.

Sincerely yours,

Assurance of Prompt Action

Dear **Name**:

I am sorry to learn of your difficulties with our **name of product**. I can work with you in two ways to resolve the problem:

1. I can send you a new **part name**, with instructions on how to replace the defective part.
2. Or you may return the entire unit to us, and we will replace the part and return the unit to you, together with reimbursement of your shipping costs.

The first alternative is faster, of course, and we believe the replacement procedure can be easily carried out by the customer. If you don't like to use a screwdriver, however, I suggest you take the second option.

Either way, we will make every effort to get you up and running again as quickly as possible. Just give me a call at **telephone number** to let me know how you would like to proceed.

We apologize for the inconvenience the defective part has caused you and thank you for your patience and understanding.

Sincerely yours,

Dear **Name**:

I have received your complaint concerning **name of product**. I am sending **Name**, one of our field representatives, to you within the month **week, etc**. He will call to set up an exact appointment date and time.

Please be assured that we will do whatever is necessary to resolve your problem quickly, fairly, and to your satisfaction.

Sincerely,

Assurance of Fair Action

Dear **Name**:

Name, president of our company, has asked me to reply to your letter of **date**, in which you describe a serious problem with **name of product**.

We understand that you are anxious for immediate action. We also wish to resolve the problem as quickly and effectively as possible. However, as you can appreciate, we are dealing with a complex situation that requires careful investigation. The following steps are necessary in order to determine the appropriate adjustment in your case:

- Step 1
- Step 2
- Step 3

Please be assured that we will proceed with our investigation as quickly as prudence and fairness permit in order to arrive at an adjustment equitable to all concerned.

Sincerely yours,

Dear **Name**:

Your letter of **date**, concerning a problem with **name of product**, has been referred to me for immediate response. Accordingly, I have initiated an investigation of your complaint. Please expect to hear from one of our field representatives within **time period**.

Like you, we are anxious to resolve this matter as quickly as considerations of prudence and fairness to all concerned will permit.

Sincerely yours,

APOLOGIES

Jump Starts . . . to Get You on Your Way

I was very unhappy to learn that the **name of product** you recently purchased from us was defective.

We have had excellent reports on **name of product**, so I am very distressed by the problem you have experienced.

When something goes wrong with one of our products, it's our job to get you up and running again as soon as possible.

Here's a brief story: On **date** you ordered **quantity and merchandise**. On **date** we shipped **different quantity and merchandise**. The wrong quantity of the wrong item. Here's the end of the story: We'll make it right.

I am sorry for the delay in your shipment.

Enclosed is my check for **$ amount**, together with my apologies for making the payment late.

This is a hard letter for me to write.

We try hard to keep our promises, and it hurts us—perhaps even as much as it hurts you—when we can't deliver.

Defective Product

Dear **Name**:

I was very unhappy to learn that the **name of product** you recently purchased from us was defective. We make every effort to ensure that merchandise reaches you in perfect condition—but even the best efforts are not always adequate.

Name of our Customer Service Department tells me that you have received a replacement. I trust that it will be free from defects and give you years of trouble-free service.

I apologize for the inconvenience you were caused, I thank you for your patience and understanding, and I invite you to call me at **telephone number** if you have any questions concerning **name of product** or any other matter.

Sincerely yours,

Dear **Name**:

The service and performance record of **name of product** is excellent, so it particularly disturbs me to learn of the difficulty you have experienced with this item.

Our customer service department has informed me that a replacement has been shipped to you. I am confident that you will experience no problems with it.

I am very sorry for any inconvenience you may have been caused, and, on behalf of **Name of company**, let me thank you for your patience and understanding.

Sincerely yours,

Faulty Service

Dear **Name**:

When something goes wrong with one of our products, it's our job to get you up and running again as soon as possible. When we fail to do that, we're well aware, we have really let you down. That's why I was very distressed to learn that the service we provided on **date** proved inadequate, and that's why I sent our senior service representative to your plant to make sure that—this time—there would not be another problem.

Name, I am very sorry for any inconvenience the problems with the unit and the servicing may have caused. I can only tell you that I am very grateful for your patience and understanding in this matter, and I want to assure you that such problems—both with our product and our service—are very rare indeed.

If you have any questions at all, please call me directly at **telephone number**.

Sincerely yours,

Dear **Name**:

I was pleased to learn that the difficulties you had with the service we performed on **name of product** have been resolved to your satisfaction. Of course, I am not pleased that you had a problem to begin with. We try to get things done right the first time. Sometimes we don't succeed.

On behalf of **Name of company**, thank you for your patience and understanding in this matter.

Sincerely,

Billing or Shipping Errors

Dear **Name**:

On **date** you ordered **quantity and product**. On **date** we promptly shipped **quantity and product**. The right quantity. The wrong item.

You called me about it, and although you had every right to be steamed, you were extraordinarily understanding and patient.

This note is an apology. It is also a thank you—for your goodwill in dealing with our mistake.

We will make every effort to ensure that your patience is not put to the test again.

Sincerely yours,

VIA FAX

Dear **Name**:

To err, they say, is human. Our human error offers you a golden opportunity to be divine and forgive us.

Here's the story.

On **date** you ordered **quantity and product**. We shipped the order promptly, only to discover that the boxes we shipped had been improperly labelled. Instead of the item you had ordered, the boxes contain **other item**.

We are shipping today the required quantity of the item you had ordered via air freight at our expense. We ask that you hold the original shipment at your dock and call us at **telephone number** so that we can arrange for a pick up.

We are very sorry to cause you the inconvenience of a handling hassle like this, and we are grateful for your understanding, patience, and cooperation.

Sincerely yours,

Delay

Dear **Name**:

In reviewing the paperwork for your recent order with us, I noticed that your shipment had been delayed by **time period**. Since we haven't heard from you concerning this, I am assuming that the delay caused you no undue inconvenience. Nevertheless, I want to take this opportunity to apologize for the delay, to thank you for your patience, and to assure you that we will do everything possible to prevent such delays in the future.

Sincerely yours,

For Slow Payment

Dear **Name**:

I enclose a check for **$ amount** in payment of your invoice number **number**. I also enclose my apology for sending the check later than either of us would have liked.

We have had some internal difficulties here, which are now resolved. Please be assured that all future invoices will be paid promptly, and please accept my thanks for your patience and understanding in this matter.

Sincerely yours,

Dear **Name**:

At long last, our check for **$ amount** is enclosed in payment of our account **number**.

I am very sorry that we're late with the payment. This was due to a number of internal problems here, which we have now resolved.

I thank you for the patience you have shown us, and I assure you that we will make all future payments on time.

Sincerely,

Missing a Deadline

Dear **Name**:

This is a very hard letter for me to write.

When we agreed to the deadline you proposed, we made a promise: to complete construction **or other procedure** by **date**. As you are all too aware, we were unable to keep that promise.

The sole cause of our being late was, it is true, beyond our control. Inclement weather or **other cause** made it impossible to push the work forward as quickly as necessary. Still, we take full responsibility for missing the deadline, and we hope you will accept one more promise from us: to do our very best to make up for lost time by devoting all available resources to completion of construction.

I deeply appreciate your understanding and your willingness to continue to work with us.

Sincerely,

Dear **Name**:

We try hard to keep our promises, and it hurts us—perhaps even as much as it hurts you—when we can't deliver. I am very sorry that we are unable to complete **name of project** by the scheduled deadline, and I am very grateful for your willingness to work with us to develop an alternative plan of completion.

Our proposed revision of the completion schedule is enclosed. I look forward to your response.

Sincerely,

Failure of a Project

Dear **Name**:

We've worked long and hard with you on **name of project**. I cannot tell you how disappointed all of us at **Name of company** are that the proposal we created together did not fly with **Name of mutual client**.

I can tell you at this point what I believe you already know: We gave the project everything we could, and we were all confident that we had produced an irresistible proposal. I am very sorry that the outcome proved us wrong.

I am sorry about that. But I am not sorry for having had the opportunity of working with you. I suggest that we take a next step. I suggest that we meet to review the proposal with an eye toward making the next one we do—and I am confident that we will try again—an unqualified success. I will give you a call next week to discuss a meeting.

Sincerely yours,

Dear **Name**:

Let's not give up. We're both disappointed after working so long and so hard on **name of project**, only to have the client take a pass. But one thing we both gained is the experience of working together. We may not have bagged a customer this time, but we've made a team. Let's not give up on that.

Best regards,

LETTERS REJECTING OR DISPUTING CLAIMS

Jump Starts . . . to Get You on Your Way

I am replying to your letter of **date**, in which you report damage to the **name of product** you purchased from us on **date**.

I am very sorry to learn that your Model 34 electric razor failed to operate after immersion in bath water. However, . . .

I am responding to your letter of **date**, in which you report that we shipped you the wrong item. I have enclosed a photocopy of your original order . . .

Your letter of **date** was referred to me for response.

I was sorry to hear that you are disappointed with the performance of your **name of product**. However, . . .

Your comments regarding **product name** have been brought to my attention.

Customer Error

Dear **Name**:

I am replying to your letter of **date**, in which you describe damage to a set of Superba dishware caused by your dishwasher. I am very sorry to hear about the damage, but, unfortunately, Superba cannot agree to your request for a refund. Warnings against attempting to wash fine Superba dishware in a dishwasher are clearly displayed on the exterior and interior shipping cartons and on a loose sheet inside each carton.

Superba not only makes no claim to dishwasher safety, but specifically and clearly warns against putting the dishware in a dishwasher.

While Superba cannot, therefore, make a full refund, I do want you to have the opportunity of enjoying our product. If you will return the damaged pieces to us, we will replace them at cost, according to the following schedule of prices:

list

We ask that you use the above list to determine your cost and enclose a check for that amount with the damaged pieces you are returning. We ask that you assume the responsibility for paying the cost of shipping the pieces to us, but we will pay the freight on the replacement shipment.

I hope this offer will be of help to you.

Sincerely,

Dear **Name**:

I am very sorry to learn that your Model 560 electric motor now fails to operate since you attempted to run it on alternating current. However, Voltaic Industries cannot accept responsibility for the damage to your motor, since the specification sheet and warning labels clearly indicate that the device operates on direct current only and that alternating current will destroy the coils.

Although we cannot be held responsible for damage caused by improper use of the Model 560, we can offer to repair the motor, including replacing the armature coil, at our cost: $54.50 for the part and $25 for labor, plus $4.50 shipping. The total cost to you will be $84.00. Alternatively, you may take the unit to any of our factory-authorized dealers for repair at a somewhat higher cost. In either case, your warranty (which does not cover damage caused by improper use) will remain in force.

Sincerely yours,

Following Customer's Orders

Dear **Name**:

I am responding to your letter of **date**, in which you state that you ordered model number 1234 but received model 2345 and are, therefore, requesting an exchange.

I have enclosed a photocopy of your original order specifying model 2345. The error, as you can see, was not ours.

Unfortunately, since model 2345 is an item we custom make only in response to an order, I cannot simply exchange it for model 1234. I can, however, make the following offer: Return your model 2345, and we will give you **$ amount** credit toward the purchase of model 1234.

Alternatively, of course, you may very well wish to keep the merchandise you have. It should serve your needs as well as our model 1234 would.

I hope you find these suggestions helpful.

Sincerely,

Dear **Name**:

Your letter of **date** was referred to me for response. I am, of course, distressed that your husband does not like the color of the carpeting you ordered. Unfortunately, his displeasure does not warrant a refund or free reinstallation from us. You placed the order and specified the color and style we supplied. That agreement included no third-party approval.

I can offer you an excellent price on new carpeting, if you wish, and our crew will remove the present carpeting at no charge. Alternatively, perhaps you will succeed in convincing your husband that you have made a superb choice in color and have installed the best carpeting in the business.

Sincerely yours,

Missed Deadline—Unavoidable Circumstances

Dear **Name**:

Name in our shipping department has asked me to respond to your letter of **date**, in which you ask for a refund of the expedited shipping fee you paid for your order number **number**. Your letter mentions that the shipment reached you within five days of your order instead of the promised three.

Please note that the entire region was hit by crippling snowstorms during the period of **date** to **date**, which grounded all flights out of **Name** Airport, making it impossible to meet the three-day deadline. Since the weather is beyond our control, and since the five-day shipping time still represents an expedited turnaround (the usual shipping time is eight days), we do not feel that a refund is appropriate. We trust that, under the circumstances, you will appreciate our position and understand our decision.

Sincerely yours,

Dear **Name**:

I have received your letter of **date** requesting the payment of a **$ amount** penalty in compensation for our having missed the deadline specified in our agreement of **date**.

While I greatly regret our having delivered late and fully appreciate the inconvenience this must have caused you, I must also direct your attention to the *force majeure* clause in our agreement. This exempts us from meeting the specified deadline in cases of certain unavoidable circumstances. The fire that swept our offices is one such instance specifically governed by the clause, and I informed you at the time of the disaster that we would likely miss the deadline on account of it.

I am very grateful for your understanding in this matter.

Sincerely yours,

Product Not Defective

Dear **Name**:

Your letter of **date** in which you describe a problem with **product name** was referred to me for response.

The "problem" you describe is not a symptom of faulty operation, but a normal product feature. Please refer to page **number** of your owner's manual for a full explanation.

Based on your letter, I can assure you that your unit is operating correctly and that no replacement or repair is called for.

Please feel free to contact me directly at **telephone number** if you have any further questions on this matter or if I can help you with any other aspect of the operation of our product.

Sincerely yours,

Services Performed as Promised

Dear **Name**:

Name has reported to me your dissatisfaction with the service performed on your automobile **or other device** on **date**. He tells me that you are concerned that some of the service items you requested were not completed, namely **list**. I reviewed the service record for your vehicle, and discovered that all of the service items were performed as you requested.

Please give me a call at **telephone number** if you are still dissatisfied or if you have any questions.

Sincerely yours,

Preventing Future Misunderstandings

Dear **Name:**

I was sorry to hear that you were disappointed with the specifications of **product name** and that it was not all that you had expected it to be. We at **Name of company** take great pride in the thoroughness of our product documentation, which lists in great detail all relevant specifications for each item we offer. I am enclosing a copy of the documentation for all **series number** models of our **product name**. I am confident that you will find it helpful to review this material before placing your next order. I am also always available— at **telephone number**—to answer any questions you may have concerning product specifications.

I'm eager to ensure that what you purchase from us is exactly what you want and meets all of your expectations.

Sincerely yours,

Dear **Name:**

Your comments regarding **product name**, which you recently returned in exchange for **product name**, have come to my attention. I understand that the specifications and recommended product application were not clear to you. Your comments prompted me to review our product documentation, and while we do include the relevant information in our product documentation, I have concluded that we could provide this information in a clearer form. Therefore, I've ordered a revision of our documentation.

Thank you very much for bringing this problem to our attention and for helping us to avoid future misunderstandings. I apologize for any inconvenience the process of making the exchange may have caused you.

Sincerely,

‌

Chapter Six

Working with Clients and Customers: Earning and Maintaining Goodwill

Step by Step . . . to What's Best for You

"Feelings," begins that dreadful song from the 1970s, "nothing more than feelings." True. Goodwill letters deal with nothing more than feelings. But it is also true that some of the people some of the time—and all of the people some of the time—are moved to action by nothing more than feelings. Motivation—to buy, sell, do a favor, whatever—is often a matter of giving your reader nothing more than the *right* feelings. Goodwill letters are not mere gestures of politeness and civility—though they do serve that function—they are the means of earning and banking positive emotional capital.

Welcome

When you acquire a new client or reactivate an old one, welcome her.

1. Express your pleasure in welcoming the customer/client.

2. Express your appreciation, conveying gratitude for the confidence the customer/client has demonstrated in you.

3. Promise to serve him to the best of your ability.

4. Invite questions and communication.

Congratulations

Use occasions of congratulation as opportunities not only to build goodwill, but to acquire new business.

1. Express the congratulations.

2. Mention your business relationship to the reader.

3. Offer help and advice.

4. Express the desire to continue a successful business partnership.

5. Optionally, close by repeating congratulations.

Thanks

Everyone appreciates a thank you. Structure yours simply and warmly.

1. Express thanks.

2. Explain how valuable the service, favor, recommendation, etc. is. Be as specific as possible ("You helped turn a potential disaster into a profitable transaction.")

3. Close by reiterating your appreciation and feeling of good fortune to be associated with the reader.

Invitation

A letter of invitation can be sent as a stand-alone item or as an accompaniment to a formal printed invitation.

1. State name of occasion and describe it.

2. Warmly express your wish that the reader will attend.

3. State response due date.

Sympathy and Comfort

Even the most intelligent and articulate people often find it difficult to say the right thing on occasions of death, serious illness, or other loss. Trite as it sounds, saying the "right thing" is mostly a matter of being yourself, of getting in touch with your feelings and speaking from them. How do you know what to say? Think about what you would like to hear in such a situation. Think about your feelings.

1. Express sorrow at hearing the news of the death or loss.

2. If this is a letter of condolence for a death, sympathize by acknowledging the emotional pain of the loss.

3. Say something good about the deceased. Share a memory, if possible.

4. Without minimizing present grief, remind the reader of the healing virtues of time.

5. Offer your help and support as much as is possible and appropriate.

Apologies

Apologizing for such things as a missed meeting, minor errors, rudeness, and the like calls for a straightforward, honest response. Take responsibility for your action, but there is no need to grovel. Don't magnify your slight or indiscretion into a major crime. The object is to minimize bad feelings—or even turn negative feelings into positive ones. Therefore, be careful not to signal to your reader that she should be *more* upset than she already is.

1. Begin with a forthright apology, which might incorporate part of your explanation for the problem.

2. Offer some form of reparation.

3. Repeat the apology and thank your reader for his patience and understanding.

WELCOME

Jump Starts . . . to Get You on Your Way

It is a pleasure to welcome you to our family of clients.

Welcome aboard!

Thanks for your business—for your trust and your confidence.

We at **Name of company** are pleased and proud that you have chosen us as your **product name** supplier.

Welcome back! We sure missed you. And now that you're back, we'll be doing everything we can to keep you with us.

A New Customer

Dear **Name**:

I am delighted to welcome you to our family of customers. We at **Name of company** know that you have a choice, and we will do everything possible to ensure that you are always pleased with the choice you have made in coming to us.

If you have any questions—now or in the course of what I am confident will be a long and mutually profitable business relationship—please don't hesitate to call me directly at **telephone number**.

Sincerely yours,

Dear **Name**:

Welcome!

We at **Name of company** are pleased and proud that you have chosen us as your **product name** supplier. We will do everything in our power to ensure that you get the best service and the greatest value in the business.

Should you have any questions or wish to discuss special needs, please give me a call anytime at **telephone number**.

Sincerely yours,

New Business from an Inactive Customer

Dear **Name**:

Welcome back! We sure missed you. And now that you're back, we'll be doing everything we can to keep you with us.

You have a choice in **type of business**, and we are very grateful that you have, once again, chosen us. We want you to be satisfied. So if you have any questions, comments, or special requests, please call me directly at **telephone number**. I'm here to help.

Welcome back.

Sincerely yours,

Dear **Name**:

We are delighted to see you back, and we intend to do our level best to make sure that you don't go away again. Please, **Name**, stay in touch: Call me directly at **telephone number** if you ever have any questions, problems, or special requests.

Best regards,

CONGRATULATIONS

Jump Starts . . . to Get You on Your Way

Everyone's singing your praises!

You're getting to be the talk of the industry.

I thought I'd better claim my place in the line of folks waiting to congratulate you.

A quick note to wish you the best of good luck in your exciting new venture.

I can't wait to see you tear into **name of project**.

I hope your back is not too tender from all the pats you've been getting.

I hear you'll be joining us old married folks pretty soon!

We've just been alerted that you now have a new son and heir. Congratulations!

Sales Success

Dear **Name**:

You're getting to be the talk of the industry, **Name**. Of course, you deserve all the credit for racking up such a great sales record for **year or quarter**. But we at **Name of company** do like to think that we helped—with prompt, personal service, a terrific product, and prices that are just right for you.

So here's to you and your continued success! And here's to the continued success of our partnership!

Best regards,

Dear **Name**:

I thought I'd better claim my place in the line of folks waiting to congratulate you. What a sales year!

We enjoy working with a winner, and we look forward to many more years of continued success as your supplier of **product name**.

All the best,

New Venture

Dear **Name**:

I was delighted to hear of your new project. I'd wish you good luck, but you've always made your own good luck—through skill, knowhow, and character. I am confident that this new venture will meet or exceed everything you expect from it.

You know that you can rely on us to meet all of the **type of product/service** demands this new venture will achieve. Just reach for your phone.

Best wishes,

Dear **Name**:

I can't wait to see what you'll do to shake up the **type of business**. And whatever you'll do, I know that you will shake things up.

You can be sure that we'll be here, ready to serve you with the **type of product/service** you'll need for this new venture. I'll be giving you a call in a week or two. I'd like to take you to lunch and talk over ways in which we might fit into your future.

Best wishes,

New Position

Dear **Name**:

I hope your back is not too tender from all the pats you've been getting. Moving up to **position** at **Name of company** is not an everyday achievement. Congratulations and best wishes.

You know, we have a similar success story to tell. Just **number** years ago, we existed only on paper. Today, we are the leading supplier of **product/service** in the area. After you've settled in, I'd be grateful for the opportunity to drop by, shake your hand, and talk to you a little about what **Name of company** can do for you now that you'll be making all the **type of decisions or type of purchases**. I'll phone you late next week.

Congratulations and all best wishes,

Personal Matters (Engagement, Marriage, Birth, Etc.)

Dear **Name**:

I hear that you'll soon be leaving the ranks of the unwed. Welcome aboard!

I've found that being married changes everything—for the better—including your commitment to your professional life. If there is anything I can do to make your job easier, now that you're taking on family responsibilities, I hope you won't hesitate to give me a call at **telephone number**.

Best wishes,

Dear **Name**:

We hear you've just had an addition to the **family name** dynasty!

Please accept the congratulations of all of us here at **Name of company**.

Best wishes,

THANK YOU LETTERS

Jump Starts . . . to Get You on Your Way

Many thanks for your recent order.

Just a note to thank you for your recent order and to express our appreciation for your having chosen us as your **name of product/service** supplier.

You have been a terrific customer, and I thought it was high time to thank you for that fact.

Many thanks for giving **Name** a demonstration of the Dynamico system we installed in your plant.

Thanks for recommending me to **Name**. It is a great feeling to have one of your clients give you such a vote of confidence.

For Being a Customer

Dear **Name**:

Just a note to thank you for your recent order and to express our appreciation for your having chosen us as your **name of product/service** supplier.

We know we have plenty of competition, and we pledge to work for you everyday to ensure that you will be happy with the choice you have made.

Again, thanks.

Sincerely yours,

Dear **Name**:

I am so pleased that you have come to us for **name of product/service**. We greatly appreciate your business, and we will work hard at all times to earn your continued confidence in us.

Sincerely yours,

For Being a Great Customer

Dear **Name**:

You have been a great customer for so long that it would be all to easy to take you for granted. That's one thing I definitely do not want to do. So I'm taking this opportunity just to thank you for all of your business, for your loyalty, your integrity, and your understanding.

We're delighted that you have chosen us as your **name of product/service** supplier year after year, and we look forward to many more years. We'll work hard for each of them, day by day, order by order.

Best regards,

Dear **Name**:

What would we do without you?

Sure, we'd survive as a company. But we'd be a lot poorer—and I don't just mean poorer in revenue. You are a pleasure to work with, and your commitment to excellence is not only refreshing, but keeps us at our best.

So I thought I'd just drop you line: Here's to many, many more years of a very rewarding relationship.

All the best,

For a Favor

Dear **Name**:

Many thanks for giving **Name** a demonstration of the Dynamico system we installed in your plant. When I called to ask if you would be kind enough to put the unit through its paces for him, I had no doubt you'd do me the favor. That's the kind of person you are. What I didn't expect is that you'd go so far out of your way to *sell* the system for us.

Name just placed his order today.

I'd like to take you out to lunch. I'll call you early next week. Maybe you can give me a few pointers on selling our systems!

Best regards,

Dear **Name**:

When I asked if I could come over and chat about **subject**, I had no idea that I would be given a free tutorial and consultation! I really appreciate your generosity in sharing your expertise and your time. I learned a great deal. You are an extraordinary teacher.

Please accept the accompanying **gift** as a very small token of my thanks.

Yours,

For a Recommendation or Referral

Dear **Name**:

The greatest feeling I get from my job is when I do it so well that one of my customers recommends my services to a valued colleague.

What a vote of confidence!

Thanks a million.

Sincerely yours,

Dear **Name**:

Nothing feels better than being told you've done a job well—except for finding out that someone you admire and respect is telling other people that you do your job well.

I am very grateful for your having recommended my services to **Name**. It means a great deal to me.

Sincerely,

INVITATION

Jump Starts . . . to Get You on Your Way

I hope you will be able to attend our annual **name of function**.

Won't you and your husband **wife** give us the pleasure of your company this year at the **Name of company** annual dinner?

I'll never forget the speech you gave at **place** in **month/year**. That's why I'm inviting you to speak at our upcoming **name of function**.

I enjoyed speaking with you the other day about our organization, the **Name of organization**.

The members of **Name of organization** have long admired your important work with **charity, etc.** and recognize that you are, in fact, one of this community's most influential voices.

Corporate Dinner (or Other Function)

Dear **Name**:

We at **Name of company** are holding our annual **name of function**, and it would give us great pleasure if you would enjoy the occasion with us.

The food and drink are always terrific, the speeches mercifully short, but the conversation very good indeed.

We would appreciate your response by **date**. Please call at **telephone number**. Of course, your wife **husband** is very welcome to join us.

Sincerely yours,

Dear **Name**:

Won't you and your husband **wife** give us the pleasure of your company this year at the **Name of company** annual dinner?

We would love to have you join us for an evening everyone enjoys.

Please respond by **date** at **telephone number**.

Sincerely yours,

To Speak

Dear **Name**:

One of my most pleasant memories is of hearing you speak at **place** in **month/year**. Your speech was lucid, delightful, and enlightening. When I met with the speakers' committee yesterday to plan our annual **name of function**, I mentioned to the group how great it would be if we could get someone like **Name of correspondent** to speak.

"Well, why don't you ask her?" one of the committee members said.

Why not indeed?

I can't tell you what a great service I would be doing for my company if I succeed in persuading you to speak. I've enclosed a flier that describes the event. The choice of subject is entirely up to you.

I know what you have to offer us. Let me tell you that we can offer you a very good meal, some excellent conversation, a speaker's honorarium in the amount of **$ amount**, and our undivided attention.

Won't you, please, think it over and give me a call at **telephone number** by **date**.

Sincerely yours,

Dear **Name**:

I hate after-dinner speeches. That's why I'm asking you to make one at our annual **name of function**.

No, I'm not a sadist.

I am asking you to speak after dinner because I know that *your* speech won't be the usual after-dinner ramble among the platitudes. When you talk, people listen—they listen and learn and enjoy.

The event takes place on **date and time** at **location**. Our theme for the evening is **theme**. In addition to a terrific meal, we are able to offer an honorarium of **$ amount**.

Please reply directly to me at **telephone number** no later than **date**.

For the sake of our minds and our digestions, I hope you'll be able to say yes.

Sincerely yours,

To Join Our Club (or Other Group)

Dear **Name**:

I enjoyed speaking with you the other day about our organization, the **Name of organization**. It is a great group of people who, I truly believe, have made and continue to make a positive difference in our community. I was delighted to learn from you that you are interested in joining us, and I discussed the matter with the membership at our most recent meeting. They have agreed to extend this invitation to you.

We would be honored if you would attend our next meeting at **time** at **location**. There you will be given full information on membership, including benefits, responsibilities, and dues, and you will be given the opportunity to make a formal application.

I look forward to seeing you there.

Sincerely yours,

Dear **Name**:

I have never been a "joiner." I don't belong to a lot of clubs. But **Name of organization** is not just another club, and I have been proud to be a member for **number** years.

I think you know the kind of work we do to advance the art and science of **name of industry/profession**. Our goals are worthwhile and no-nonsense.

Name, I've known you long enough to be confident that **Name of organization** is right for you and that you are very right for **Name of organization**. I've mentioned you many times to fellow members, and we all agree: it's time we got you on board.

I would be delighted if you would come to our next meeting at **time** at **location**. You will be given the opportunity of sitting in on a meeting and then chatting with some of the members. If you like, you may make a formal application for membership at that time.

I hope to see you there.

All the best,

To Accept an Honorary Position

Dear **Name**:

The members of **Name of organization** have long admired your important work with **charity, etc.** and recognize that you are, in fact, one of this community's most influential voices. We would be deeply gratified if you would accept our invitation to become honorary chairman **or other position** of **Name of organization**. As president of the organization and on behalf of the membership, I hereby formally extend the invitation to you.

I believe that you are quite familiar with what we do and what we stand for. However, I would be pleased to discuss our organization with you and to enumerate the few responsibilities the honorary position entails. I will call you next week in the hope that you can work a lunch meeting with me into your busy schedule.

In the meantime, I ask that you give serious thought to our invitation.

Sincerely yours,

Dear **Name**:

You know who you are and what you've done—how much you've accomplished on behalf of **charity, political organization, etc.** So I don't have to explain why, on behalf of **Name of organization**, I am asking you to accept this invitation to serve as honorary chairman of our annual fund drive.

The position requires nothing more or less than that you lend your name and endorsement to this most worthwhile cause.

I will call you within the next several days to arrange a meeting with you to discuss the position and to answer any questions you may have about **Name of organization** and the details of the drive. In the meantime, please give our invitation serious thought. Your participation would be a great honor and help to us.

Sincerely yours,

To Accept an Award

Dear **Name**:

Each year **Name of organization** presents its **Name of award** to individuals who have demonstrated an extraordinary commitment to **cause**. It is my pleasure to inform you that the Awards Committee has voted to confer the **Name of award** for **year** on you in recognition of your long record of achievement and accomplishment.

We would be greatly honored if you would consent to accept the award and to attend the annual awards dinner, which will be held on the evening of **date** at **location**.

I ask that you telephone me at **telephone number** to indicate your acceptance of the award and your willingness to attend the dinner.

Sincerely yours,

Dear **Name**:

It is my great honor and pleasure to inform you that **Name of organization** has voted to present you with its annual **Name of award**. As you know, the **Name of award** is presented to those individuals who have made an extraordinary contribution to **cause, profession, etc.** Our voting board unanimously agreed that your work in the following areas—**list**—amply merits our recognition.

We would be honored if you would accept this award, which will be presented to you at our annual award dinner. This will be held at **location** on **date and time**.

I ask that you write or telephone me (at **telephone number**) to indicate your acceptance of the award and your availability to attend the award dinner.

Please accept my congratulations on this honor.

Sincerely yours,

SYMPATHY AND COMFORT

Jump Starts . . . to Get You on Your Way

All of us here at **Name of company** are saddened by the death of your **job title, Name**.

No one is ever ready for death.

Name and I wish to express our heartfelt sympathy to you and your family.

Your son **Daughter, husband, etc.** was impossible not to like.

Words at a time like this offer too little comfort.

I learned only today of your mother's **father's, wife's, etc.** death.

No one can replace the loss you have suffered, and only one who has experienced such a loss can fully understand what you are going through.

Time, far more than anything I can say now, will console you for the loss of your husband **wife, mother, etc.**

I have just heard the sad news.

I wish I knew the magic words that could comfort you at a time like this.

Death of a Business Associate

Dear **Name**:

I was very sorry to learn of the passing of your president **or other officer/associate, Name**. I've done business with **Name** for **number** years, and it was always a pleasure and a privilege. He was astute, generous, and honorable. I know how much you will miss him as a person and as a business leader, and I fully sympathize with your loss.

If there is anything I can do to help you during what I'm sure will prove to be some difficult days to come, please don't hesitate to call on me.

Sincerely yours,

Dear **Name**:

It was a shock to hear of the death of **Name**. As you know, he and I worked together for many years—pleasurable and profitable years. I know that you will miss **Name** at least as much as I will.

The coming days, weeks, and months are bound to be difficult for you. Please call me if I can be of any help.

Sincerely yours,

Death of a Business Friend

Dear **Name**:

Name, as you know, was far more to me than a business associate. She was a dear and good friend, and I will miss her very much. I sympathize deeply with you, who have lost not only a friend as well, but a vital member of your management team. Perhaps it will be some comfort to you—as it is to me—to know that **Name** will live on, in the legacy of leadership she leaves your firm and in the memories of friendship she leaves in our hearts.

If there is anything I can do to help you during what I'm sure will prove to be some difficult days to come, please don't hesitate to call on me.

Sincerely yours,

Dear **Name**:

Name was a good friend to both of us—for me, a good friend first, and a valued business associate second. As hard as this loss is for me, I realize that you have lost not only a friend, but a key member of your management team.

Nothing can replace the loss of our friend, but I know that he had full confidence in you, that he always regarded you as a full partner in business, and that, therefore, even without his guidance and experience, you will carry your company on to continued, even greater success.

I want you to know that I am here for you, ready to help in any way I can during the difficult days to come.

Sincerely yours,

Dear **Name**:

I wanted to write to express my condolences on your loss. But then I realized that **Name** has left you—left us—more than his death has taken away.

To me he was a fine friend and a great business associate, who has left wonderful memories and a strong professional legacy. To you, he has bequeathed a love and warmth that I am sure are everlasting.

I am sorry for the loss. but I am thankful for what remains to us.

Sincerely yours,

Illness of a Business Associate

Dear **Name**:

I was very sorry to hear from our mutual friend **Name** that you are in the hospital. I hope that your recovery will be swift, and that I'll soon be hearing your familiar voice again when I call the **Name of department** at **Name of company**.

Get well!

Sincerely yours,

Dear **Name**:

Name tells me that you are laid up. All that bed rest must be pretty tough on an old workaholic like you. Better get well quickly and start shaking 'em up again at the office.

All the best,

Illness of a Business Friend

Dear **Name**:

Well, **Name**, some people will go to any lengths to avoid work. But don't you think a hospital stay is overdoing it a bit?

Get well quick. Rumor is your company needs you!

Seriously: I hope you're feeling better soon, and if there is anything I can do to help out while you're laid up, don't hesitate to give me a call.

All the best,

Dear **Name**:

How can you do this to me? Sure, your company needs you, but what about me? You're the only person I know whose golf game I can beat! What am I supposed to do now?

Get back to work so that we can get together on the links—please!

Best regards,

To the Bereaved Family

Dear **Name**:

I am so very sorry to hear of the death of your husband. I worked with **Name** for many, many happy years. I'm sure that the fine qualities he displayed in business—generosity, wisdom, and understanding—were the same ones that his family members had known. So my sympathy for you is deep and heartfelt.

I will remember him with great pleasure and warmth.

Sincerely yours,

Property Loss or Damage

Dear **Name**:

I was very distressed to learn of the fire **or other disaster** that hit your offices. It's a shock, I'm sure, but I've known you for a good long time now, and I am confident that you will come out of this even stronger than before. That is the kind of person you are.

If there is anything I can do to help you out during this difficult time, please do not hesitate to call on me.

Sincerely yours,

Dear **Name**:

You've taken a terrible blow. Thank goodness it happened to you.

I mean that. Because anyone else would have caved in. You, I know, will not only pull through and survive, but will be stronger for the experience.

In the meantime, if there is anything I can do to help out, please call my office.

Sincerely,

On Other Losses

Dear **Name**:

I was just reading in the **Name of newsletter/publication** that **Name of company** is closing its doors. I know they were one of your biggest clients, and I've no doubt that their packing it in did not come as welcome news to you.

You have a fine company, and I know that you'll weather this loss and emerge from it stronger than ever. If you'd like to get together over lunch to discuss some strategies and ideas for the future, why don't you give me a call. I'd like to see you.

Sincerely yours,

Belated Condolences

Dear **Name**:

I returned this morning from my vacation to the sad news that **Name** had died **number** days ago. I hope that you will accept these belated condolences on the loss to yourself and to your firm. **Name**, as you know, was a fine man, with whom it was an honor and a pleasure to do business.

Sincerely yours,

Dear **Name**:

I just learned this morning of the passing of **Name**. I have been out of the country, and the sad news had not reached me.

Please accept my sincere condolences, however belated, on what I know is a personal as well as business loss.

Sincerely yours,

APOLOGIES

Jump Starts . . . to Get You on Your Way

I am very sorry that my bout with the flu kept me from attending the meeting last **day**.

I really messed up this time, and I am very sorry.

We are both lucky that you caught my mistake before I made the pair of us look dumb.

There are few things more offensive and irritating than feeling as if you've been snubbed. Imagine, then, how I felt when I heard that you had left several messages for me at the convention—and had received no response.

I am going to tell you straight: I had no right to lose my temper like that last **day**.

Missed Meeting or Appointment

Dear **Name**:

I am very sorry that illness **or other reason** prevented me from attending the **date** meeting.

I have thoroughly reviewed the notes from the meeting, which was obviously very lively and productive. I'll phone you within a few days to discuss some of the points.

Again, I apologize for missing the meeting, but I am pleased that it went so well—even without me!

Sincerely,

Dear **Name**:

Some folks respect a man who admits his mistakes. Others just think he's a jerk. I'll take my chances.

I messed up. As I explained over the phone, I wrote down the wrong date for our scheduled meeting and, I'm afraid, left you hanging.

I wanted to apologize to you in writing, and to thank you for your understanding and for your willingness to reschedule. This time, I assure you, I've got the right date *engraved* in my book!

Sincerely yours,

Inaccurate Information

Dear **Name**:

It is lucky for all of us that you are sharp and alert. As you pointed out, the figures I quoted for **name of project** were inaccurate. I'm very relieved that you caught the error before acting on the basis of the figures.

Enclosed is a revised report with all the correct information.

Please accept my apologies for having supplied incorrect information. I was unaware that an update had already been made. Next time, I'll ask my staff more questions before releasing the figures.

I appreciate your understanding.

Sincerely yours,

Dear **Name**:

As they used to say on the TV quiz shows, *You're right! You're right! You're absolutely right!* The only trouble with this situation is that *I'm wrong! I'm absolutely wrong!*

I gave you the wrong information concerning **name of product/project**, and at least one of us was sharp enough to realize it.

The correct information is: **supply.**

I am grateful for the correction, and I thank you for not giving vent to the irritation and anger my error so richly merits.

Best regards,

Ignoring a Customer

Dear **Name**:

There are few things more offensive and irritating than feeling as if you've been snubbed. Imagine, then, how I felt when I heard that you had left several messages for me at the convention—and had received no response.

It turns out that the people at the information desk misfiled your messages to me. I never received them. Had I even known that you were attending the convention, of course, I would have sought *you* out.

I will be in your area during **dates**, and I hope you will let me take you out to dinner, where we can have a good talk.

I'm very sorry for the mix up.

Sincerely yours,

Bad Behavior or Rude Treatment

Dear **Name** and **Name**:

It's true what they say: I really *did* hate myself in the morning. I only hope that *you* can find it in your hearts not to hate me. My behavior, I realize, was deplorable, tiresome, and downright rude. I promise you that you will not be subjected to a similar display again.

I hope that you will accept my sincere apology.

Regretfully,

Dear **Name**:

I wouldn't blame you if you throw away this letter without reading it. My behavior on **date** was way, way out of line. I had no right to blow my stack like that. It was inappropriate, it was hurtful, and it was entirely unwarranted.

I could explain to you that I have been under a great deal of pressure lately—but, then, who of us isn't? No, what I did was just plain wrong, and I am very sorry for it. I hope you can find it in your heart to forgive me.

With regret,

Chapter Seven

Working with Suppliers and Vendors: Placing Orders, Making Requests, Rejecting Proposals

Step by Step . . . to What's Best for You

The bulk of your dealings with suppliers and vendors is handled through phone calls or by filling out forms that are utterly devoid of personality. Letters are not always necessary, but they can be of invaluable aid in expediting orders and service and in communicating that certain touch of humanity that may be absent from a phone call and that certainly won't be found in an order form. A good letter to a vendor or supplier can transform a business transaction from an exchange of cash, parts, dates, and numbers to an interaction between human beings. And that brings us to the human nature of business. We may like to think that we are "businesslike" and that businesses deal best with other businesses. The truth is that businesses are run by human beings, and human beings deal most effectively with other human beings. Humanizing even the most straightforward transactions does not mean making them warm and fuzzy and sloppy. It means giving yourself an edge by introducing the personal touch, making your vendor or supplier feel like he *knows* you—even if he has never met you in person.

Letters Requesting Information

Even simple letters requesting information provide an opportunity for injecting your personal presence:

1. Introduce yourself and your company very briefly.

2. Request the required information.

3. Underscore your interest in top quality, best price, quick turn-around, and so on.

4. If you are eager to act, say so. Ask the vendor to expedite the information.

Soliciting Bids

Letters soliciting bids—or cover letters accompanying RFP's—should be businesslike (that is, objective and efficient), but, again, stress your special requirements, your high regard for quality, your need to be able to depend on your supplier 100 percent.

1. Introduce yourself and your company very briefly. If necessary, include a longer description or refer to an enclosure.

2. State the particulars of the project (referring to all necessary enclosures).

3. State any format or information requirements you may have for the bid.

4. In a more subjective tone, underscore your company's commitment to quality, etc.

5. You may mention that other "top vendors" have been asked to bid and that you must adhere to a stated deadline.

6. Express your appreciation for a carefully prepared bid quickly and efficiently delivered.

7. Invite questions.

Letters Securing Credit and Other Funds

Even in cases where a vendor supplies credit application forms, a good cover letter can give you an edge. The effective cover letter is an opportunity to draw the reader's attention to highlights in your credit record and financial statement. Its tone can also reflect your seriousness about your business and remind the lender that he is dealing with more than just a set of numbers. He is dealing with a living, breathing person.

1. If this is an inquiry, introduce yourself (including your title) and your company. If this is a cover letter accompanying a completed application, simply point out that you are returning the completed application.

2. If this is an inquiry, ask for the required information. If it is a cover letter, point out any highlights in the financial statement. Address any potential problems (for example, a record of a late payment).

3. In an inquiry letter, make it clear that you wish to establish a credit relationship quickly and that, therefore, you require the information as soon as possible. Do much the same in a cover letter, making it clear that you are eager to place your first credit order and that you would appreciate the vendor expediting your application.

4. Close all letters of this type by inviting questions and making clear your readiness to supply additional information.

Cover Letters to Accompany Orders

Often, sending a cover letter with an order is not absolutely necessary; however, doing so can be a sign of courtesy and can also secure an extra measure of performance. Letters are also useful when your order is especially complex or requires special handling.

1. Explain what you have enclosed (for example, a purchase order for a certain quantity of merchandise).

2. State what kind of service you expect ("Our customers rely on us for prompt, dependable service. We are, therefore, depending on you . . . ").

3. Invite questions.

Letters Requesting Favors

Most vendors actually welcome the opportunity to do you a favor, to give you special service or performance. Most vendors welcome the opportunity to demonstrate excellence. Capitalize on this natural tendency when you write a letter requesting a favor or extra special handling of an order.

1. State the nature of the favor. If appropriate, introduce your request by affirming your relationship with the vendor ("We've worked together so long that . . .").

2. Motivate your vendor by explaining the reason for the favor. Make it clear that you are offering the vendor a chance to help you, an opportunity to strengthen the business relationship.

3. Acknowledge that you are asking for extra effort and that you are very appreciative of it.

Only the confirmed sadist enjoys writing letters rejecting proposals. However, you should not go to artificial lengths to soften the blow. The kindest rejection is one that honestly gives reasons for turning down the proposal. At least the vendor or applicant can learn something from it. If possible and appropriate, offer alternatives (for example, modify the proposal and resubmit it).

1. Thank the reader for his interest and/or find some common ground for agreement.

2. Enumerate the reasons for rejection or refusal.

3. Clearly state the rejection or refusal.

4. Thank the reader again, offer an honest, helpful alternative (if possible), and (if appropriate) close with best wishes for success.

LETTERS REQUESTING INFORMATION ABOUT PRODUCTS OR SERVICES

Jump Starts . . . to Get You on Your Way

Please send me specification sheets and a price list for **name of product**.

I need information on the following products: **list**.

I am the president **or other position** of **Name of company**, a small, high quality **type of firm** in **location**.

Name of company, a long-established dealer in **type of merchandise**, is looking for a great supplier of **product/service**.

We are looking for the best.

Requesting Specification Sheet/Price List

Dear **Name**:

Please send me specification sheets and a price list for **name of product**. I am looking at lines from several vendors, and I need to make my decision quickly, so I would greatly appreciate your expediting delivery of this information.

Please send it to:

Name

Title

Name of company

Address

Fax

Sincerely yours,

FAX

To: **Name**

Name of company

Fax number

From: **Name**

Name of company

Fax number

Please fax to me as quickly as possible a price list for **product line**.

I greatly appreciate your immediate response.

Dear **Name**:

I need information on **types of products** you offer. Let me give you an idea of what my requirements are. Then send me specification sheets and a price list for the products you think would best suit my situation.

Here's what I need:

List

If you have any questions, please call me at **telephone number**.

You've made the final cut of suppliers I am looking at. I'm facing a decision deadline, so I would appreciate anything you can do to expedite delivery of the information I've requested.

Sincerely yours,

Specifying Service Needs

Dear **Name**:

I am the president **or other position** of **Name of company**, a small **type of firm** in **location**. We are currently soliciting proposals from a variety of **type of firm** for **service**.

What we require is:

list

In addition to these specific requirements, we are looking for a firm that is flexible, dependable, and willing to customize stock services to suit our needs. We place a high premium on communication, and we will expect the firm we work with to be responsive to our changing requirements.

We want to begin **service** no later than **date**, which means that we will need to have all proposals in hand by **date**. Therefore, we appreciate your expediting delivery of the proposal to us.

If you have any questions, please call me at **telephone number**.

Sincerely,

Dear **Name**:

Name of company, a mid-size **type of business** firm located in **location**, is looking for a company to handle **service**. Your firm comes to us highly recommended from **Name** at **Name of company**, so we anticipate a great proposal from you.

Please give me a call at **telephone number** at your earliest convenience to set up a conference at which I can outline our needs and give you all the information you need to make your proposal.

Sincerely yours,

SOLICITING BIDS

Jump Starts . . . to Get You on Your Way

Enclosed is a complete set of specifications for **item(s)**, which we are planning to purchase. Please furnish your bid for supplying this merchandise in the quantities indicated.

Name of company, a **type of business** serving the **geographical area,** is soliciting bids for **name of project or product.**

I was highly impressed by your presentation on **date,** and I would welcome your submission of a bid on **name of project.**

You come to us highly recommended as a supplier of **product.**

Name of **Name of company** recommended you as a fine supplier of **product.**

Form Letters

Re: Our reference number

Dear Account Executive:

We have enclosed specifications for **item(s),** which we wish to purchase in quantities of **number.** Please furnish your bid for supplying these quantities and include a statement of your credit and customer support policies.

We are soliciting bids from a number of fine suppliers, and we ask, therefore, that you submit your bid no later than **date** so that we can fully evaluate all proposals.

Please call if you have any questions regarding the specifications.

Sincerely,

Re: **Our reference number**

Dear **Account Executive:**

Name of company, a **type of business** serving the **geographical area,** is soliciting bids for **name of project or product.** You will find a specification sheet enclosed. In addition to the requirements set forth there, you should be aware that our evaluation of your bid will take into particular consideration three things:

1. Quality of product

2. Quality of service

3. Price

You are in company with a number of excellent suppliers, from whom we have solicited bids. We must review all proposals thoroughly, and we ask, therefore, that you submit your bid no later than **date**. We cannot grant any extensions.

Please call me at **telephone number** if you have any questions concerning the specifications.

Sincerely,

Custom Letters

After Presentation

Re: **Our reference number**

Dear **Name**:

Your presentation on **date** made quite an impression on us, and we would welcome your bid on **name of project** per the specification sheet enclosed.

You should know that we have solicited bids from a number of very fine suppliers. The complexity of this project makes it imperative that we review all proposals very carefully, so we must ask that you submit your bid no later than **date**. We cannot grant any extensions.

Please call if you have any questions concerning the specifications. We look forward to receiving your bid.

Sincerely,

On Recommendation

Re: **Our reference number**

Dear **Name**:

Name of **Name of company** speaks very highly of you as a fine supplier of **product**. I've known **Name** for **number** years, during which time I've learned to value his opinion. So, based on his recommendation, I'd like you to bid on the items described on the enclosed spec sheet. In addition to furnishing prices on the quantities indicated, please give me run-on prices for additional 1,000s.

I believe the specifications are straightforward, but don't hesitate to call me at **telephone number** if you have any questions. Our production start-up deadline is **date**, so we need to have your bid no later than **date**.

Sincerely,

LETTERS SECURING CREDIT AND OTHER FUNDS

Jump Starts . . . to Get You on Your Way

I am shopping for money.

I am the chief financial officer of **Name of company**, a mid-size manufacturer of **types of products**. We are currently surveying potential suppliers of **item**. A key to our operation is a sustained credit arrangement with our principal suppliers.

I am pleased to enclose the information and documents you requested.

Your request for **documents** has arrived, and I am currently gathering the material for you.

We have thoroughly reviewed the credit terms you propose.

Requesting Information about Policies and Terms

Dear **Name**:

I am the president of **Name of company**, a **type of business** located in **location**. I am shopping for money, looking for a line of credit in the amount of **$ amount**. Please send me a statement of your customary policies and terms governing lines of credit in this range, together with any other information you think would be useful.

After I review this information, I may well contact you to discuss financial options with your institution.

Sincerely yours,

Dear **Name**:

I am the chief financial officer of **Name of company**, a mid-size manufacturer of **types of products**. We are currently surveying potential suppliers of **item**. A key to our operation is a sustained credit arrangement with our principal suppliers. Accordingly, please send me a statement of your customary policies and terms, together with any other information you think would be useful.

I am soliciting such information from a wide variety of suppliers. Based on my review of their policies, I hope to make a choice of a few firms to open negotiations with.

Sincerely yours,

Responding to Requests for Financial Information

Dear **Name of loan officer**:

I am delighted to send the enclosed documents you requested on **date** pursuant to our loan application, **number**:

- **list documents**
- etc.
- etc.

- **etc.**

Another document, **name or description**, which you also requested, will come to you under separate cover directly from our firm's attorneys, **Name of law firm**, no later than **date**.

For my peace of mind, I will check in with you early next week to ensure that you have all of the documents you need.

Sincerely yours,

Re: **Loan Application Number**

Dear **Name of loan officer**:

Here are the financial statements you requested on **date**. I am, quite frankly, proud to send them to you, since they are prime evidence of my firm's good health.

You will note one negative quarter, **date**, which resulted from the purchase of new equipment.

Please call me if you have any questions.

Sincerely yours,

Re: **Loan Application Number**

Dear **Name of loan officer**:

I am writing to let you know that **number** of the documents you requested—**list documents**—are unavailable.

Document name/description was destroyed in a fire on **date**, and **document names/descriptions** are missing. I believe that the documents I have enclosed, however, contain substantially the same information as the documents you requested, and I trust these substitutes will suffice.

If you have any questions concerning the documents, please don't hesitate to call me at **telephone number**.

Sincerely yours,

Re: **Loan Application Number**

Dear **Name of loan officer**:

Your request for **documents** has arrived. I am gathering the material now, and I will send it out to you, via **method of delivery**, no later than **date**.

I will call to confirm their safe arrival.

Sincerely,

Negotiating Terms

Your reference number : **number**

Our reference number : **number**

Dear **Name**:

We have carefully reviewed the proposed credit terms you sent on date. We need a repayment schedule more conveniently tied to our order-and-delivery cycle. I've enclosed a detailed alternative to the terms you sent. Your year-end bottom line is, of course, unchanged, but the modifications we suggest will make things much easier for us during the course of the year.

You might want to give **Name, title/position** at **Name of company** a call. We currently have a similar arrangement with this firm, and I know that **Name** would be happy to talk to you about it.

In any event, please call me just as soon as you have had a chance to evaluate our proposal. As you know, we are facing some supply deadlines, and we need to resolve our financial relationship quickly. I would, then, appreciate your prompt attention to this matter.

Sincerely yours,

Overcoming Reservations: New Business

Re: **Loan Application Number**

Dear **Name of loan officer**:

Thank you for your reply to our application for a loan or **line of credit**. Of course, I am disappointed that you did not feel you could make the loan at this time, but I certainly understand your reservations in the matter. Ours is, as you point out, a new business.

While I do understand your reservations, I also believe that other factors peculiar to our situation merit your reconsidering our application.

I ask you to take note of our exceptional growth in a short period and that you consider the great demand for the service we perform **product(s) we supply**. We are a rapidly growing company in a rapidly growing industry. I also ask that you review, once again, the personnel profiles of our staff; we are uniquely qualified to serve our markets.

I understand and appreciate the necessity for rules and guidelines. In money matters, I respect a conservative approach. However, I also appreciate flexibility and a willingness to weigh potential risks against potential benefits, even when guidelines must be interpreted creatively.

Please, therefore, review our loan application in this light. Of course, I am available for further conversation on this matter. Please call me at **telephone number**. I appreciate your thoughtful reconsideration.

Sincerely yours,

Overcoming Reservations: New Venture

Dear **Name**:

Many thanks for our meeting yesterday. The conversation was stimulating, and the reservations you expressed concerning your financial support for **name of project** are certainly understandable. They deserve careful consideration and a considered response.

Any new venture involves risk, of course. But I do want to remind you that we are not flying blind on this one. If you review the back-up material I sent you, you will see no fewer than **number** scenarios that record situations very similar to what we propose. In each case, investors realized a substantial profit.

Of course, as they say in all investment brochures, past performance is no guarantee of the future. And I certainly can make no guarantees—other than a guarantee that we have carefully thought through every conceivable contingency, as summarized in the prospectus, and we are confident that we have plans in place to counter virtually anything that might go wrong.

Obviously, **Name,** I want to convince you that **name of project** is a good investment. But the last thing I want to do is pressure you. Please take a few days to reexamine the material I left with you. I'll call early next week to see where you're at and to answer any new questions that may have occurred to you.

Sincerely yours,

Overcoming Reservations: New Product Line

Re: **Loan Application Number**

Dear **Name of loan officer**:

It occurred to me that you might find a timely follow-up letter helpful in reviewing our application for a production loan to help us launch our new product line.

You indicated during our discussion that your loan board is often reluctant to finance new product startups. I must confess, that put me on the spot. I certainly couldn't deny that we were starting up a new line. But what I wish I had pointed out—and will take the opportunity to point out now—is that, while **name of product** is new, our firm does have extensive experience with similar products, including **list**.

I've enclosed detailed sales reports on these product lines, which go into much greater depth than the financial statements we submitted as part of the loan application. If you look over these reports, you will see a consistent pattern of customer acceptance. We have, in short, an enviable batting average, and there is every reason to anticipate similar success with the new product. We aren't, after all, reinventing the wheel.

Please give me a call if you have any questions or if you would like me to supply additional information.

Sincerely yours,

Overcoming Reservations: Slow Payment

Re: **Loan Application Number**

Dear **Name of loan officer:**

This is a response to your request for an explanation of slow payment on our corporate **Name of credit card.**

The payment in question was due on **date** and made on **date**. Our company has only two principals, and from **date** to **date**, both of us were out of the country. Neither of us was present when the bill arrived, and in the backlog of work that had accumulated on our return, this bill was, quite simply, overlooked. This, of course, was regrettable, but I ask that you take note of the following:

1. The payment was indeed late, but was made only **number** days beyond the thirty-day limit.

2. We have held **Name of credit card** for **number** years; this is the single instance of a late payment.

3. The instance of late payment occurred **number** years ago. Since then, we have maintained the account in a current status.

I trust this addresses your concerns. Please call me if you have any further questions or need additional information.

Sincerely,

Re: **Loan Application Number**

Dear **Name of loan officer**:

This is to explain the incidents of "slow payment" you noted in the credit report you secured pursuant to our loan application.

You will notice that the late payments occurred during a single period, from **date** to **date**. It was during this time that we lost three of our major clients—through, I might add, circumstances beyond our control. **Name of company** did not succeed in obtaining anticipated funding for a project contracted with us, **Name of company** petitioned for Chapter 11 bankruptcy on **date**, and **Name of company** closed its branch in this area.

The result of these misfortunes was a sharp drop in available cash. During the emergency, we secured the cooperation of **Names of creditor officers and their respective firms**, who agreed to deferred payments. You might like to contact them at **telephone numbers**, respectively.

All of these accounts are now current and up to date.

I trust that this addresses your question adequately, and I respectfully direct your attention to our otherwise overwhelmingly exemplary credit history. As our financial statements indicate, we have long since recovered from past difficulties.

Sincerely yours,

Soliciting References

Dear **Name**:

We've enjoyed a credit relationship with you for **number** years now. I am writing to ask you the favor of furnishing a credit reference to **Name of vendor/lender**, with whom we are applying for a line of credit.

I've enclosed the necessary form—it's quite brief—together with an addressed and stamped envelope.

I greatly appreciate your taking the time to help us out in this matter. Please call me if you have any questions.

Sincerely,

Dear **Name**:

Because we have enjoyed a great credit relationship with you for some **number** years, I have taken the liberty of using your firm as a credit reference for a line of credit **or loan** we are applying for with **Name of bank/lender**. You need not furnish a letter or fill out any forms, but you might get a telephone call from **Name** at **Name of bank/lender**. I'd appreciate your putting in a good word for us.

Sincerely yours,

Securing a Guarantor

Dear **Name**:

We have enjoyed a long and profitable business relationship built on mutual trust. There are not many business associates of whom I would make the request that follows.

We have applied for a major loan in the amount of **$ amount** from **Name of bank/lender**. The lender is inclined to make the loan, provided that we secure a guarantor for **percentage** amount of it. I am hoping that you will consider providing the necessary guarantee.

In return for this service, we will pay your firm a premium of **$ amount** over a **number**-month period, beginning **date**.

I have enclosed, for your examination, copies of the loan agreement, together with copies of the supporting documentation (including recent financial statements) we furnished the lender.

I will telephone you early next week, after you have had time to review the request. Of course, if you have any questions before then, please don't hesitate to call me at **telephone number**.

Sincerely yours,

COVER LETTERS TO ACCOMPANY ORDERS

Jump Starts . . . to Get You on Your Way

We are pleased to enclose our purchase order for **quantity items** at the quoted price of **$ amount** each.

Our purchase order is attached.

I am delighted to place the enclosed order with you.

Here is another order from **Name of company**!

Here is our work order for **name of service**. We look forward to seeing you on **date**.

Products (One-time)

Dear **Name**:

We are pleased to enclose our purchase order for **quantity items** at the quoted price of **$ amount** each.

Our customers rely on us for prompt, dependable service. Therefore, we are depending on you to fill the order as expeditiously as possible.

Sincerely yours,

To:

From:

Re: Purchase Order **#number**

Below is our purchase order for **quantity items** at the price confirmed by telephone on **date**.

If you are unable to fill this order as specified, please contact **Name** at **telephone number** immediately.

purchase order

Products (Ongoing)

Dear **Name**:

We are delighted to place our order for **quantity items** at the quoted price of **$ amount** each. A formal purchase order is enclosed.

We are an organization that thrives on building a close relationship with our customers. This requires an equally close relationship with our suppliers. We look forward to forging such a relationship with you.

Sincerely yours,

Dear **Name**:

Here is another order from **Name of company**! Our schedule is tight on this one, so we are especially relying on your customary fast and efficient service.

Please call me right away at **telephone number** if you have any questions.

Best regards,

Services (One-time)

Dear **Name**:

Our work order for **name of service** is enclosed, and we look forward to seeing you on **date**.

I believe that you'll find us quite easy to work with, but we do maintain high standards of quality. I'm including this note with the work order so that I can direct your attention to the following points concerning your work with us:

list

If you have any questions before you come out, please don't hesitate to call me at **telephone number**.

Sincerely,

Dear **Name**:

Here is the work order for **name of service** we discussed on the phone on **date**.

As I mentioned, we expect the best from the people we work with, but I'm sure you'll find us reasonable and most cooperative. There are **number** points I did not make during our conversation. Please note the following:

list

I look forward to seeing you on **date**.

Sincerely yours,

Service (Ongoing)

Dear **Name**:

As always, it's a pleasure to have you working with us. The usual specifications apply, with the following additions and exceptions:

list

Please review the enclosed work order carefully for the details, and don't hesitate to call if you have any questions.

Sincerely yours,

Dear **Name**:

Here is the usual work order for **name of service**—with **number** of additions for this time only. While you are here, please pay special attention to the following:

list

I'd also appreciate it if you checked in with me before you start work on **date**, in case I have any last-minute changes.

Best regards,

LETTERS REQUESTING FAVORS

Jump Starts . . . to Get You on Your Way

We are looking down the barrel of a very tough deadline.

Can we count on you?

I realize that nobody likes a nervous, nagging client, but I'm willing to risk being thought of as just that.

I really need your help on this one.

This one calls for very special handling.

Our client has just informed us that he is moving up his start-up date from **date** to **date**.

You are always very particular with our shipments, but this one's more complicated than usual.

I'd like to ask a special favor of you.

Extra-fast Delivery

Dear **Name**:

You'll notice that we've specified expedited service on the enclosed purchase order. Well, this note is to let you know that we *really* mean it.

We're facing a monster deadline, and we can use all the help we can get. Please, do whatever you can to expedite this one.

I am grateful for your extra effort.

Sincerely yours,

Dear **Name**:

I'm offering you a genuine opportunity to be a real-life hero. See the word *RUSH* stamped on the enclosed purchase order? I know you've seen it before. But this time it's different. This time, WE REALLY MEAN IT!

We—well, I—grossly underestimated the quantity of **item** we need to fill our current orders, and now I'm in need of a rescue. Please be a hero and do everything in your power to expedite this order.

Many thanks to you.

Best regards,

Pledge to Hold Deadline

Dear **Name**:

I realize that nobody likes a nervous, nagging client, but I'm willing to risk being thought of as just that.

It is imperative that we complete this project by **date**, which means that you must absolutely meet your deadline date of **date**. There is no margin for error here, and I must be able to count on you 100 percent.

I am confident that you will not let me down.

Sincerely,

Dear **Name**:

It is a pleasure to be working with you again. I'm sending you this note to underscore just how vital it is that we meet the deadline on this project. There is absolutely no fat built into the schedule.

We've grown comfortably accustomed to counting on you 100 percent. We really need everything you can give us this time around.

Best regards,

Shortened Deadline

Dear **Name**:

Our client has just informed us that he is moving up his start-up date from **date** to **date**. I told him that we'd move heaven and earth to meet his new deadline.

I need to start by moving you.

I am confident I can meet my client's revised requirements if you can complete your work by **date** instead of **date**. If you can accommodate us, I am prepared to offer a bonus of **$ amount**. Even so, I know it is a lot to ask. But, as you can appreciate, a lot is riding on this for us.

Please give me a call at **telephone number** no later than **date** to let me know if the revised deadline is doable for you.

Sincerely yours,

Dear **Name**:

I've just put my neck on the block. I hope you'll be there to stop the ax—or you might just have to pick up my head.

Our client pushed up our deadline from **date** to **date**. What did I tell him? I told him "No problem."

Of course, I was assuming that you could make the same answer to me when I ask you to push up your delivery time from **date** to **date**. What about it?

Please call or fax your confirmation. Or just plan to drop by for the execution.

Best regards,

Special Handling

Dear **Name**:

The enclosed purchase order specifies special handling of our shipment, which I thought best to bring to your attention.

Please note that we are asking for this shipment to be split as follows:

list.

We appreciate your extra attention to this order and these instructions.

Sincerely,

Dear **Name**:

You folks are always careful with our shipments, but this one's a bit complicated. Please note that we are asking you to split the shipment as follows: **list**.

If any of this is unclear, please give me a call at **telephone number** right away.

Sincerely yours,

Personal Supervision of a Special Order

Dear **Name**:

I'd like to ask a special favor of you. We've just placed a major order for **quantity items**, and I would be very grateful if you personally supervised it. We are working with a very demanding client, and I can use all the special help I can get.

Best regards,

Dear **Name**:

We've worked together long enough for you to know that I'm not the nervous type. But the enclosed order is particularly complicated and involves a great deal of custom work. I know the people in your shop are very, very good at what they do. But, as a personal favor to me, could you supervise this one with extra care?

I can use all the help on this that I can get.

Best regards,

Odd-Lot Shipment

Dear **Name**:

I know that odd lot orders are something of a pain, but I ask that you do us a favor by filling this one.

We have a special project that requires **quantity items** and no more, and I do not anticipate ever requiring this item again. We cannot afford to stock merchandise we'll never use. So, it would help us greatly if you would fill this odd lot at a pro-rated price.

Please give me a call to discuss the order.

Sincerely yours,

Dear **Name**:

The enclosed order is for an odd lot, which I hope you will be able to fill. I just cannot afford to stock more of **item** than I am ordering here.

Please call me only if this order presents a problem.

Sincerely yours,

Change Payment Schedule

Dear **Name**:

We are planning to reorder **quantity** of **item** some time before **date**. As usual, we want to take delivery in **number** shipments. However, we would like to modify payment terms this time around.

For our last order, your terms specified one-half payment of the total price in advance of the first shipment. The total balance was due after we received the last shipment. This puts a terrific strain on our cash flow, and I'd like to suggest an alternative.

We propose to pay with our order one-half the charges for the first shipment, and the balance for that shipment when it is delivered. **Number** days before the second consignment is due to ship, we will pay onehalf, followed by the balance for that consignment when it is delivered, and so on through the final shipment.

This plan has two effects. It will greatly improve our cash flow, and, we believe, it will improve yours as well. You will not be obliged to wait until the last delivery to receive the balance due.

This seems like a very sane alternative to me. What's your take on it? Please give me a call to discuss it.

Sincerely,

Dear **Name**:

This is one of those times a fella needs a friend.

I can't tell you how happy I was when we worked out the payment schedule for our order, **number** dated **date**. I'd set up the payments to mesh perfectly with what we had scheduled with our client. Things were great, and life was good.

Now, this morning, our client sent me a proposal for a revised payment schedule (enclosed). I have to tell you, this client is a big one for us, and we want to do whatever we can to accommodate him.

That's where you come in, my friend.

Can you accommodate us by agreeing to a new payment schedule? We suggest payment due dates **number** business days after each of our client's revised dates, which are given on the enclosed payment schedule.

I'll call to confirm your agreement—or, if necessary, to discuss the matter further—by **date**. Thanks for giving it some thought. Your cooperation will be a great help to us.

Sincerely,

LETTERS REJECTING PROPOSALS

Jump Starts . . . to Get You on Your Way

Many thanks for your proposal for **name of project**.

Thanks for submitting your proposal so promptly. Unfortunately, your numbers make it clear that this project would be prohibitively expensive.

Your proposal is most impressive, but I am afraid that it is not for us.

We have read your proposal with great interest, but, unfortunately, we have concluded that it is inappropriate for our market.

After long and careful consideration of proposals from various vendors for **name of project/product**, we have concluded that what you offer is not quite right for us.

Too Expensive

Dear **Name**:

Thank you for submitting your proposal for **name of project**. Unfortunately, your proposal makes it clear that the project would be prohibitively expensive. We cannot, therefore, proceed.

Please be assured that we appreciate your prompt attention to our request for a proposal, and we will keep you in mind for future projects.

Sincerely,

Dear **Name**:

Your proposal for **name of project** is very impressive and has occasioned a great deal of thought here. Unfortunately, after thoroughly costing the project out, we have concluded that it is prohibitively expensive.

I am returning the proposal to you with our thanks, and we will certainly keep you in mind for future projects.

Sincerely yours,

Inappropriate

Dear **Name**:

Thank you for your project proposal for **name/type of project**. We read the proposal with great interest, but have concluded that it is inappropriate for our market **needs, customers, etc.**.

We appreciate your thinking of us.

Sincerely,

Dear **Name**:

Thank you for letting us see your proposal for **name/type of project**. Unfortunately, what you propose lies well beyond our area of specialization and is not, therefore, right for us.

Sincerely yours,

Not Quite Right

Dear **Name**:

After long and careful consideration of proposals from various vendors for **name of project/product**, we have concluded that what you offer is not quite right for us, and we have elected to go with the proposal of another vendor.

We appreciate your taking the time to prepare and submit the proposal.

Sincerely yours,

Competition Is Superior

Dear **Name**:

Competition for this project was not just lively, it was downright fierce. We received many very fine proposals, yours among them. However, we could only go with one—which offered the very best combination of service, product, and price.

Thanks for taking the time to prepare your very impressive proposal.

Sincerely yours,

Market Too Specialized

Dear **Name**:

I have received and reviewed your proposal to create a **name of product**. The idea is a very interesting one, but I am convinced that the market for such a product is, at this time, too narrow, specialized, and limited to warrant the investment necessary to put your proposal into production.

I'd be happy to go into greater detail, if you like. Give me a call.

Sincerely yours,

Does Not Meet Specifications

Dear **Name**:

We have completed our review of your proposal to supply **Name of product**. Unfortunately, the equipment you propose does not meet our minimum specifications. There is still time before our **date** deadline for considering proposals. We invite you to reexamine our spec sheet and submit a revised proposal.

Sincerely yours,

Dear **Name**:

Your proposal is very impressive, but the merchandise you have available does not meet the specifications outlined in our RFP. We invite you to reexamine the RFP and, if you can supply more appropriate merchandise, please resubmit your proposal before the deadline of **date**.

Sincerely yours,

Inadequate Warranty

Dear **Name**:

Thank you for your proposal to supply **name of product**. While there is much that we like about what you propose, your warranty terms are inadequate. Please consult our specification requirements once again. If you can revise your warranty to meet these requirements, we will be pleased to reconsider your proposal.

Sincerely yours,

Dear **Name**:

Your product looks great. Unfortunately, the warranty you offer falls well below our minimum guidelines, which specify **terms**. We will not consider purchasing additional coverage, but if you can extend the standard warranty as specified, we will be delighted to reconsider your proposal.

Sincerely yours,

Working with Suppliers and Vendors: Complaints, Apologies, Thanks, and Recommendations

Step by Step . . . to What's Best for You

Letters of Complaint

The object of a complaint is not to shame your reader or make him feel bad. The object of a complaint is to improve a situation or rectify an error and, in the process, strengthen, rather than erode, your relationship with the supplier or vendor.

The effective letter of complaint works like this:

1. Clearly and succinctly state the nature of the problem. Include such important details as duration or frequency of a problem or error. It is important to begin the letter with *facts* rather than an emotional statement ("You guys are killing me!").

2. After stating the facts, tell your reader what effect the problem is having on your business.

3. Propose a solution.

4. Close by affirming that you want to work with the vendor or supplier to correct the problem or rectify the error.

Letters of Apology

When you're on the other end of a problem, an apology is called for. Apologies to vendors and suppliers concern erroneous complaints, misunderstandings over orders and the like, and financial issues such as slow payment. As with any apology, avoid telling the reader how bad he *should* feel.

1. State what you are apologizing for.

2. Explain the problem or error.

3. Propose reparation or remedy.

4. Thank the reader for her patience and understanding.

Thank You Letters

Effective letters also capitalize on the good things that happen between you and your suppliers. You may think that placing a new order is ample reward for good service, but it is always a good idea to put your feelings into words by thanking a vendor for exceptional service.

1. Thank the vendor for something specific ("for responding so efficiently to our request for expedited service . . .").

2. Make it clear that you appreciate the reader's efforts and that you do not take them for granted.

3. Affirm your eagerness to work together again.

Letters of Recommendation

Business offers many win-win situations, if you know how to recognize them or how to create them. The opportunity to recommend a vendor's services to others presents a win-win-win scenario. Your vendor wins by getting new business; your reader wins by gaining the services of a good vendor; and you win by earning the gratitude of both your reader and the vendor. Of course, you should not make recommendations lightly, but a well-deserved recommendation should not be a chore or an obligation for you. It is an opportunity.

1. Introduce the recommendation by building on your relationship with or knowledge of your reader. ("I know that you are always on the lookout for a good supplier of . . . ").

2. Make the recommendation. It is often effective to begin with the duration of your association with the vendor, then try to mention a few relevant specifics.

3. Invite questions.

4. Suggest that your reader contact the vendor.

LETTERS OF COMPLAINT

Jump Starts . . . to Get You on Your Way

This is not the first time I've had to write to you about **problem**.

It's happened again. Your shipping department sent us the wrong parts for **item**.

On **date** I ordered **quantity merchandise** from you. I was promised delivery by **date**. I have yet to receive the shipment.

To:

From:

Re: Order Number _____

This order was received incomplete, lacking the following items:

list

The **name of item** we ordered from you on **date** was received on **date**, with the following parts damaged in shipment:

list

We have done a lot of business together, so I feel I can—and should— speak frankly with you.

Delayed Delivery

Dear **Name**:

Repeatedly during the past **period of time, Name of company** has shipped our orders anywhere from **number** to **number** days late. Occasional late shipments are understandable and, I suppose, unavoidable. But your practice of shipping later than promised is becoming intolerable. We simply cannot keep adjusting our schedules and disappointing our customers.

I need two things from you at this point—

First: Please send me a letter of explanation detailing the reasons for your pattern of late shipment and outlining a plan for preventing late shipments in the future. I will expect this letter no later than **date**.

Second: Start making your shipments on time.

We want to work with you to resolve this problem, but, above all, we need to work with suppliers on whom we can depend.

Sincerely yours,

Dear **Name**:

We're all familiar with the concept of a chain reaction. Something happens at one end of a process, and the other end is affected. One reaction sets off another, and that one another, and pretty soon you've got a very big explosion.

I'm afraid that's what's happening to us. Your company has been consistently late in making shipments to us, which has meant that we, in turn, have sometimes been unable to keep our promises.

We can't go on this way. Let's stop the chain reaction right now—*before* the explosion.

I'd like to set up a meeting with you before **date** to discuss the reasons for the late shipments and to hear your plan for making all future shipments on time. Please give me a call at **telephone number** as soon as possible.

We like your product and your price, but we need to be able to depend on you 100 percent.

Sincerely yours,

Failure to Fill Order

Dear **Name**:

On **date** I placed an order for **number items** with **Name** in your Customer Service Department. I was promised delivery by **date**. When **date** came and went, I called Customer Service to find out what the problem was.

Imagine my surprise when I was told that you have no record of my order!

I have placed the order again, and I am sending you this note in the hope that I will not be the victim of another error. I am pleased with your product, and I am inclined to continue doing business with you in the future. I would be more comfortable doing additional business with you, however, if I felt that I could rely on your people to see to it that my orders were placed and accurately filled. I would appreciate your looking into the problem I experienced and sending me an explanation of the incident within the next **period of time**.

Sincerely yours,

Dear **Name**:

On **date** I placed an order for **number items**. The confirmation number for this order was **number**. When the promised delivery date of **date** passed, I called your fulfillment department, gave them the order number, and was told that there was no record of such a number.

It gets worse.

This is the second **third, etc.** time this has happened to me in dealing with you.

Once is an accident. Twice, as far as I am concerned, is a habit.

I have placed my order again, but, I must tell you, I have begun investigating alternative suppliers. It would greatly boost my confidence in your firm if you would send me a letter of explanation, which includes what you plan to do to ensure that no more of my orders are mysteriously lost.

Sincerely yours,

Incomplete Order

To:

From:

Re: Order Number _____

This order was received incomplete, lacking the following items:

list

Please note that the invoice accompanying the shipment lists the missing items. The incomplete shipment has caused us considerable inconvenience, and we ask that you ship the missing items without delay.

To:

From:

Re: Order Number _____

This order was received incomplete, lacking the following items:

list

Please note that the invoice accompanying the shipment includes charges for the missing items. I intend to render payment only for the goods I have received. Please cancel my order for the missing items listed above.

Goods Damaged In Shipment

Dear **Name**:

The **name of item** we ordered from you on **date** was received on **date**. The following parts were received damaged—we assume in shipping:

list

On receipt of replacements for these parts, we will make arrangements with you for the return of the damaged items.

You will probably want to know that our Receiving Department reports that the merchandise was packed without adequate cushioning material. This may have been an oversight on the part of your shipping department. If not, we suggest that you reevaluate your damage-prevention procedures.

Sincerely yours,

To:

From:

Re: Goods Damaged in Shipping

Attached is a copy of the shipping invoice for our order **number**, which we received on **date**. The items check-marked were received in a badly damaged condition. Please ship replacements to us immediately. On receipt of the replacements, we will make arrangements to return the damaged items to you.

Wrong Part Shipped

To:

From:

Re: Wrong Part Shipped, Order Number _____

I am returning herewith part number **number**, which we received on **date**. We had ordered part number **number**.

This error has caused us considerable inconvenience, and we would therefore appreciate your expediting delivery of the correct part, part number **number**.

Repeated Shipping Errors

Dear **Name**:

We've been doing business with you for a long time, now, and I feel I can speak frankly with you.

The performance of your shipping department over the past **number** months has been, in a word, poor. Of **number** shipments we received since **date**, **number** have been late by at least **number** days; **number** have been incomplete; and **number** have included items we did not order.

These errors have cost us time and effort and have inconvenienced our customers. They have simply got to stop happening.

I'd like to hear what you've got to say about this situation, how you account for it, and how you plan to deal with it. A written response is not necessary, but I do expect a phone call at your earliest convenience.

You've got one unhappy customer here.

Sincerely yours,

Dear **Name**:

During this quarter **or other time period** we have placed **number** orders with you. Of that number, **number** included errors: incorrect quantities, incomplete shipments, wrong items, and unauthorized substitutions.

These habitual mistakes have cost us money, time, and effort. I'm sure they have cost you plenty of the same as well. Neither of us can continue to tolerate this situation. Please give me a call at **telephone number** to discuss the problem. If we are going to continue doing business together, I need to hear your plan for correcting this very serious, very costly problem.

I look forward to speaking with you.

Sincerely yours,

Faulty Product

Dear **Name**:

Enclosed please find one **name of product**, which I am returning for warranty repair or replacement. The unit suffers from the following problems: **describe**.

I use this product almost every day, and I cannot afford to be without it for long. I would therefore be grateful for all that you can do to expedite repair or replacement.

Sincerely yours,

Dear **Name**:

This is the second **third, etc. name of product** I have returned to you because of manufacturing faults. The problems with this unit include **list**.

I am willing, yet one more time, to accept a replacement, but I reserve the right to a complete refund if I find the replacement unsatisfactory.

Might I respectfully suggest that you thoroughly review your manufacturing and quality control procedures?

Sincerely yours,

Repeated Quality-Control Problems

Dear **Name**:

I have been installing **name of product** for **number** years now. Since **date**, I have received **number** complaints from my customers and have had to replace **number** units. This has led me to the unavoidable conclusion that too many faulty units are being shipped, which means that you have a breakdown in your quality-control procedures.

I strongly urge you to reevaluate your quality-control program in order to determine where the breakdown is occurring. These repeated problems are making my customers unhappy, which means they are making me *very* unhappy.

Please give me a call or drop me a note at your earliest convenience in response to this complaint. I would especially like to know how you plan to improve your quality control. This situation cannot be ignored. You can't afford it, and I can't afford it.

Sincerely yours,

Billing Error

Dear **Name**:

Enclosed is my check for **$ amount**, the price (including shipping) you quoted for **number items**, which we received on **date**. The invoice accompanying the shipment indicated a total charge of **$ amount**, which I assume is in error.

Sincerely yours,

Dear **Name**:

I am returning the enclosed invoice unpaid because the amount charged—**$ amount**—differs sharply from the price I was quoted on **date**. I assume the invoice is in error. Please send me a corrected invoice.

Sincerely yours,

Misinformation

Dear **Name**:

On **date** I called your Customer Service Department to obtain information on **name of product**. I needed specifically to know if **name of product** could be used for the following applications: **list**. **Name**, in customer service, assured me that **name of product** was fully suited to these applications.

Based on this information, I purchased the unit and was surprised and dismayed when I discovered, after reading the owner's manual, that **name of product** cannot be used for **list applications**.

I am returning the unit for a full refund. But I must also tell you that this misinformation has cost me time and created a substantial inconvenience. Had **Name** simply referred to the owner's manual, he could have steered me in the right direction.

I have the option of ordering **name of product**, which will satisfy my requirements, from you or from any one of your competitors. What can you do to convince me to order from you instead?

Sincerely yours,

Misrepresentation

Dear **Name**:

Your advertisement for **cleaning product**, published in **Magazine** on **date** states that it will "remove grease stains from all synthetic fabrics." On the strength of the ad, I purchased **cleaning product** and used it on a grease-stained polyester shirt. Not only did it fail to remove the stain, it darkened and spread the stain, completely ruining the shirt.

I believe that you have misrepresented your product, and I ask that you refund the **$ amount** spent on it, plus pay me **$ amount** for the shirt. If necessary, I am willing to send you the shirt for your examination.

I anticipate your reply by **date**. If I don't hear from you, I will forward a copy of this complaint to the local Better Business Bureau.

Sincerely yours,

Discourtesy

Dear **Name**:

I work hard in a business that runs on deadlines. I do not need the added pressure of discourteous treatment when I place an order with your firm.

On **date**, I called your Shipping Department to check up on the status of an order placed on **date**. The clerk to whom I spoke—he refused to give me his name—was evasive and claimed that he did not have the time to check up on my order. When I insisted that the information was absolutely necessary, he simply replied that he couldn't help me, and he hung up.

This behavior is inexcusable.

If we are to continue doing business together, I suggest you speak to this employee and convince him of the importance of supplying customers with the information they request when they request it. I believe I am also owed an apology, and I must inform you that I will not tolerate this treatment a second time.

Sincerely yours,

Repeated Billing Errors

Dear **Name**:

I am tired of having to audit your invoices.

Since **date**, I have placed **number** of orders with you. In no fewer than **number** instances, you have billed me incorrectly.

I simply can no longer afford the time and inconvenience involved in ferreting out your errors. If you wish to retain me as a customer, I strongly urge you to examine your billing procedures in order to find out just what is going wrong.

Everyone makes occasional errors, but mistakes committed with such regularity suggest that something very basic is going very wrong. If it would help, I am very willing to discuss the problem with you in detail.

Sincerely yours,

Dear **Name**:

I am returning your **date** invoice unpaid. It lists **number** items I neither ordered nor received. I've indicated these by check marks on the invoice.

Your firm has sent me a good many erroneous invoices in the past. I used to review them, correct them, and send you a check. I do not intend to do that any longer. Any problem invoices I receive will be returned to you for correction first.

Please take some time to examine your billing procedures.

Sincerely yours,

LETTERS OF APOLOGY

Jump Starts . . . to Get You on Your Way

Man, is my face red!

Let me put it this way: I screwed up.

I have something better than an apology for having let this invoice go over thirty days. It's a check for the balance due.

Few things are more infuriating than a returned check.

I hate complaining. I *really* hate complaining when it turns out that I was all wrong.

Erroneous Complaint

Dear **Name**:

The only thing more embarrassing than making a mistake is mistakenly blaming someone else for a mistake.

I am very sorry that I raked you over the coals for **incident**, which, it is now quite apparent, was not your fault at all. I hope you can forgive me for having been unpleasant and unjust.

Sincerely yours,

Dear **Name**:

I have to admit that I was rather proud of the letter I wrote you complaining about errors in your report **or other matter**. I sent the letter off—and only after I had put it into the mail did I think of reviewing my records. As it turned out, of course, your report was completely accurate. I was the one making the mistakes.

If I could physically retract my letter, I would. Since I can't, the best I can offer you is my apology for the unwarranted scolding. If it makes you feel any better, why not turn around and write *me* a nasty letter?

Best regards,

Misunderstandings

Dear **Name**:

I wish I'd learn to listen—and I bet you wish I'd learn, too. I am very sorry that I wasted your time and made extra work for you by misinterpreting your request **requirements, question, order, etc.**.

Now that I understand what you need, I'll move ahead on the project as quickly as possible.

I hope I have not caused you too much aggravation.

Sincerely yours,

Dear **Name**:

I am very sorry that I failed to make our credit policy **or other topic** clear to you. Misunderstandings over financial matters are potentially very destructive, and I am therefore most grateful for your understanding and cooperation in this instance.

Let's stay in close touch to avoid any similar misunderstandings in the future.

Sincerely,

Slow Payment

Dear **Name**:

I have something better than an apology for having let this invoice go over thirty days. It's a check for the balance due.

We have had some personnel difficulties here, which caused delay in paying some of our bills. The problem is now fully resolved, and I assure you that future invoices will be paid promptly.

I greatly appreciate your patience and understanding in this matter.

Sincerely yours,

Dear **Name**:

Here's one I bet you've never heard: The check is in the mail.

Honest.

No, my dog didn't eat your invoice. But my filing system did. And I just now resurrected the bill.

Please accept my apologies for any inconvenience this delay may have caused. I promise to be more careful in the future.

Sincerely yours,

Returned (Bounced) Check

Dear **Name**:

You are very understanding. Few things are more infuriating than catching a bounced check, and you had every right to be angry. I greatly appreciate your patience, graciousness, and good humor.

I can assure you that I won't put your good nature to this test again.

A check—and it's a good one!—to cover bank fees is enclosed.

Sincerely yours,

Dear **Name**:

I am sorry—and very embarrassed—to have put you through the trouble and inconvenience of having a check returned. You are very kind to take the incident in such good humor.

The enclosed check (a perfectly good one) is in payment of your bank charges and handling fee.

Sincerely,

THANK YOU LETTERS

Jump Starts . . . to Get You on Your Way

People keep telling me about the Good Old Days—when you got first-class service from a vendor you could trust. For me, working with you, these *are* the Good Old Days.

I've been meaning to write this letter for some time now. It's just to thank you for always being there when we need you.

I want to thank you for responding so efficiently to our request for expedited service on the **Name** project.

When our **name of product** broke down on **date**, I was ready to kick the thing—and I didn't have too many kind words in mind about your company. But you responded to the problem so quickly and efficiently that it was impossible to stay angry.

Thanks for coming to the rescue.

Thanks for the good advice.

Thanks for lending a helping hand.

As the old saying goes, "A friend in need . . ." Whoever said that could have been talking about you.

Thanks, **Name**, for all your hard work on the **name of project**.

Good Service

Dear **Name**:

A lot of folks say that you just can't get first-class treatment in business these days. They're wrong, and you've proven it.

I want to thank you for the extra effort you made to complete **name of project** not merely on schedule, but ahead of schedule. You've done a super job, and I look forward to working with you again soon.

Sincerely yours,

Dear **Name**:

Too often, people doing business together communicate only to order or reply or complain. What I intend to do now is to thank—to thank you for providing great service over the past **period of time**.

I've learned to take your terrific performance as routine, but I don't want to make the mistake of taking you for granted. So, again, thanks, and I look forward to many more years of doing business together.

Sincerely yours,

Favored Treatment or Special Service

Dear **Name**:

I want to thank you for responding so efficiently to our request for expedited service on the **Name** project. We were in a tight spot, and, quite simply, you saved the day. It's not every company that would go the extra mile.

In addition to thanking you, I suppose I should be congratulating myself on having had the good sense to pick you as our partner in this project!

You can be sure that I look forward to working with you again.

Sincerely,

Dear **Name**:

In our business, we're so accustomed to talking about competition that we forget how much depends on cooperation. Without your special cooperation, we could not have completed **name of project** successfully, let alone on schedule. Your extra effort made all the difference.

We *will* be working together again, often.

Sincerely yours,

Prompt Attention to Complaint

Dear **Name**:

I'd be lying if I told you that I wasn't upset about the problem we had with **name of product**. Nobody likes problems. But, after having to complain, I am pleased to have the opportunity to praise.

Once we alerted you to the problem, your people responded with speed, accuracy, and courtesy to make things right. You did a fine job with the fix and got us up and running with a minimum of delay. Thanks for standing by your product and your customer.

Sincerely yours,

Dear **Name**:

When our **name of product** broke down on **date**, I was ready to kick the thing—and I didn't have too many kind words in mind about your company. But you responded to the problem so quickly and efficiently that it was impossible to stay angry. Nobody likes the things they buy to break down, but I certainly do appreciate a company that stands by its product *and* its customers.

Sincerely,

LETTERS OF RECOMMENDATION— SERVICES OR PRODUCTS

Jump Starts . . . to Get You on Your Way

I understand that you are in the market for **service or product**.

Name tells me that you are looking for a good **type of vendor**. I've got just the outfit for you.

Yes, I can certainly recommend a good **vendor**.

I'm getting tired of hearing you complain about **vendor**. Have you thought about taking your business elsewhere? I am very happy with the firm I use.

To Customers and Clients

Dear **Name**:

Name tells me that you are in the market for **name of product or service**. If that is the case, it gives me an opportunity to help you out by connecting you with a business associate and friend who happens to be the best supplier of **name of product or service** I know. **Name of company** is reliable, courteous, and reasonable. You will find that they care about their customers and really work for you.

Why not give **Name of contact** a call, and tell him I sent you? If you're serious about **name of product or service**, you'll want to check them out.

Sincerely,

To Other Business Associates

Dear **Name**:

I'm very glad that you asked me to recommend a good **type of business**. We've been working with **Name of firm** for **number** years now and have found them to be economical, efficient, helpful, and generally a great pleasure to work with. We rely on them, and they have never let us down. I can recommend them without reservation.

Sincerely,

Dear **Name**:

In answer to your note asking me to recommend a good supplier of **name of product**, it does happen that I am very pleased with a company I've been using for years now, **Name of company**. Their prices are great, their product is excellent, and they treat their customers very well.

I suggest you call **Name** at **telephone number**, and, as the saying goes, tell him I sent you.

Sincerely yours,

Chapter Nine

Working with the Business Community and the Public

Step by Step . . . to What's Best for You

The letters in this section help make it possible for your business to be a good citizen and neighbor, both within the business and professional community and in the community at large.

Letters Requesting Favors

Often, we need to ask favors of an everyday nature from business colleagues. Such requests can be made on the phone, but a letter accomplishes three things a phone call cannot. First, it gives your reader a chance to consider your request at some leisure rather than be tempted to come up with an off-the-cuff response in the course of a telephone conversation. Second, putting your request in the form of a letter makes the request seem all the more important. Finally, the letter makes the request an almost ceremonial occasion; by formalizing the request, it flatters and honors the reader.

1. State occasion of request ("We're thinking about finding new attorneys . . . ").

2. State your reason for coming to the reader with the request. ("As I recall, you are quite pleased with your current counsel. . .").

3. Make the request.

4. Close by expressing appreciation for whatever help the reader chooses to give.

Letters Raising Charitable Funds

Businesses often participate in community affairs by helping to raise funds. Effective fund-raising letters can take many forms, but the most effective spring from your own belief in the cause you are representing.

1. Present the need or problem the organization addresses.

2. Present the solution the organization offers.

3. Talk about your relation to the community and the organization. (Some effective letters begin with this: The writer establishes his sense of responsibility to the community.)

4. Make the pitch: How can the reader help?

5. Pose the rhetorical question: Wouldn't it be great to take care of this problem, address this need, help this community?

6. Invite action. Tell the reader what to do and how to do it.

Letters Declining Charitable Requests

Being a good citizen does not mean contributing to every charity or cause that solicits you. The goal is to decline the request without alienating any part of your community.

1. Acknowledge receiving the solicitation.

2. Decline the request. Usually, you will want to preface this with some expression of regret.

3. Give a succinct but firm reason for declining the request.

4. Only if appropriate, suggest that the reader solicit you again at a later time or under other, specified conditions.

5. Thank the reader for his understanding.

Letters Responding to Complaints

Answering complaints from your neighbors range from simple replies concerning situations that are easily addressed to major responses entailing profound consequences and requiring the advice and aid of legal counsel and others. The letters here deal with everyday matters. As with many ostensibly negative situations, an effective response can turn a problem into a positive step in building a healthy relationship between your business and the community.

1. Express your serious concern about the complaint.

2. State your policies and practices aimed at addressing the source of the complaint (for example, your policy on limiting noise pollution).

3. Propose action or state action already taken. If you dispute the complaint, state that here, together with your reasons for disputing it.

4. Invite a dialogue, perhaps a community meeting. Invite constructive advice.

5. Thank the reader for patience and understanding. Reinforce the idea that you are eager to work cooperatively to resolve the problem.

Letters Creating Goodwill

Why wait for a complaint to forge a stronger relationship with your community? Goodwill letters address various common concerns of the community to which you belong.

1. State your policy of community concern.

2. State the community-related issue.

3. Propose action, announce a community meeting, or simply invite interested community members to your place of business.

LETTERS REQUESTING FAVORS FROM BUSINESS ASSOCIATES

Jump Starts . . . to Get You on Your Way

We are thinking about putting in a **type of system/device** like the one you recently installed. I would be grateful for an opportunity to talk with you about the system.

Our current **contract for type of service** is about to expire, and I thought I should take the occasion to shop around a bit.

I have always been impressed with your voice mail system whenever I call. I'd like to come by and talk to you about it.

Can you give me some advice on **service or product**?

I have a cooperative information-sharing proposal to suggest to you.

Shakespeare's Polonius said it—"Neither a borrower nor a lender be"— but who cares about Polonius when you really need to borrow something?

Plant Visit

Dear **Name**:

We have just installed a **type of equipment** in our **Name** plant, and I understand that you have used this system for some **number** years.

I will be in your area during **dates**, and I was wondering if I might invite myself for a visit to your operation. We have had some interesting experiences with the equipment, and I believe that it would benefit us both to share information. If this seems like a good idea to you, please call me at **telephone number**, and we can set the date.

I look forward to hearing from you.

Sincerely yours,

Referral: Legal Services

Dear **Name**:

We're thinking about finding new attorneys to represent our firm. During the **number** years I've known and worked with you, I've come to greatly value your opinions and judgment. That's why I'm writing to ask you to recommend top-notch legal services.

As I recall, you are quite pleased with your current counsel. Could you give me the name of someone to speak to at that firm? Or is there another firm you are impressed with?

I'd certainly appreciate hearing your thoughts on the matter.

Sincerely yours,

Referral: Building Maintenance Service

Dear **Name**:

Our current building maintenance contract is about to expire, and, since we're not very happy with the company we've been working with, we are looking for a new building maintenance service. Your shop always looks terrific. Would be so kind as to tell me who services your building and to give me the name of someone to contact at the firm?

I know how busy you are, and I appreciate your taking the time to give me this information.

Sincerely,

Referral: Telephone Answering Service

Dear **Name**:

My practice has finally outgrown my answering machine, and it's time to hire myself a good—or, better yet, a great—answering service. I've always been impressed with your service whenever they pick up my calls to you. Are they as good as they sound? Would you mind giving me a call with the name of a contact person there?

I look forward to hearing from you.

Sincerely yours,

Recommendation: Copying Machine

Dear **Name**:

I have always envied your knack for buying just the right equipment. I thought it high time to stop envying you and start taking advantage of your expertise instead.

I'm in the market for a good copying machine—a general-purpose, high-volume workhorse—and I am completely bewildered by the choices out there. Can you help?

I have two questions. First: What machine do you use? Second: Do you recommend that machine—or something else?

I'd appreciate it if you'd take a moment to ponder these queries and then call me at **telephone number** with your considered opinion.

I look forward to hearing from you.

Sincerely yours,

Share Customer Information

Dear **Name**:

It was a great pleasure meeting you and speaking with you at **occasion**. In thinking about our conversation, it occurred to me that our businesses are largely complementary, and, to a great extent, we share the same customer base. Since this is the case, it seems to me worthwhile to discuss the possibility of sharing customer data with one another.

I realize that we tend to guard such information very closely. It is, after all, the life blood of our businesses. But in our case, since we are not in competition, I believe that we can only benefit by sharing information.

I suggest we get together to discuss the details. I have the following dates open and available: **dates**. If you would like to pursue this idea—and I hope you will—please call me at **telephone number** to arrange a meeting on one of these days or on an alternative date of your choosing.

I look forward to hearing from you.

Sincerely yours,

Borrow Equipment

Dear **Name**:

Can you help us?

We have contracted for a major **type** job, set to begin on **date**. We own one **piece of equipment**. We'll need two to get the job done. I had assumed that this equipment would be available for rental or lease, but I have just discovered that nothing is available anywhere near our start-up date.

Would it be possible to borrow yours?

We would be pleased to pay you the going rental rate of **$ amount** per day.

Could you give me a call at **telephone number** as soon as possible to let me know if the equipment is available? Of course, we will pick it up and return it at our expense.

I look forward to hearing from you at your earliest convenience.

Sincerely yours,

Cooperation in Achieving Common Goal—Appeal to Tax Commission

Dear **Name**:

Doubtless you have heard a great deal of talk in our business community about the proposed reassessment of commercial property taxes. In case you are not familiar with the issues, I've enclosed a press release our organization, **Name of organization**, has prepared.

What it comes down to is this: Reassessment is likely to mean higher taxes—from **percent amount** to **percent amount**—for every business in our area.

I am writing to ask you to attend a meeting of business persons in the **Name** area on **date** for the purpose of drafting an appeal to the tax commission. The meeting is vitally important, for we have strength only if we all pull together on this issue. We need to forge a united front and work together.

I hope I can count on your attendance at the meeting, which will be held at **location** at **time** on **date**.

Sincerely yours,

Cooperation in Achieving Common Goal—Complaint to Chamber of Commerce

Dear **Name**:

If you are like most business people in **location**, you can't be very happy with our Chamber of Commerce. I've heard a lot of folks complain for a long time.

And now I have a suggestion.

Let's stop complaining here and there, at this time and that, and get together with one voice so that the Chamber of Commerce cannot fail to hear us.

I will be coming around to your business within the next week or two with a petition, and I'm writing to you now to secure your support for it. It's time to join together and get things done.

I hope—I believe—I can count on you, and I look forward to calling on you.

Sincerely yours,

Cooperation in Achieving Common Goal—Attend Zoning Commission Meeting

Dear **Name**:

I like it here in **Name of community/neighborhood**. Business is good here. I don't want to move.

I suspect you feel the same way. And that's why I'm writing to you.

Like it or not, we may soon have no choice but to leave **Name of community/neighborhood**.

As you may have heard, the Zoning Commission is holding a hearing on rezoning **Name of community/neighborhood**, and there is a very real possibility that businesses like ours will be sent packing.

Right now, we do have a choice. We can sit back, do nothing, and wait for whatever decision is handed down.

Or we can get together, formulate a common agenda, attend the upcoming Zoning Commission meeting on **date**, and make our united position known.

I hope that I can count on you to attend a get-together for businesses in our area, which will be held at **location** at **time** on **date**. Let's discuss, decide, and get ready for the Zoning Commission meeting.

I want to stay here, and I'm betting you feel the same way.

Sincerely yours,

LETTERS RAISING CHARITABLE FUNDS

Jump Starts . . . to Get You on Your Way

I owe this community a great deal.

I believe in this community, and I believe in my professional colleagues who live and work in this community.

I am writing to leaders of our business community on behalf of **name of charity**.

Look around us. We're buried in garbage. Let's do something about it.

We are the fortunate ones.

How many letters do you get that begin, "I have a problem"? This letter begins differently. *We* have a problem.

I am proud to have been chosen to represent **Name of organization** as chairman of its **year** fund drive.

Charity Drive—Letters to Business Associates

Dear **Name**:

Our town has given me much since I started doing business here in **year**. Now I think it's time I gave something back. So I'm pledging on behalf of my business **$ amount** for **name of cause**.

Okay. So why am I telling you this?

Because I believe that your relationship to our community is very much like mine. It is a great place, full of generous, caring folks like you. I believe that you, too, will want to give back to this community by helping it address some of its most urgent needs, including **list charitable needs/projects**.

How about it? Won't you write a check for **$ amount** or whatever you feel appropriate?

A return envelope is enclosed.

Sincerely,

Dear **Name**:

I am writing to leaders of our business community on behalf of **Name of charity**. The folks at this organization have told me about some very urgent needs, needs that are going unmet because of a critical lack of funding. These include:

- **list**

I won't kid you. The fine people at **Name of charity** need some real money to do what has to be done—at least **$ amount** to provide the services I just mentioned.

The fact is, the government is not going to help, and I don't know of any multibillionaire waiting in the wings.

The fact is, it's all up to us. We have to help. And we have to help now.

Won't you write a check for **$ amount** or whatever you think appropriate and enclose it in the return envelope?

Help us help.

Sincerely,

Charity Drive—Letter to Neighbors

Dear **Name**:

I am proud that **Name of organization** has asked me to direct its fundraising efforts to build a new **name of project** for our community.

We've all talked a great deal over the years about how **name of community** needs a new **name of project**. Now we have an opportunity to stop talking and start giving.

We need a total of **$ amount** for construction and staffing costs. If each of us in this community gives just **$ amount**, we will reach our goal.

And if you can give even more we'll reach our goal sooner, and we'll have a headstart on funding for the following year.

I have enclosed a brochure that details the proposed **name of project**. If you have any questions, you may call **Name of organization representative** at **telephone number** or you can speak to me directly, at **telephone number**.

Sincerely yours,

LETTERS DECLINING CHARITABLE REQUESTS

Jump Starts . . . To Get You on Your Way

Thank you for telling me about **Name of charity**. Unfortunately, our funds are too limited to allow a contribution at this time.

It is very difficult to turn down your request, but I have no choice.

Your organization's efforts to fund name of program are highly commendable and, certainly, you are addressing a vital community need.

I take your request for a contribution to **Name of cause** very seriously, which is why I am responding personally.

Thank you for your letter about **Name of cause**. While I agree that cause is worth contributing to, I must tell you that I strongly differ with the policies of your organization in addressing this cause.

Funds Limited

Dear **Name**:

I was very impressed by your recent appeal for a donation to **Name of charity**, and I wanted to reply to you personally.

Unfortunately, our funds are too limited to allow us to make a contribution at this time. However, I am convinced that your cause is worthwhile, and I will keep it in mind for a donation at a later date, when we have the discretionary funds to devote to it.

Sincerely yours,

Funds Otherwise Committed

Dear **Name**:

It is difficult to turn down a request from **Name of organization**, but I'm afraid that I must. Our firm is active—financially and in terms of a commitment of time—in a number of community groups, and we simply have neither the excess funds nor the free time to devote to another organization. I regret this fact, but I know that an organization as worthwhile as yours will attract many supporters who can furnish the hours and the cash the **Name of organization** deserves.

Sincerely yours,

Request Made after Budget Deadline

Dear **Name**:

Your organization's efforts to fund **name of program** are highly commendable and, certainly, you are addressing a vital community need. I only wish that you had contacted **Name of company** earlier in the year. Our budget for community giving has already been allocated, and, particularly in these difficult times, I am sure you can appreciate the importance of remaining within the limits of a budget.

We allocate our charitable budget early in **month**. I invite you to contact us next **month**, when we will be able to give your program serious consideration.

Sincerely,

No Wish to Support Program

Dear **Name**:

You don't have to convince me that **Name of cause** is worth contributing to. But, in all frankness, I have to tell you that I strongly differ with the policies of your organization, specifically **list**.

I cannot, therefore, agree to make the donation you ask for.

Sincerely yours,

LETTERS RESPONDING TO COMPLAINTS

Jump Starts . . . to Get You on Your Way

I am distressed to hear that you have been inconvenienced by **activity or operation**.

I received your letter regarding **complaint**, and while I appreciate your feelings in the matter, I believe that you are being unfair.

I have received your letter of **date** concerning what you call the "impact" of our truck activity on local traffic conditions.

Your letter of **date** regarding an "offensive odor" you detected near our plant has been forwarded to me.

We at **Name of company** share your concern regarding **issue**.

Noise

Dear **Name**:

I am very sorry to hear that you have been disturbed by the noise of **activity or operation**. We make every effort to respect our neighbors and keep noise levels at a minimum. Of course, in our business—and in a commercially zoned area—a certain amount of noise is unavoidable.

However, I have spoken to our crews about your complaint, and I have reminded them of our policy of working as quietly as possible.

I thank you for your patience with us, and I believe you will notice a positive difference in noise level.

Sincerely yours,

Parking Problems

Dear **Name**:

I received your letter regarding the parking situation in our neighborhood. It is true that, like almost everyone else in this area, our employees park their cars on the street, and it is also an inescapable fact that more cars mean fewer available parking spaces. However, I have to question two aspects of your complaint. First, how can you determine which of the many cars parked on area streets belong to our employees? Second, of our **number** employees, **number** drive to work. I don't believe that this number of vehicles has a very significant impact on the parking situation here.

Name, I don't deny that parking is tight in this neighborhood. Our own employees remark on that fact. I do not believe, however, that we are in any significant way responsible for the problem. Perhaps the most constructive thing to do is set up a meeting with you and other concerned residents of the neighborhood in order to discuss how we might work together to petition the city to provide more parking in the neighborhood.

Why don't you give me a call at your convenience, so that we can discuss how, where, and when to arrange such a meeting?

Sincerely yours,

Traffic Problems

Dear **Name**:

I have received your letter of **date** concerning what you call the "impact" of our truck activity on local traffic conditions.

Like everyone else in this area, we want to promote efficient traffic patterns. It is as important to us as it is to you to attract customers and to get goods in and out of the area as quickly and as efficiently as possible. Therefore, I have asked my shipping and receiving department to study our trucking operation with an eye toward doing whatever we can to improve the situation.

Sincerely yours,

Offensive Odor

Dear **Name**:

Your letter of **date** regarding an "offensive odor" you detected near our plant has been forwarded to me.

We are unaware of any odor—offensive or otherwise—produced in or near our plant. No process we perform produces any appreciable odor.

These facts notwithstanding, I have asked our plant manager to make a thorough investigation to determine if any unusual activity had taken place on the day in question.

I will write you with information about the outcome of our investigation.

Sincerely yours,

Hire More Neighborhood People

Dear **Name**:

Like you, I am greatly concerned about the welfare of our neighborhood. After all, this is where I work. However, I am not sure what you mean by "hire more neighborhood people." The fact is that, at present, **percent amount** of our employees live within **number** miles of this plant.

That seems to me a very significant percentage. Furthermore, we advertise all openings in the neighborhood newspaper and post them on our signboard facing **Name** Street. In short, we give the people of this neighborhood ample notice of all openings.

Name, I believe we are very responsible to our neighbors. I cannot, of course, make living in this neighborhood a requirement of employment. That would be discriminatory. Aside from this radical—and illegal—step, if you have any ideas about how I might increase local hiring even beyond its present high rate, I would be pleased to listen to them.

Sincerely yours,

LETTERS CREATING GOODWILL

Jump Starts . . . to Get You on Your Way

We at **Name of company** do our best to be good citizens of this community. But we believe our best can always be better, and we need your help.

As a member of **Name of community/neighborhood**, we are concerned about **issue/problem**.

You are invited to a community get-together!

Thank you for your letter alerting us to the problem of children playing in our parking lot after closing time.

We'd like you to be our guest.

Name of company is throwing a good old-fashioned block party.

Inviting Community Comment

Dear Neighbor:

We at **Name of company** do our best to be good citizens of this community. But we believe our best can always be better, and we need your help.

You are invited to meet with the management of **Name of company** from **time** to **time** on **date** at our main location, **address**. We're eager to hear from you what you like and don't like about how we operate in **community**. It's an open, frank forum for discussion, strictly informal, and coffee and soft drinks will be served.

We hope to see you there.

Sincerely yours,

Neighborhood Meeting

Dear Neighbor:

All of us who live or work in **Name of community** are deeply concerned about **issue**. Many of us at **Name of company** have been hearing a lot of anxious talk about the subject, and we thought it would be useful for as many folks in the neighborhood as possible to get together for a community discussion.

We'd like to provide a forum for that discussion.

On **date** at **time** at **location**, **Name of company** will host an open meeting on **issue**. We believe that such a meeting is the first major step in effectively addressing **issue**, and we hope you'll attend.

Sincerely,

Security Concerns

Dear **Name**:

Thank you for your letter alerting us to the problem of children playing in our parking lot after closing time. We agree that this presents a security and safety problem—both for us and the children of the community. We plan to install higher fences and a gate, which will be locked after 6:30 P.M. and on weekends.

We appreciate your concern and your assistance.

Sincerely yours,

Chapter Ten

Working with Government and Regulatory Agencies

Step by Step . . . to What's Best for You

Faceless, heartless, devoid of humanity: a great bureaucratic machine. That's how most of us tend to think about government. Of course, governments—federal, state, local—are run by people. And this is where effective letters come in. Human beings respond to courtesy and to an acknowledgment that they are, in fact, more than cogs in a machine. Adding the personal touch of a cover letter to otherwise impersonal forms gives you an edge that just might coax a faster response of a higher quality than might otherwise be expected. This does not mean that you should send a long friendly letter with an application for a U.S. Small Business Administration Loan. Do get to your point quickly, and don't force the clerk or official to labor over what is, after all, a routine request. But let him know that you are a human being in a transaction with another human being.

1. If this is an inquiry, briefly describe your business and what you are requesting. If this is a cover letter, list the material enclosed. Point out anything exceptional about the material (for example, incomplete information that will arrive later).

2. Give clear mailing instructions and supply a phone number.

3. Close with a friendly plea for expedited service.

GETTING STARTED: LETTERS TO ACCOMPANY LICENSE AND PERMIT APPLICATIONS

Jump Starts . . . to Get You on Your Way

I am planning to open a **type of business**, employing **number** persons, in **name of community**. I would appreciate your sending me official information . . .

Enclosed are the completed **forms/numbers** required to apply for **type of permit**, the necessary documentation your department requested, and my check for **$ amount** to cover the application and permit fee.

Enclosed is all of the material you requested—**list material requested**—in your letter of **date**.

GETTING STARTED: COVER LETTERS TO ACCOMPANY AP-PLICATIONS

Local Business Licenses—Requesting Information

Licensing Agency, etc.

Appropriate Division

Address

Re: Small business licensing information

Dear Sir or Madam:

I am planning to open a **type of business**, employing **number** persons, in **Name of community**. I would appreciate your sending me official information on what licenses and permits are required, how to obtain them, the cost of obtaining them, and all necessary forms for obtaining them.

Please send the information to me at:

- **Name and address**

My telephone number is **telephone number**.

As I am planning to begin operating by **date**, I would be very grateful for your prompt response to this request.

Sincerely,

Cover Letters—Local Permits

Permit Department
Appropriate Division
Address
Re: Application for **permit type**

Dear Sir or Madam:

Enclosed are the completed **forms/numbers** required to apply for **type of permit,** the necessary documentation your department requested, and my check for **$ amount** to cover the application and permit fee.

If you have any questions about the enclosed materials, please call me at **telephone number**.

I appreciate your prompt attention to my application.

Sincerely,

Providing Additional Information Requested

Permit Department
Appropriate Division
Address
VIA CERTIFIED MAIL, RETURN RECEIPT REQUESTED
Re: Additional Material Requested Pursuant to **type of** Application **number**
Dear Sir or Madam:

Enclosed is all of the material you requested—**list material requested**—in your letter of **date**.

I trust that this material satisfactorily completes my application, but if you have any questions, please call me at **telephone number**. I do hope to begin operating no later than **date**. I would be very grateful for your efforts to expedite processing of the permit.

Sincerely,

GETTING MONEY: LETTERS TO ACCOMPANY LOAN APPLICATIONS AND INQUIRIES

Jump Starts . . . to Get You on Your Way

Please send me "Business Loans from the SBA," "Your Business and the SBA," and "Business Development Pamphlets" (Form 115A).

Kindly send Form 115B, "Business Development Booklets," to the following address:

I enclose completed forms, together with the necessary documents from my bank, to complete my application for SBA-guaranteed financing.

Small Business Administration Loans—Requesting Information

Small Business Administration
1441 L Street, NW
Washington, DC 20416

Dear Sir or Madam:

Please send me "Business Loans from the SBA," "Your Business and the SBA," and "Business Development Pamphlets" (Form 115A).

I am the owner of a small business, and I am actively looking for financing, so I would be very grateful for your prompt response.

Please send the material to

Name and address

Sincerely,

Superintendent of Documents

Government Printing Office

Washington, DC 20402

Dear Sir or Madam:

Kindly send Form 115B, "Business Development Booklets," to the following address:

Name and address

Sincerely,

Local office
U.S. Small Business Administration
address

Dear Sir or Madam:

Please send me the forms and documentation required to apply for SBA-guaranteed bank financing. I am the owner of a small business, which produces annual revenues under **$ amount**. My firm employs **number** people in addition to myself.

Please send the material to:

Name and address

Sincerely,

Small Business Administration Loans—Providing Information

Local office
Small Business Administration
address

Dear Sir or Madam:

I enclose completed forms, together with the necessary documents from my bank, to complete my application for SBA-guaranteed financing.

I have taken the time to ensure that the forms are as detailed as possible. Should you have any questions, however, you may call me at **telephone number**. The loan officer responsible for my account at **Name of bank** is **Name**, whose direct line is **telephone number**.

I appreciate your prompt attention to my application.

Sincerely yours,

Loans from Local Development Agencies—Requesting Information and Applications

Local Development Agency

Dear Sir or Madam:

I own a **type of business** in **community**. Our gross income is less than **$ amount** and we employ **number** people in addition to myself. Our firm has been operating in **Name of community** since **year**.

I would appreciate your sending me all available information on small business development programs that may be applicable to my case. If you have any questions, please call me at **telephone number**.

Thank you for your prompt response.

Sincerely,

Local Development Agency

Dear Sir or Madam:

I recently received in the mail your bulletin **title or number,** which mentions the availability of **name of program** for small businesses like mine. Kindly send me form **number,** which is mentioned in the bulletin, together with any other information or documents I need in order to apply for **name of program**.

I am grateful for your prompt response.

Sincerely,

Local Development Agency

Dear Sir or Madam:

Enclosed are the completed application materials for **type of loan, name of program**. I've been careful to answer all of your questions very fully, but please do call me if you need any further information. You may reach me at **telephone number**.

We are committed to doing business in this community and to growing with it. It would be a great help to us if you could expedite processing of the enclosed application.

Sincerely,

PART III

INSIDE BUSINESS

Chapter Eleven

Communicating with Employees: Personnel Issues

Step by Step . . . to What's Best for You

Communication with employees runs the gamut of emotion and encompasses a wide range of experience. True, depending on the size of your business, much communication with employees is simply a matter of talking face to face or shouting down the hall. But even the smallest business—one that employs a single person in addition to the owner—needs to put some of this communication in writing. Memories are short and very fallible, and, especially in an age clogged with litigation and regulation, adequate documentation is an absolute necessity.

Hiring

Letters concerning hiring include responses to applications, invitations to apply, or requests for additional information. Keep these letters as positive as possible without misleading the reader or giving false hopes. The response to an application requires that you:

1. Acknowledge that the application has been received. This can be in the form of a thank you.

2. Advise the reader of the action you are taking: You will review the application and be in touch by a certain date or if the application warrants a follow-up. You will keep the application on file. You are interested and require more information or an interview.

3. Thank the applicant for her interest in the company.

Rejecting Applications for Employment

Rejecting employment applications is never a pleasant task. It is important that you be clear in your rejection. Supply as detailed a reason for the rejection as you can, since this will be of some use to the applicant and will tend to avoid alienating him. Be as objective as possible, avoiding all reference to personality and character. Keep the letter job-related.

1. Thank the reader for his application.

2. Inform the reader that you have completed your review of his application.

3. State the rejection.

4. Clearly state the reasons for the rejection.

5. If appropriate, invite reapplication at a future time or "when a more suitable position becomes available," or when some other condition is met.

6. Express appreciation for the reader's interest in your firm.

Evaluations

A written evaluation of employee performance is very helpful to document employee development, to help your employees do the best work they can, to help determine salary adjustments, and to justify other actions. Whatever documentary purposes these letters serve, you should write them *to* the employee in question rather than *for* the record. Without falsifying the situation, do all you can to emphasize the positive. Build on the employee's sense of self-worth and pride. Don't use the evaluation letter as an occasion for threats and ultimatums. Your object is to develop, not to tear down.

1. Emphasize the team. Begin, if possible, by including the plural pronoun. Try not to define a "me" versus a "you."

2. Affirm the continuity of the relationship ("As always . . .").

3. Enumerate the positives.

4. Enumerate the negatives—if possible, as areas that "could use improvement" or would "benefit from further development."

5. Thank the employee for her contribution to the team.

6. Invite questions and discussion.

Recommendations

There are occasions when a former employee—or even a current employee—will approach you for a letter of recommendation. Assuming the recommendation is warranted, there is good reason to write an effective letter. It is not just in the employee's best interest, but in your own as well. Depending on the size of your community and the nature of your business, the professional world you inhabit can be quite small. It pays to extend your influence as widely and as happily through that world as possible.

1. State your pleasure in recommending the employee.

2. Give details of your working relationship with him, including most recent position, years on the job, promotions, and so on. It is best to avoid mention of salary figures, since this is a matter between you and the employee on the one hand and between the employee and the prospective employer on the other. Do highlight particular projects and accomplishments—the more specific, the better.

3. Assure the reader that she will find working with this employee a rewarding experience.

4. If you are willing to discuss the recommendation further, invite the reader to contact you.

Thank You

As it is a good idea to thank vendors and suppliers for special effort or simply for working well with you over an extended period, so letters of thanks or commendation are effective tools for employee management. There is no mystery about these letters: Everyone enjoys a good pat on the back, an acknowledgment that they are appreciated. Such letters will not "spoil" an employee; on the contrary, they strengthen the bond between employer and employee and generally improve performance.

1. Observe that another successful (or challenging) year has ended or that a project has been completed successfully.

2. Acknowledge the reader's role in the year's work or in making the project a success.

3. Thank her.

4. End by looking forward to more years and more successful projects.

Apologies

It is critically important that your employees or the personnel you supervise trust your judgment, expertise, and experience. But it is equally important that they understand that you are also human and fallible and that you admit your errors. At the very least, you want to create a working atmosphere in which personnel feel free to come to you with constructive criticism. Federal Aviation Authority studies have shown that many accidents, resulting from pilot error, could have been prevented had the co-pilot pointed out the error. However, airline crews are trained to regard the captain as an absolute authority whose decisions must not be questioned. To be sure, if you are the owner of a business or the manager of a firm or department, your authority must be clear. But to foster an atmosphere of unquestioning obedience is to invite disaster. As with any letter of apology, those written to employees should not be abject. Don't magnify your error out of proportion, but do own up to it and simply apologize for it.

1. State the context of the apology—the event, the error, the unwarranted criticism or reprimand.

2. State that you were wrong or mistaken.

3. Apologize.

4. Express your appreciation of the reader's understanding and willingness to forgive.

Reprimands

Letters of reprimand serve two important purposes. They provide creative, constructive criticism to correct or improve a situation and aid in the development of an employee. They also serve as a documentary record of employee performance. This record is invaluable as a rationale for declining a request for a salary increase or promotion or, in extreme cases, as backup for termination. Assuming you wish to retain the employee, the tone of a letter of reprimand should be as positive and constructive as the situation permits. Explain the nature of the problem, suggest ways in which the situation can be improved or corrected, invite the employee to discuss the situation with you. Do not attack the employee personally. Do not make threats—but do, as appropriate, advise the employee of possible consequences if an infraction is repeated or a situation goes unremedied.

1. If possible and appropriate, begin by acknowledging the generally positive nature of the reader's performance.

2. State the nature of the problem, infraction, or issue.

3. Explain the effect of the reader's performance on the welfare of the company.

4. Suggest remedies, appropriate steps to resolve the situation, and/or a conference with you.

5. Advise the reader of consequences to himself if the infraction is repeated or the situation goes unresolved.

6. Assure the reader of your willingness to work with him to correct the problem.

Refusing Employee Requests

Letters refusing salary increase, promotion, or such things as a change in work hours, additional break time, equipment, and so on are difficult to write well, but they are essential to managing personnel creatively, balancing what employees want with what the firm is able prudently to provide. Like letters of praise and thanks, these letters also have as their object the development and maintenance of a sense of community and teamwork. The key to refusal—without alienating the reader—is explanation and persuasion.

1. Acknowledge receiving and reviewing the request.

2. State the rejection; usually this should be prefaced with some expression of regret ("Unfortunately, . . .").

3. Explain the reasons for the refusal, with emphasis on the company as a whole and the reader as a vital part of the team.

4. If possible, propose a compromise or alternative, or propose a time and conditions that might allow the request to be granted.

5. Thank the reader for her understanding and cooperation, and sincerely acknowledge your gratitude for both.

Responding to Complaints

Few things will more strongly or more immediately affect the employer-employee or supervisor-subordinate relationship than how you respond to a complaint. A letter is the ideal format for such a response because it shows that you take the complaint seriously, it avoids the emotional misunderstandings and failures of articulation that can occur in merely verbal exchanges, and it records and documents the nature of the complaint, your understanding of the complaint, your responsiveness to the complaint, and the proposed action. In the event of further difficulties or of legal allegations, such documentation is invaluable.

1. Acknowledge receiving and reviewing the complaint.

2. If at all possible and appropriate, thank the reader for bringing the matter to your attention.

3. Propose action, which might simply be a call for a meeting, discussion, or mediation. If you dispute the complaint or are unable or unwilling to propose a remedy, state this and explain the basis of this response.

4. Affirm your willingness to work together to address and resolve the complaint or to arrive at an alternative solution.

Accepting Resignations

No resignation should be accepted without some form of documentation. It is not enough for the employee to say "I quit" and for you to reply,

"Okay." Even if the employee does not resign in writing, you should acknowledge the resignation in a letter written to him and copied into your files. As with most ostensibly pro-forma business documents, the letter accepting a resignation can and should be modified to serve as means of expressing productive emotions—congratulations or regret—or of inviting additional action—reconsideration or later return.

1. Acknowledge the resignation.

2. Accept it with congratulations, regret, etc.

3. If appropriate, share a memory, comment on years of service, and so on.

4. If appropriate, invite reconsideration or later return.

5. Wish the reader success in his new position or endeavor.

Terminations

The principal reason for writing a *letter* of termination may seem obvious. Termination is the one action that absolutely requires careful documentation. However, even the letter of termination can be positive and creative, preserving as much as possible—in this small world of business—your firm's relationship with the former employee. As with most "negative" letters, the key element is explanation. At bare minimum, for purposes of documentation, you must:

1. Announce the action.

2. State the effective date.

3. List reasons for the action.

4. Advise the reader of the disposition of his final check, addressing such issues as vacation pay due, severance pay due, removal of personal belongings, and so on.

Many employers will want to do more than this, expressing regret, satisfaction with performance, and offering some form of assistance (for example, letters of recommendation) in finding the reader a new position.

HIRING LETTERS

Jump Starts . . . to Get You on Your Way

Thank you for responding to our announcement of a **type of position** position at **Name of company**.

Thank you for sending us your resume. At this time, we have no appropriate positions open, but we will keep your resume on file.

We have received your resume, which we will keep on file. We will advise you of a suitable opening, should one become available.

This will confirm the salary offer I made at the time of our interview on **date**.

It is my great pleasure to welcome you to **Name of company**.

Name or **Name of company** tells me that you may be interested in moving from your present position. **Name** spoke so highly of you that I am eager for the opportunity of speaking with you in person.

Name of company invites your application letter and resume for the position of **name of position**.

Responding to Applications: Immediate Position

Dear **Name**:

Thank you for responding to our announcement of a **type of position** position at **Name of company**.

Please be assured that your application will be evaluated thoroughly and thoughtfully. We expect this process to take approximately **time period**. In the meantime, should there be a change in your employment status, we would appreciate your letting us know.

Thank you for your interest in **Name of company**.

Sincerely yours,

Dear **Name**:

Thank you for sending your application and resume in response to our announcement of a **type of position** position at **Name of company**.

We want to ensure ample time to evaluate each candidate, so we do not anticipate having an answer for you before **date**. We ask that you refrain from inquiring about the status of your application before then. However, should your employment situation change before you hear from us, please do let us know.

We appreciate your interest in **Name of company**.

Sincerely yours,

Responding to Applications: Future Opening

Dear **Name**:

Thank you for sending us your resume. As our announcement specified, we anticipate that the position of **name of position** will become available by **date**. The application period will close on **date**, at which time we will evaluate all qualified applicants and notify those we wish to interview by **date**. In the meantime, should your employment status change, we would appreciate your informing us.

Thanks for your interest in **Name of company**.

Sincerely yours,

Responding to Applications: Will Keep On File

Dear **Name**:

Thank you for sending us your resume. At this time, we have no appropriate positions open, but we will keep your resume on file, and we encourage you to keep us up to date on your status and availability.

Sincerely yours,

Responding to Application: Need Additional Information

Dear **Name**:

Thank you for sending us your resume pursuant to your application for **name of position** at **Name of company**.

Your education and professional background suggest that this job may well be for you. However, we do need some additional information before we can proceed further on your application. Specifically, please provide greater detail on your experience at **Name of company**, specifying three or four key projects in which you played a principal role. Include a brief description of each project, your involvement in it, as well as what you accomplished—and failed to accomplish.

We are in the final stage of evaluating applications, so it is important that we receive this additional information no later than **date**.

Sincerely yours,

Inviting Application and Resume

Dear **Name**:

Just the other day, I was speaking with **Name** of **Name of company** about our staffing needs in the area of **job area**. Without a moment's hesitation, he mentioned your name. Indeed, you have quite a fan in **Name**.

With the good press he gave you, I don't see how I could fail to ask if you are interested in working for **Name of company** as a **title**. If the possibility appeals to you, please send, to my attention, a full resume.

I enclose a description of the position we have open. If you have any questions before you send me your resume, please do call.

Sincerely yours,

Dear **Name**:

Name of company invites your application letter and resume for the position of **name of position**. A complete job description, with experience requirements and salary levels, is enclosed.

The position is available now, and we will accept no applications after **date**.

Please address all materials to **name, department, address, etc.**.

Name of company is an equal opportunity employer.

Sincerely,

Confirming Job Offer

Dear **Name**:

It is my pleasure to welcome you to **Name of company**.

This letter formally confirms our offer to you of a position as **name of position** to begin on **date** and in accordance with the following terms:

1. Your employment is subject to a probation period of **number weeks/months**, during which time we may terminate your employment without notice or with payment in lieu of notice.

2. Your gross cash salary will be **$ amount** per year, payable **weekly/every two weeks**. Salary is subject to review by **date**.

3. Fringe benefits include: **list**.

4. It is company policy to issue bonuses from time to time for exceptional performance. Your supervisor will discuss with you the criteria for the payment of bonuses at appropriate intervals during your employment.

5. Your working hours are **time** a.m. to **time** p.m., Monday through Friday, with **minutes** off for lunch and two **number**-minute coffee breaks each day.

6. All overtime work must be requested and authorized by your supervisor. Normally, overtime will be compensated at the rate of time and a half.

7. You have **number** weeks' paid vacation per year. Vacation time must be reserved **number weeks/months** in advance. However, no vacation time may be taken during the probationary period.

8. Your employment duties are listed in the job description marked "Exhibit A" and attached to this letter.

9. You acknowledge that any confidential information learned in the course of your employment constitutes trade secrets, which you agree not to disclose to anybody outside of this firm both during and after your term of employment. You acknowledge this as a binding pledge.

If the above accurately represents your understanding of the terms of our offer of employment, please sign and date one copy of this letter and return it to me.

We are delighted to have you working with us, and we look forward to seeing you on the **date**.

Sincerely,

Accepted:

_____

(signature)   (date)

Confirming Salary Offers

Dear **Name**:

This will confirm the salary offer I made at the time of our interview on **date**.

It is understood and agreed that your starting annual salary will be **$ amount**, in addition to the following fringe benefits and bonus provisions: **specify**.

Please acknowledge your acceptance of this offer by signing and dating one copy of this letter and returning it to me.

And welcome aboard!

Sincerely yours,

Accepted:

_____

(signature)   (date)

REJECTING APPLICATIONS FOR EMPLOYMENT

Jump Starts . . . to Get You on Your Way

Thank you for sending us your resume and letter. They are both very impressive. At this time, however, **Name of company** has no suitable positions available.

After carefully reviewing your resume, our selection committee has determined that your background and skills, while most impressive, are not best suited to the position available.

Thank you for submitting your resume to us. While your educational background is certainly impressive, suggesting a most promising future, the present position requires a person with some years of practical experience in the field.

Few things are more frustrating than being told that you are "over-qualified" for a job—but, I'm afraid, that is precisely the case in the present situation.

No Suitable Position Currently Available

Dear **Name**:

Thank you for sending us your resume and letter. They are both very impressive. At this time, however, **Name of company** has no suitable positions open.

We appreciate your interest in **Name of company**.

Sincerely yours,

Skills Unsuited to Position

Dear **Name**:

Thank you for your application for the position of **name of position** at **Name of company**.

After carefully reviewing your resume, our selection committee has determined that your background and skills, while most impressive, are not best suited to this position. Therefore, we cannot pursue your application further.

We wish you the best of luck in securing a position appropriate to your fine credentials.

Sincerely yours,

Inadequate Experience

Dear **Name**:

Thank you for your application for the position of **name of position** at **Name of company**.

Your educational background is impressive, and we believe you have a promising future. However, the present position demands a person thoroughly experienced in the field, and, at this stage in your career, your experience is not sufficient. We cannot, therefore, pursue your application further.

Please accept our wishes for the best of luck in finding an appropriate position. Thanks for your interest in **Name of company**.

Sincerely yours,

Over-qualified

Dear **Name**:

Thanks for sending us your resume and application for the position of **name of position** here at **Name of company**.

Few things are more frustrating than being told that you are "over-qualified" for a job—but, I'm afraid, that is precisely the case in the present situation. The position we have available is strictly at the entry level and is not, therefore, appropriate for a person of your extensive experience. I cannot, therefore, pursue your application further.

I am confident that a person with your fine qualifications will be successful in securing an appropriate and rewarding position.

Sincerely yours,

EVALUATIONS

Jump Starts . . . to Get You on Your Way

Another great year has come to an end—and, as usual, you've played a big part in bringing it to a successful conclusion.

I just wanted to let you know: You have made a big difference here at **Name of company**.

This letter is not a reprimand or a threat or collection of my personal gripes.

I hope that you realize how much I value your contribution to **Name of company**. Please bear in mind as I outline a few areas in which, I believe, your performance could be developed further and improved.

Well, we have come to the end of **name of project**. I want to thank you for all your hard work on it.

Year-end Letter

Dear **Name**:

Let's congratulate ourselves on completing another successful year.

As always, I have greatly enjoyed working with you. Your performance in general has been top notch, and I particularly appreciate the fine work you did on the following projects: **list**.

I believe that you would agree with me that **name of project** was less successful than the others. We have already gone over the problems with that project, and we have agreed that, in the future, you will devote more care to **list items**.

Of course, I realize that you cannot hit a homerun every time you come up to bat. Your average this past year, as it has been every year, was outstanding. I am confident that, together, we can work to make it even better.

Thanks for your effort, cooperation, and loyalty.

Sincerely yours,

Room For Improvement

Dear **Name**:

Let me begin by telling you what this letter is *not*.

It is not a reprimand.

It is not a warning.

It is not a threat.

It is not meant to make you feel bad.

What I want to communicate to you is feedback from two customers concerning your handling of their accounts. **Name** and **Name** both mentioned to me—in casual conversation—that they thought you were efficient, but that you weren't giving them 100 percent. They did not feel you were always responsive and available.

Name, I know how hard you work. I also know that you have a lot of accounts and that you cannot let any one account monopolize your time. Nevertheless, **Name** and **Name** are, as you know, big clients, and I suggest you think about how you might manage, in the first place, to give them more of your time and, even more important, to give them the *feeling* that you are absolutely, 100 percent committed to them and their needs.

I think, after all, that what we are primarily dealing with here are feelings, impressions. That's where you could use a little work. It's not enough to do your job, to service your accounts. You need to give each of them the feeling that nobody means more to you. I hope you'll think about this important point.

Sincerely yours,

Dear **Name**:

I greatly value your work here at **Name of company**, which is why I feel that I can be frank in mentioning two areas in which your performance could use improvement.

You have an excellent record in turning up sales leads, but I believe that you could be more consistent and systematic in following up all of your leads. I've actually had people you've contacted call me to ask for information you promised. Don't get me wrong: I'm grateful for the inquiries. But I shouldn't be the one following through, and you should be getting back to these potential customers rather than putting them in the position of calling us.

You also need to follow up *after* the sale. The best source of new customers for any business is the pool of current customers. By all means, go prospecting; but start with the prospects who have already had experience with us.

Please understand that I think you are doing an excellent job. These suggestions are meant not so much to address deficiencies as they are intended to guide you in honing the ample skills you already possess.

I'd be happy to talk any of this over with you, if you wish.

Sincerely yours,

Special Project

Dear **Name**:

Well, we have come to the end of **name of project**. I want to thank you for all your hard work on it. I believe it will pay off.

Before either of us becomes numb from too many pats on the back, however, I want to meet with you to discuss the following aspects of the project, to talk about what went right and what could have gone better, and to consider alternatives for the future. Specifically I would like to discuss: **list**.

Please give me a call as soon as possible to set up a meeting time.

Sincerely yours,

RECOMMENDATIONS

Jump Starts . . . to Get You on Your Way

It is a pleasure to recommend **Name** to you. We worked together for **number** years, from **year** to **year**.

It is a pleasure to recommend **Name** for **name of position** at your firm. We have employed **Name** repeatedly on a temporary basis, as our needs warranted.

People like **Name** don't come along every day.

When **Name** asked me to write a letter of recommendation, I agreed without hesitation.

There aren't many people in whom I place absolute confidence. **Name** is one of those few.

We have engaged the services of **Name** on **number** occasions, most recently in **month**. He is an outstanding **title of profession/skill**, who completes a job on time and with a minimum of fanfare.

I have to admit, it's hard for me to write this letter. **Name** is the kind of free-lancer you really want to keep all to yourself.

Longtime, Regular Employee

Dear **Name**:

It is with very mixed emotions that I recommend **Name** to you. I don't mean that I'm uncertain about my recommendation. **Name** is a superb employee, a hard worker, bright, and personable. My emotions are mixed because, on the one hand, I am not in a position to offer **Name** the kind of promotion he deserves, but, on the other hand, by recommending him to you for a position that seems tailor-made for him, I'll be losing the services of a terrific person.

Still, I don't want to hold **Name** back, and the opportunity you offer is a valuable one.

It's a valuable opportunity for both of you. People like **Name** don't come along every day. He was, for example, instrumental in the successful completion of **list projects** and is especially skilled at **list skills**. As you can see, I trust him with a wide variety of assignments. He has never failed to deliver anything other than first-rate work.

Sad as I'll be to see **Name** leave, I must recommend him to you without reservation or hesitation.

Sincerely yours,

Temporary Employee

Dear **Name**:

It is a pleasure to recommend **Name** for **name of position** at your firm. We have employed **Name** repeatedly on a temporary basis, as our needs warranted. She is the kind of person who comes into a new situation, sizes it up instantly, and digs in. **Name** is intelligent, a quick study, and very personable. I recommend her without hesitation.

Sincerely yours,

Dear **Name**:

I am delighted to recommend to you **Name** for **name of position** at your firm. We have worked with **Name number** times over the past **number years, months** on a temporary basis. As you know, in many ways, temporary assignments are the most demanding, requiring the employee to come into an unfamiliar situation and get up to speed with a minimum of delay and without tying up your permanent staff. Let me assure you that **Name** has always fit in here as if he'd been with us for thirty years.

Name is fast, efficient, a hard worker, and very easy to get along with. I recommend him to you highly, and I invite you to call me at **telephone number** if you need any further information.

Sincerely,

Free-lance

Dear **Name**:

We have engaged the services of **Name** on **number** occasions, most recently in **Month**. He is an outstanding **title of profession/skill**, who completes a job on time and with a minimum of fanfare. He worked on the following projects for us: **list**. In each case, we were thoroughly satisfied in regard to quality, timeliness of completion, and price.

I recommend **Name** without reservation. You'll enjoy working with him.

Sincerely yours,

Dear **Name**:

I have to admit, it's hard for me to write this letter. **Name** is the kind of free-lancer you really want to keep all to yourself. But, for her sake as well as yours, I guess I'm willing to share.

Name has worked with us on **list projects**, which includes some of our most sensitive accounts. She is thoroughly skilled, takes great pride in her work, and always finishes on time and as promised, even in the most trying circumstances. She is flexible—doesn't so much as bat an eye when we ask her to make last-minute changes—and, while I know she manages a large client list for herself, we never had the feeling we were being asked to take a back seat to anyone.

Name is a real find. You'll enjoy working with her.

If you'd like any more details, just give me a call.

Sincerely yours,

THANK YOU

Jump Starts . . . to Get You on Your Way

I don't want this year to slip by without acknowledging the contribution you have made to this firm.

It has been one hell of a year. Thanks in large part to you, we've come through it not only unscathed, but richer.

You have racked up quite a sales record this quarter.

I want to thank you for your willingness to defer a much-deserved salary increase during what has proven to be very difficult times for this company.

Just a note to thank you for putting in overtime when we desperately needed it.

I wanted to let you know as soon as I could just how pleased we are with **name of project**. You and your team did a marvelous job, and you were a pleasure to work with.

At Year's End

Dear **Name**:

I couldn't let the year lapse without taking this opportunity of thanking you for having done a great job—day in, day out, spring, summer, fall, and winter. It's very special people like you that make it possible to run a productive, profitable business.

For yourself, I wish you a happy and prosperous New Year. For all of us, as a company, I *know* that, because of your good work, we *will* have just such a New Year.

Sincerely yours,

Dear **Name**:

Well, we've been through another challenging year together—challenging, but, thanks to your help, productive and profitable. We don't take you for granted, **Name**, and I just wanted you to know that.

Have a happy and prosperous New Year. With your help again, we are confident that *our* New Year will be great.

Best wishes,

Exceptional Performance

Dear **Name**:

Bagging the **Name** account was quite an accomplishment. Then going on to snare the **Name**, **Name**, and **Name** accounts in addition to that—well, it's almost too much to believe.

But you did it.

Thanks—not just for exceptional performance, but for making exceptional performance your routine.

Best regards,

Dear **Name**:

What's that old poem—"They Said It Couldn't Be Done"? That's what I think of when I review the marvelous job you've done on **name of project**. Schedules were impossibly tight, problems were plentiful, and the client was demanding. They said it couldn't be done—but, thanks in large part to your fine work, we did it, and the client is delighted.

Best regards,

Deferring Request for Salary Increase

Dear **Name**:

I want to thank you for your tremendously understanding and unselfish willingness to defer your request for a salary increase during these difficult times for us.

It's hard for us, and, I know, it was hard for you to put off asking for a much-deserved raise.

Please rest assured that I will put through a salary increase just as soon as we have safely navigated the very perilous waters in which we find ourselves at present.

Sincerely yours,

Overtime

Dear **Name**:

I know how devoted you are to your family. That's one of the things I most admire and respect about you.

So I am that much more aware of what a sacrifice your recent overtime represents, and I want to thank you for it. Your hard work brought us through a difficult and demanding period, and I am deeply grateful for your dedication.

Best regards,

Dear **Name**:

Just a note to thank you for putting in overtime when we desperately needed it. You came through eagerly and uncomplainingly—and at a time of year when most of us would like extra time off, not on, the job.

Thanks for being there when the team needed you.

Sincerely yours,

Special Project

Dear **Name**:

At long last we have completed **name of project**. I am pleased, and our client is delighted. The project, of course, was a team effort—but you were a key member of that team, and much of our success is due to your fine work.

We all appreciate what you did and congratulate you on it. Thanks.

Sincerely yours,

Dear **Name**:

I wanted to let you know as soon as I could just how pleased we are with **name of project**. You and your team did a marvelous job, and you were a pleasure to work with.

I very much look forward to working with you again. I hope it will be soon.

Best regards,

Bringing in New Business

Dear **Name**:

If you've read our quarterly report, you'll see that we've been growing.

A significant part of that growth has been due to employees like you, who aren't content just to serve the clients we have, but who work overtime to bring in new business. You've been responsible for introducing **number** accounts to our services, and that is a significant accomplishment.

Thanks for helping us grow.

Best regards,

Dear **Name**:

This year you've brought into **Name of company** no fewer than **number** new clients. These are the kind of numbers we like to get, and they are the kind of numbers we need in order to develop and grow as a company.

Thanks for your innovative hard work and your great skill in representing **Name of company**.

Best wishes,

Reviving an Inactive Customer

Dear **Name**:

Regarding **Name of customer**: He once was lost, but now is found. And *you* found him.

We can't afford to lose customers, and when they stray, it's well worth the special effort necessary to bring them back. You've made that effort, and we're all grateful to you for it.

Thanks for bringing us **Name of customer** back where he belongs.

All best,

Dear **Name**:

You just don't give up, do you?

I was pleasantly surprised to see a new order from **Name**, but I was not surprised to see that you were the one who got her back. I am very grateful that you made the extra effort to revive what has been a most productive account.

Nice work.

Best regards,

APOLOGIES

Jump Starts . . . to Get You on Your Way

I was way off base.

I gave you a very hard time about **issue, project, etc.** the other day. Then, only after I had opened my big mouth, did I think to review the file.

I have just completed a thorough investigation of the incident of **date**. It is now quite clear and apparent that I acted prematurely in reprimanding you.

I am not going to tell you that postponing your much-deserved raise was as hard on me as it is on you.

Please accept my profound apology for issuing you an incorrectly calculated payroll check.

Undeserved Criticism

Dear **Name**:

If it is human to err and divine to forgive, I'm offering you a shot at divinity. I gave you a very hard time about **issue, project, etc.** the other day. Then, only after I had opened my big mouth, did I think to review the file.

Let me tell you something you already know: You did nothing wrong, and certainly nothing to merit the criticism I made.

I'm sorry for speaking out prematurely and mistakenly, and I am particularly sorry if my remarks caused you any anxiety or irritation.

Best regards,

Undeserved Reprimand

Dear **Name**:

Regarding the incident of **date**, my office has completed a thorough investigation, and it is now painfully clear to me that I acted prematurely in issuing a reprimand.

It is now apparent that you were in no way responsible for any part of the incident.

I have written a detailed report, which is attached, correcting my error and withdrawing the reprimand. A copy of the report will be filed with your employment record, together with this letter.

Finally, I want to extend to you my personal apology for issuing this completely unwarranted reprimand. It was simple human error—a mistake—but with painful consequences for you. I can only trust to your generous nature to forgive me.

Sincerely yours,

Poor Working Conditions

Dear Colleagues:

The remodeling project currently under way in our offices has meant that all of us have had to put up with a lot of inconvenience. Our jobs are hard enough under the best of circumstances. Having to work around construction crews makes the work that much more difficult.

I want to take this opportunity to apologize for the protracted inconvenience and to thank you for your patience and good humor under adverse circumstances.

The work will be finished soon.

Sincerely yours,

Necessity of Postponing a Raise

Dear **Name**:

I am not going to tell you that postponing your much-deserved raise was as hard on me as it is on you.

It's much, much harder on you, and I am very sorry for that.

I am grateful for your understanding and willingness to hold on until we are in a financial position to put the salary increase into effect.

Sincerely yours,

Payroll Problem

Dear **Name**:

Few things are more disquieting than to receive a paycheck for less than you expected. I am very sorry that this happened to you.

A keypunch error resulted in a misplaced digit, and our computer simply spit out what we had inadvertently told it to.

Enclosed is a check for the correct amount. Please accept it with our apologies and our thanks for your patience and understanding in this matter.

Sincerely,

Postponement of Vacation

Dear **Name**:

I know how much you were looking forward to your vacation, for which you are long overdue. I can only apologize to you for asking you to postpone your plans and express my gratitude for your willingness to do so.

We need you at this critical juncture, and, as usual, you have come through with high spirits and good humor.

Sorry—and thanks.

Sincerely yours,

REPRIMANDS

Jump Starts . . . to Get You on Your Way

We have worked together for a very long time, so I feel that I can speak frankly with you.

I was very disturbed to receive a report that, since **date**, you have failed to update the files in your division.

I was distressed to see that you reported for work late on **date**—for the _**nth** time this month **quarter, etc.**.

I don't want to make the folks in this office feel like they've got to punch a clock. However, we are a team, and, as a team, we depend on everyone being where they are supposed to be when they are supposed to be there.

We need to get together to talk about your recent performance evaluations.

I received a phone call yesterday, **date**, that distressed me very much. One of your customers, who was (understandably) angry enough to take her business elsewhere, described some very rude treatment from you, including what I would consider abusive language.

This firm thrives on creativity and initiative, but it also operates on a solid understanding of who exercises final authority over certain decisions.

A small company like ours is a lot like a family. We cannot operate happily and efficiently by threats, coercion, yelling, and complaining. What keeps us going is an attitude of cooperation.

Habitual Lateness

Dear **Name**:

I was distressed to see that you reported for work late on **date**—for the _nth time this month **quarter, etc.**

Name, we try to be reasonable and understanding at **Name of company**. There are occasions when it is simply unavoidable to be late. Traffic is bad, you have a last-minute emergency at home, whatever. But your lateness, I think you'll agree, has become an unwelcome habit.

Name, we depend on your being here at regular hours. We need you here. You are a valuable part of this operation.

I ask that you make whatever adjustments are necessary in your morning routine to get here on time. If there is a problem I should know about, please come in and talk to me right away. I am confident we can work together to make any necessary adjustments.

Sincerely yours,

Dear **Name**:

We need to talk about your frequent—even habitual—late mornings this past **month, etc**.

The team in this office needs you, and we need to be able to rely on you to be where you are supposed to be when you are supposed to be there. It's that simple.

If there is a problem or situation I should know about, please come in and talk to me about it. Maybe I can help. But, whatever the cause of your being late, we must resolve it without delay.

Sincerely yours,

Early Departure

Dear **Name**:

You are valuable to us. We need you. And that means we need you when you are supposed to be here.

Lately, that's been a problem.

Since **date**, you have left at least one-half hour **or other period** early no fewer than **number** times. **Name**, none of us punches a clock here, and I don't sit in my office with one eye on you and the other on the clock. But you are expected to report to work on time and remain at work—and available to all of us—until at least **hour** o'clock.

If there is some problem I should know about, please come in and let me in on it. Let's work together on it. Otherwise, I must insist that, except in cases of emergency, you remain in the office and available until regular closing hours.

Sincerely yours,

Dear **Name**:

I don't believe in punching a clock, and I have never run this office with sign-in and sign-out sheets and the like. There are times when coming in late or leaving early is unavoidable. But, **Name**, during the past few **months or other time period**, you have been routinely leaving the office a good half-hour **or other period** early.

Name, it is not that I am trying to squeeze every last ounce of work out of you. But we are a team here, and we need to function as one. We need to be in place and available *routinely and dependably* from **hour** o'clock to **hour** o'clock. Anything less than this, and you are letting down the team. It's unfair, and it's no way to do business.

Do we need to get together to discuss your schedule? Perhaps you would like to start earlier in order to leave earlier? It can be worked out. If there is something I should know about, please, let's discuss it. Otherwise, take this letter as my instruction to plan on leaving the office no earlier than **hour** o'clock.

Sincerely,

Too Many Sick Days

Dear **Name**:

I have never felt comfortable establishing an absolute limit on the number of "sick days" an employee may take. After all, how can you predict how many days you might be sick?

However, I do rely on employees to use sick days only when absolutely necessary, and if an illness is chronic, I expect the employee to discuss the situation with me.

Name, you are a valuable part of this operation. I need to be able to depend on you—and that means, in significant part, to depend on your presence. Since **date**, you have reported yourself sick no fewer than **number** times. I cannot afford to be without you on such a regular, chronic basis.

Name, if you have a medical condition—or some other problem —I should know about, let's discuss it in strictest confidence. Otherwise, I must tell you that I feel you are abusing your sick day privileges, and this rate of absence simply cannot continue. We cannot do business this way.

Sincerely yours,

Dear **Name**:

During the past **time period** you have called in sick **number** times. That is an average of **number** per week. Please be advised that I consider this excessive. It is a great hardship on all of us to be without your services on such a regular basis.

Name, if you are suffering from a chronic medical condition I should know about, we must discuss a way of scheduling your time more effectively to cope with it. Any such discussion, of course, would be in the strictest confidence. In the absence of such a condition, I have no choice but to conclude that you are abusing your sick-leave privileges, and I must inform you that such abuse is resulting in far too high a rate of absence.

Sincerely yours,

Rude to a Customer

Dear **Name**:

I received a phone call yesterday, **date**, that distressed me very much. One of your customers, who was (understandably) angry enough to take her business elsewhere, described some very rude treatment from you, including what I would consider abusive language.

I want to talk to you about this incident and, especially, to hear your side of the encounter. Without prejudging, however, I must remind you that ours is a service-oriented operation. We have to treat each and every customer as someone very special to us. And, indeed, each customer *is* special. Each customer, one by one, keeps us in business and pays our salaries.

With this in mind, please see me in my office at **time** on **date** to discuss your interaction with this customer.

Sincerely yours,

Repeated Rudeness to Customers

Dear **Name**:

Our store not only offers top-quality merchandise, but top-quality service. That is how we have attracted a loyal clientele in this community. Unfortunately, we have received **number** customer complaints during the last **number** months about curt and even rude treatment from you. I am sure that you realize we cannot afford salespersons who treat our customers with anything less than the utmost courtesy, and I trust that, having been informed of these complaints, you will require no additional reminders from me.

Sincerely yours,

Rude to Fellow Employees

Dear **Name**:

One of the most basic ingredients in a successful business operation is mutual respect among everyone in the shop. Problems come up, and arguments arise, of course, but, underneath it all, we thrive on respect for ourselves and for others.

This is why I am very disturbed by several comments and complaints that have crossed my desk regarding your attitude toward your colleagues. Specifically, **number** incidents of rudeness, including impolite or downright abusive language, have been reported to me.

Name, I have always been pleased with the quality of your work. But, good as that is, we cannot function as a business in an atmosphere of rudeness, short temper, or bad attitude.

Let me hear your side of this story. Please come into my office for a conversation about this issue at **time** on **date**.

Sincerely yours,

Sloppy Appearance

Dear **Name**:

We sell a number of products and services here at **Name of company**. But there is one product we must sell before we can promote anything else: confidence. Our customers must be comfortable dealing with us. They must believe in us. We begin to sell confidence by our appearance. It is important that we look professional and successful. It is important that we look like we care.

Name, we have never had a formal dress code around here, but we have always depended on our employees to dress with taste and, above all, to dress neatly. It is all part of the package we are selling. Lately, your clothes have been wrinkled, shirts occasionally unlaundered, tie loose. I don't ask that you go out and purchase a new wardrobe, but I do ask that you make an extra effort to see to it that the clothing you wear is clean and neatly pressed. It is important that you wear a necktie and that you keep it neatly tied. All of this sends the right message to our customers, and we can afford nothing less than to send the right message.

Sincerely yours,

Insubordination

Dear **Name**:

When you started your employment here, you agreed to take direction from and carry out assignments made by your designated supervisors. On **date**, **name**, **job title**, assigned you to **perform task**. You refused because, you said, you didn't think the job was worth doing.

At **Name of company**, the last thing we want is an army of unthinking robot employees. Legitimate objections and alternatives are always welcome. A simple refusal to perform assigned work, however, constitutes insubordination and is not acceptable.

If you would like to discuss this incident with me, either in the presence of **Name of supervisor** or with me alone, my door is open to you. Otherwise, please regard this letter as a reprimand and a warning. If you are not willing to live up to the obligations of your employment agreement, you must be willing to recognize that **Name of company** cannot and will not long retain your services.

Sincerely yours,

Uncooperative Attitude

Dear **Name**:

A small company like ours is a lot like a family. We cannot operate happily and efficiently by threats, coercion, yelling, and complaining. What keeps us going is an attitude of cooperation.

I cannot emphasize this enough: Without a cooperative attitude from everyone, we simply cannot survive.

That's why I'm writing you this note. Of late, you have been short-tempered, uncommunicative, and uncooperative. I am thinking, in particular, of the following incidents:

list

Name, behavior like this is not characteristic of you. If you are having a problem you would like to discuss with me, let's get together. Otherwise, I can only advise you to work on your attitude. We cannot continue on this course.

Sincerely,

Inadequate Record Keeping

Dear **Name**:

No one is more aware than I that we move fast around here. It is not only tempting to cut corners, but, sometimes, it seems absolutely necessary. Whatever else we must do to get the job done, however, there is one corner we cannot afford to cut. We must always take the time to keep accurate and full records in strict accordance with company policy as set out in the *Employee Handbook*.

I was very disturbed last week when I asked you for the file on **Name of project/customer** and found that the following necessary records were either missing or incomplete: **list**. We cannot do business on this basis.

I want you to begin reviewing your files, one by one, and bring each of them up to company standards in terms of completeness of records. You need not drop everything to do this, but I do want to see a proposed schedule of completion. I'll expect to have this document no later than **date**.

I appreciate your prompt, careful, and thorough attention to this very important matter.

Sincerely yours,

Repeated Errors

Dear **Name**:

Occasional mistakes are human, but a pattern of error is a quality control problem, which we cannot afford to ignore. I have attached to this letter a summary of error reports generated by Customer Service concerning your accounts. In and of themselves, none of the errors is of great consequence, but, taken together, they form a pattern of carelessness that must be addressed.

I want you to review your customary processing procedures to ensure that your routine meets the requirements of company policy. Following this self-review, I ask that you submit a report to me no later than **date**, in which you detail 1) what exactly has been going wrong, 2) why it has been going wrong, and 3) what measures you propose to take in order to reduce your rate of error.

Name, you are a fine and very productive **name of position**. I am confident that, by meeting these errors head-on, you will be able to improve your overall performance and turn in a consistently outstanding job. If there is anything you feel I can do to help in this matter, you know that my door is always open to you.

Sincerely yours,

Disclosing Privileged Information

Dear **Name**:

I will begin by leveling with you. I am not happy to find myself obliged to remind you that you hold a position of significant sensitivity and confidence. I enjoyed seeing you at the annual trade convention reception last night, but I was very distressed to overhear you talking—even in the broadest terms—about our upcoming line of **products**.

Under no circumstances is such information, no matter how vague and general, a topic of casual conversation. To take such information outside of the company is at best squandering a portion of our investment in present research and future markets. At worst, it is theft and, in either case, grounds for dismissal.

Yes, it really *is* that serious.

I don't believe that your careless conversation did any serious damage. But it verged on doing so, and it was improper, unwise, and dangerous.

Please accept this letter as an official reprimand and as a warning. Future indiscretions will not be tolerated, and I will have no other choice than to act in strict accordance with company policy and the terms of your employment. Discussing privileged information with unauthorized persons—let alone potential competitors—is ample reason for dismissal.

Sincerely yours,

Violation of No-Smoking Policy

Dear **Name**:

We at **Name of company** are very serious about our policy prohibiting smoking in the office. While we appreciate your personal rights, including the right to choose to smoke, we must protect the rights of others to a clean-air environment. Smoking, as you know, not only affects your health, but the health of those who are exposed to "second-hand" smoke. You can choose to smoke or not to smoke. Those around you have no choice in the matter of breathing.

Therefore, to protect the health of all—and to ensure the comfort of all—I must insist that you adhere to our no smoking policy in this office.

Sincerely yours,

REFUSING REQUEST FOR A RAISE

Jump Starts . . . to Get You on Your Way

You have been doing a most impressive job since you began here just **number** months ago. But that's precisely the point. Here at **Name of company** we review salaries only after an employee has been with us a full year.

I have received your request for a salary increase. Before we review your compensation status, however, I believe it is necessary to review your job performance.

I agree, **Name**, you deserve more money. I only wish our current revenue level would allow me to give it to you.

I have carefully reviewed your request for a salary increase of **percent amount**.

Much as I would like to oblige you immediately in the matter of a salary increase, our cash situation makes that impossible.

Length of Employment Too Brief

Dear **Name**:

I am delighted with the work you have been doing for us, but you began here just **months** ago, on **date**, and it is therefore inappropriate to review your salary at this time. Company policy specifies a salary review only after an employee has been with us for at least one year **or other period**. Your review is scheduled for **date**. I certainly can tell you that, assuming you maintain or, better yet, improve upon your present level of performance through that period, I will be inclined to review your salary status most favorably.

Sincerely yours,

Performance Does Not Merit Increase

Dear **Name**:

I have received your request for a salary increase. Before we review your compensation status, however, I believe it is necessary to review your job performance.

I will put it bluntly. Your present level of performance does not merit a raise at this time for the following reasons:

item

item

item

item

item

I would be happy to sit down with you to review these issues, along with any others you may care to raise. Together, I believe we can create a plan for bringing your performance to a level that will permit me to consider a timely salary increase.

Sincerely yours,

Dear **Name**:

I agree that it would be a great thing if I could increase your current salary. What's stopping me?

You. Or, rather, your performance.

Let's take your request for a salary increase as our opportunity to sit down together and discuss your performance over the past **time period**. Let's talk about what's going right—and what could be going better. Let's talk about how *you* can give yourself the raise you want. Please drop by and make an appointment.

Sincerely,

Revenues Inadequate

Dear **Name**:

You're preaching to the converted when you tell me you deserve a raise. I couldn't agree with you more, and I only wish that we had achieved the level of revenue this quarter to make such a raise possible.

I hope you realize that I greatly value your contribution to this company. I feel confident that, with your continued innovative and excellent work, we will reach the level of income necessary to give you the increase you merit.

I suggest that we review the situation at the end of the next quarter. Let's hope for the best.

Sincerely,

Dear **Name**:

It hurts me to tell you that I am unable to satisfy your request for a salary increase at this time. Our current revenue levels leave me nothing for salary increases. Please be assured that this in no way reflects on your performance. I value your services greatly. Perhaps, with your continued good work, we will reach the level of revenue necessary for me to increase your compensation.

Shall we review the situation again next quarter?

Sincerely,

Salary Appropriate to Position

Dear **Name**:

I have given your recent comments about the level of your salary a great deal of thought. Let me say that I fully understand your desire for a higher salary. I also appreciate the fact that you work hard and well. However, two factors prevent my increasing the level of your compensation at this time.

First, company revenues do not warrant consideration of a salary increase other than at the time of a regular salary review. Your salary review is scheduled for **date**.

Second, the level of your salary is well within the range of the industry standard for your position. During your salary review, we may well wish to talk about your prospects for promotion, which, I believe, offers you the best prospects for substantial salary increase.

Sincerely yours,

Compromise: Lesser Amount

Dear **Name**:

I have carefully reviewed your request for a salary increase of **percent amount**. While I am persuaded that an increase is merited, the fact that you have been with us only **time period**, together with our current less-than-ideal revenue situation, suggests to me that the figure you propose is inappropriately high. I would be pleased to raise your salary by **lesser percent amount** now, with a promised review in **number** months.

Unless I hear otherwise from you, I will assume that the figure is satisfactory for the present, and I will order the necessary modifications in your payroll status.

Sincerely yours,

Compromise: Increase Deferred

Dear **Name**:

Much as I would like to oblige you immediately in the matter of a salary increase, our cash situation makes that impossible. I am convinced, however, that you do indeed merit the increase, and I ask that you accept my promise that, as of **date**, your salary will be raised to **$ amount**.

I truly regret that circumstances do not permit me to make the raise effective immediately.

Sincerely yours,

Compromise: More Vacation Days

Dear **Name**:

I have thoroughly reviewed your request for a salary increase. I believe that the level of compensation for your position is appropriate at this time, and I cannot rationalize increasing it. I am willing, however, to increase the number of vacation days to which you are entitled from **number** to **number**.

This is effective immediately.

Sincerely yours,

TURNING DOWN REQUEST FOR PROMOTION

Jump Starts . . . to Get You on Your Way

I have given your request for a promotion from **position** to **position** a great deal of thought.

After a careful review of your request for a promotion, I am sorry to say that I cannot take that action at present.

I've given the matter of your promotion careful consideration. I have concluded that, at present, your performance does not suggest that a promotion would be appropriate.

I have received your request for a promotion. At this time, however, I can offer you no appropriate position.

Thank you for your letter requesting consideration for the position of **name of position**. I only wish that our financial picture permitted us to fund this position at the present time.

Length of Employment Too Brief

Dear **Name**:

I have reviewed your request for a promotion from position of **position** to that of **position**. I appreciate your ambition, enthusiasm, and commitment to this firm. However, since you have been with us only since **date**, a promotion is premature at this time. The earliest I could reasonably consider promotion—provided a position is available, of course—is **date**. Let's see where we stand at that time and defer the question of promotion until then.

Sincerely yours,

Lack of Seniority

Dear **Name**:

I have received and reviewed your request for promotion from **position** to **position**. **Name**, you are a valued member of the team here, and I hope to bring you along—both in terms of salary and responsibility—as quickly as possible. However, our policy is guided, in significant part, by seniority status. At this time, you lack the seniority necessary for promotion to **position**. It would be unfair and inappropriate for me to jump you ahead of others whose commitment to the firm is as great as yours and whose length of service with it is even greater.

Sincerely yours,

Performance Does Not Merit Promotion

Dear **Name**:

I have completed my review of your request for promotion from your present position to **position**. While there is much to commend about your performance in **present position**, I do not find that you have consistently exhibited the qualities that indicate you are ready for promotion at this time. I would like to see several months of consistent improvement in **list areas** before I reconsider the matter of promotion.

Perhaps you would like to drop by my office to discuss your performance and formulate a strategy for improving it to the point where promotion is called for.

Sincerely yours,

Not Filling Position at This Time

Dear **Name**:

I have received your request for promotion from **present position** to **position**. You make sound arguments for promotion, and I am indeed pleased with your performance and accomplishments. At present, however, we have decided that the needs of the firm do not warrant filling the **name of position** position. Furthermore, there are no plans to fill it in the immediate future. What I'd like to do is get together with you to discuss alternatives to the promotion you have requested. Please give me a call to set up an appointment for a conference.

Sincerely yours,

Revenue Inadequate to Fill Position at This Time

Dear **Name**:

Thank you for your letter requesting consideration for the position of **name of position**. I only wish that our financial picture permitted us to fund this position at the present time, but the fact is that we do not have the money available for it. There is no question about your qualifications for the position. My problem is that, just now, the position is not mine to offer.

Management will be reviewing the need for the position in **number** months. Pending the outcome of that review, I shall reconsider your request. If the position becomes available at that time, you are number one in line for it.

Sincerely yours,

REFUSING OTHER REQUESTS

Jump Starts . . . to Get You on Your Way

I have reviewed your request for **subject of request**. Unfortunately, our needs at this time do not permit my obliging you at present.

After having carefully reviewed your request for a personal computer, I have concluded that your day-to-day needs do not call for one.

I regret that I cannot make the changes in your work schedule that you requested.

As you know, our current workload is unusually heavy. For this reason, I cannot agree to the proposed changes in your vacation schedule.

I have reviewed your request to be assigned a private office, and I am sorry to tell you that I have concluded that such an assignment is inappropriate for the following reasons: **list.**

Change in Hours

To:

From:

Re: Request for change in working hours

I have reviewed your request for a change in your working hours. Unfortunately, our needs at this time require your availability as presently scheduled. I suggest you discuss the matter with some of your colleagues. Perhaps one of them who is working the kind of hours that you would like might be willing to swap schedules with you. If you can arrange this, I will be happy to make the necessary changes in your work schedule.

Additional Coffee Break

To:

From:

Re: Request for additional coffee break

I have received and studied your request for the introduction of an additional coffee break in the early afternoon. I believe that a third coffee break would cut too deeply into our productive time and is not, therefore, appropriate for us. Employees who feel the need for an additional break are welcome to get up, stretch, and have a cup of coffee on their own. But an additional formal coffee break, especially at the hour you suggest, would take too much time from everyone's schedule.

Personal Computer or Other Equipment

To:

From:

Re: Request for a personal computer

After having carefully reviewed your request for a personal computer, I have concluded that your day-to-day needs do not call for one. You do little word processing and no accounting, and you do not need real-time access to the computer network. For the rare occasion when you need access to a computer, one is available in the **area** area.

If you feel that I am overlooking some aspect of your job in making this assessment, please don't hesitate to drop by my office for a discussion.

Private Office

Dear **Name**:

I have reviewed your request to be assigned a private office, and I am sorry to tell you that I have concluded that such an assignment is inappropriate for the following reasons:

1. The position of **position** does not require client conferences or other private meetings.

2. Other employees who hold positions equivalent to yours are not assigned private offices.

3. Our building facilities are strictly limited.

4. Our construction and remodeling budget is insufficient to fund the construction of additional private office space.

I don't expect you'll be overjoyed by this decision, but I trust that you can understand and appreciate its appropriateness.

Sincerely yours,

Reserved Parking Space

Dear **Name**:

I have reviewed your request for a reserved parking space. As you know, such spaces are at a very high premium here, and are generally assigned only to very senior personnel and, as required by local ordinances, to holders of a handicapped permit.

At this time, we have far fewer reserved spaces than applicants for them. After assigning the handicapped spaces as necessary, I have assigned the remaining available spaces according to seniority. I'm afraid you haven't been here quite long enough to jump to the head of the line, and, therefore, I have no choice but to decline your request.

I appreciate your understanding that the available spaces are limited.

Sincerely yours,

RESPONDING TO COMPLAINTS

Jump Starts . . . to Get You on Your Way

I have given your recent complaints regarding **subject of complaint** a great deal of careful thought.

I must agree with you that your work load is indeed heavy, and I have always greatly admired and appreciated your willingness to take it on.

I am very pleased that you feel comfortable coming to me with your concerns about **subject**.

I appreciate the problems that you face.

Thank you for bringing **complaint** to my attention.

I was distressed to learn of the friction between you and **Name**, but I am pleased that you came to me to discuss the problem.

I have received and reviewed your joint memo concerning the inadequacies of our employee facilities.

I have received and reviewed your report of an unsafe condition in **place, operation, etc.**. In response, I have ordered the following steps to be taken immediately: **list.**

Work Load Too Heavy

Dear **Name**:

I must agree with you that your work load is indeed heavy, and I have always greatly admired and appreciated your willingness to take it on.

We are faced with a problem of limited funding that precludes our hiring additional personnel anytime soon. This does not mean that I intend simply to ignore your complaint. I suggest we get together with the supervisors of the other departments to discuss short-term, immediate strategies by which we might distribute work more evenly, at least until such time that company revenues will permit us to hire some additional people.

I will notify you within a few days of the time and place of this brainstorming session.

Sincerely yours,

Dear **Name**:

I appreciate your honesty and openness in sharing with me your concerns about the level of your current work load. Based on your remarks, I am persuaded that you are, indeed, carrying a very heavy load—probably too heavy to sustain on a routine basis. Accordingly, I am reviewing our staffing needs. I will be calling on you shortly for your suggestions regarding the possibility of adding staff and instituting other measures that will ensure that your work load is more appropriate.

Sincerely yours,

Incompatible Fellow Employee

Dear **Name**:

Let me begin by telling you how pleased I am that you came to me to discuss your differences with **Name**. I don't, of course, mean that I am pleased that you have these differences, but that you approached the problem rationally by bringing it to my attention.

I have reviewed your personnel file and that of **Name**. You are both fine employees, and, I must tell you, there is no record of any complaints or negative comments concerning **Name**.

I suggest we take one of two courses. Either the two of you work your problem out together in the same rational spirit in which you approached me, or both of you come to my office for a three-way discussion of the problem. If you prefer the latter course, I will arrange it in the least-threatening manner I can.

Please advise me of your decision.

Sincerely yours,

Incompatible Supervisor

Dear **Name**:

I was distressed to learn of the friction between you and **Name**, but I am pleased that you came to me to discuss the problem.

Name has been with the firm for **number** years, and he has a fine record. Indeed, you are both very valuable to this company, and I am eager for you to work well together. Toward this end, I can suggest two courses. I can sit down for a talk with **Name** to get his side of this story—and, indeed, to ascertain whether he is even aware of any problem. Then he and I can discuss solutions. Or, if you prefer, the two of you can sit down with me for a three-way conversation about the situation, and we can work on the issues together.

I will take no action until I hear from you.

Sincerely yours,

Facilities Inadequate

To:

From:

Re: Inadequate employee facilities

I have received and reviewed your joint memo concerning the inadequacies of our employee facilities. Let me begin by thanking all of you for taking the time to inform me in a detailed and reasonable manner about the deficiencies you find. The memo is very helpful.

I wish I could respond by telling you that I can address all of the issues you raise and totally refurbish the facilities.

Unfortunately, I cannot. Our funding for the physical plant is limited—far too limited to make all the changes you list. However, I am convinced by your memo that improvements are needed. I suggest that the employees choose a delegation of three or four representatives to meet with me in order to determine which items on your "want list" are most urgent. Based on that evaluation and the available funds, we can determine just what changes can be made now, which ones can be put off until a later date, and which can be shelved indefinitely.

If this is agreeable to you, please have a representative give me a call so that we can set up a meeting.

Unsafe Condition

To:

From:

Re: Unsafe condition in **place. operation, etc.**

I have received and reviewed your report of an unsafe condition in **place, operation, etc.**. In response, I have ordered the following steps to be taken immediately:

list

In addition, I have asked **Name** to investigate the situation and make a detailed report no later than **date**. Based on that report, and in consultation with the appropriate managers, I will determine what longterm, permanent safety measures are required, advisable, and appropriate.

ACCEPTING RESIGNATIONS

Jump Starts . . . to Get You on Your Way

Congratulations on your new position.

I have received your letter of resignation, and while I am sorry to see you leave us, I appreciate your reasons for doing so.

I am thrilled for you—though I'd be lying if I said I was happy to see you go.

It is regretfully that I accept your resignation, and, even as I do accept it, I ask that you give the matter further thought.

I am very sorry that our failure to reach agreement on the level of compensation **or other issue** has prompted your decision to leave **Name of company**.

I have received and accept your resignation, dated **date**, from the position of **name of position**, effective immediately **or on date**.

Congratulatory

Dear **Name**:

Congratulations on your new appointment at **Name of company**. It is a big step in your career, and I know that you will do a tremendous job.

My happiness for you is, of course, tempered by my regret at seeing you leave us, but you must go where the appropriate opportunities lie.

I wish you all good fortune and every success.

Sincerely yours,

Dear **Name**:

I am thrilled for you—though I'd be lying if I said I was happy to see you go.

I do understand that you have been offered an opportunity impossible to refuse. I only wish that we could offer you something similar.

Please know that you leave **Name of company** with our very best wishes for every success. As a personal favor, I ask that you keep in touch.

All best,

With Regret

Dear **Name**:

I accept your resignation with regret, and I wish that I could convince you to stay with us. I understand, however, that you believe that the needs of your career warrant a change.

You have done a marvelous job here, and I wish you success in your new endeavors.

Sincerely yours,

Dear **Name**:

I am very sorry that our failure to reach agreement on the level of compensation **or other issue** has prompted your decision to leave **Name of company**. I do understand that you see the move as necessary, and I therefore accept your resignation with my thanks for the fine job you have done here.

Best of luck in your new endeavor.

Sincerely yours,

Under Unfavorable Circumstances

Dear **Name**:

I have received and accept your resignation, dated **date**, from the position of **name of position**, effective immediately **or on date**.

You are requested to remove your personal belongings from your office by **time and/or date**. **Name** will be available to assist you in this, if you wish.

Your separation from this company will be governed by the terms set forth in **employee manual, contract, etc..**

Sincerely,

Inviting Reconsideration

Dear **Name**:

I acknowledge and accept your resignation, dated **date**, with considerable regret. I appreciate that you see leaving this company and joining another as an important career move. Ultimately, of course, that determination must rest with your judgment. But, as we discussed, there is considerable room for upward movement here at **Name of company**, and, while I accept your resignation, I do ask that you give the matter one last, long thought.

We will not be moving to fill your position before **date**. If you reconsider before that time, our door is wide open. If not, let me wish you the best of good fortune in what promises to be a continued brilliant career.

Sincerely yours,

Dear **Name**:

I have no choice but to accept your resignation, dated **date**. However, I want it clearly understood that I accept it with regret and I ask you, yet again, to reconsider this decision.

I do not intend to place an ad to fill your position before **date**. Please use that time to think over your move. Feel free to come in and talk to me. If you change your mind and wish to continue with us, we are prepared to welcome you back.

Sincerely yours,

Inviting Return

Dear **Name**:

I am not pleased to see you go, **Name**, but I won't hold you back from a career move that does, at this time, seem propitious. I only wish we had the equivalent to offer you now.

This is not to say that, some day, a suitable and inviting upper-level position won't be available. When that day comes, I intend to track you down and ask you to return.

Make it easier on me by keeping in touch.

Good luck and best wishes.

Sincerely,

Dear **Name**:

I accept your resignation of **date**, and I bid you farewell and godspeed.

But I don't expect that you'll be gone forever. Your needs will change, as will ours, and I am hopeful that a suitable position will one day open up here and lure you back to us. In the meantime, best of luck in your new position.

Please keep in touch.

Sincerely,

TERMINATIONS

Jump Starts . . . to Get You on Your Way

This letter is to advise you that, as of **date**, you are to consider yourself on **number**-month probation.

This is a hard letter to write and, I am all too certain, an even harder one to receive.

I am sorry to be the one to tell you this, but **Name of company** no longer requires your services.

I regret having to tell you this, but due to a sharp decrease in orders, I am compelled to terminate your services effective two weeks from the date of this letter.

Cutbacks at the corporate level have made it necessary for **Name of company** to reduce personnel.

We regret to inform you that your employment with **Name of company** is terminated, effective two weeks from the date of this letter.

Probationary Status

Dear **Name**:

On **date(s)**, I issued **a** reprimands for **list infraction(s)**. You were duly advised that any repetition of these infractions would be deemed sufficient grounds for dismissal.

On **date**, you **describe infraction**.

This letter is to advise you that, commencing this date, you are on a probationary status, which will continue through **date**. During this period, any infractions of company rules or failure to discharge the responsibilities of your employment will result in summary dismissal.

Sincerely yours,

Dear **Name**:

This letter is to advise you that, as of **date**, you are to consider yourself on **number**-month probation. During this period, **Name of company** reserves the right to dismiss you for cause in the event of any infraction of company rules and regulations or any failure to discharge your responsibilities adequately and in a timely manner.

I regret that this probation action is necessary, but the actions for which you were reprimanded on **date(s)** are of such serious nature that nothing less than probation is warranted.

Sincerely yours,

Plant Closing

Dear **Name**:

This is a hard letter to write and, I am all too certain, an even harder one to receive.

On **date**, we received word from corporate management that this plant will be closed, effective **date**. That date will also be the final day of your employment at **Name of company**.

There is, of course, not much to be happy about in this news. But the single saving grace is that you do have **number** months **or weeks** to seek other employment. As you conduct your job search, please do not hesitate to call on me for assistance and for letters of recommendation.

I have greatly enjoyed working with you.

Sincerely,

Company Cutbacks

Dear **Name**:

Cutbacks at the corporate level have made it necessary for **Name of company** to reduce personnel. I am sorry to be the one to tell you this, but you are among the employees who are being let go.

Your employment here will cease two weeks **or other period** from the date of this letter. Your final check will be issued at that time and will include any vacation pay to which you may be entitled.

Please feel free to call on this office for references and letters of recommendation, and we wish you the best of luck in your search for suitable employment.

Sincerely yours,

Dear **Name**:

I have been directed to reduce personnel in this office by **percentage** percent on the basis of seniority, beginning, of course, with those most recently hired. I am very sorry to tell you that you are among the employees I am compelled to lay off.

In lieu of two weeks' notice, a severance check in the amount of **$ amount** accompanies this letter. This amount includes all salary due to date, together with appropriate vacation pay, and a severance payment in the sum of **$ amount**.

Please remove your personal belongings from your office by the end of the day.

I regret the sudden nature of this action, which in no way reflects on your performance here. Accordingly, I encourage you to use this employment experience on your resume and to call on me for letters of recommendation. I wish you luck in speedily finding suitable employment.

Sincerely yours,

Inadequate Revenue

Dear **Name**:

I regret having to tell you this, but due to a sharp decrease in our revenues, I am forced to terminate your services effective two weeks from the date of this letter.

It was very painful for me to make this decision, and I have enjoyed working with you, but the funds for your position simply are not available.

Please do not hesitate to call on me for recommendations, and be assured that you will be the first person I call if our financial situation improves to the point that I can once again fund your position.

Your final check, which will be issued on **date**, will include any vacation pay to which you may be entitled.

Best of luck in securing new employment.

Sincerely,

Poor Performance

Dear **Name**:

We regret to inform you that your employment with **Name of company** is terminated, effective two weeks from the date of this letter. Our decision is based on your inadequate performance in the following areas: **list**.

During the two-week notice period, you will be expected to perform your regular duties. Your final salary check will be issued on **date**, together with any vacation pay to which you may be entitled.

Very truly yours,

Dear **Name**:

I am sorry to inform you that your services are no longer required at **Name of company**.

My decision is based on an evaluation of your performance, which has led me to conclude that you are not right for **Name of company**, and **Name of company** is not right for you.

A severance check in the amount of **$ amount** accompanies this letter. It represents the full amount to which you are entitled through the end of today, **date**, and includes all regular pay, unused vacation pay, and a severance sum of **$ amount**. The severance payment is made in lieu of notice, and you are requested to remove your personal effects from this building by the end of the regular work day.

Sincerely yours,

Negligence

Dear **Name**:

I regret to inform you that your record of negligence and failure to perform your assigned duties makes it necessary for me to terminate your employment with **Name of company**.

A check for **$ amount** is enclosed. It reflects your salary due to date, in addition to payment for **number** vacation days to which you are entitled, and a severance amount of **$ amount**, which is given in lieu of notice.

Please vacate the premises immediately with your personal possessions.

Very truly yours,

Personal Friend

Dear **Name**:

We have been good friends for as long as you have worked here, which makes this an extremely difficult task. After a great deal of thought and study, I have concluded that it would be in your best interest and that of **Name of company** to terminate your employment here effective two weeks from the date of this letter. I see no alternative.

Based on your years of employment, you will draw full salary for **number** months, which I hope will give you sufficient time to secure another position.

You can rely on me to help in your job search in any way that I can.

Sincerely,

Longtime Employee

Dear **Name**:

I am very sorry to be the one to tell you this, but your services at **Name of company** are no longer required.

Your employment here will cease effective two weeks from the date of this letter. However, **Name of company** will continue to pay you your regular salary, plus fringe benefits, for a period of **number** months, as determined by your years of service.

The decision to terminate your employment was made for the following reasons:

item

item

item

item

I feel confident that the company's severance package will provide sufficient time for you to find another suitable position, and I wish you good luck in a speedy search.

Sincerely yours,

Mandatory Retirement

Dear **Name**:

We've come to the end of a long and profitable relationship. On **date**, you will be **number** years old, the mandatory retirement age here at **Name of company**. It is measure of your dedication and commitment that you have chosen to work up to and through your birthday.

As you know, we've planned a little party for you. After that, I'd like you to join me in my office for a parting drink.

In the meantime, I ask that you review the accompanying pension and retirement documents and drop by and see me if you have any questions concerning this material. **Name** has agreed to assist you in helping to remove your personal belongings from your office over the next few days.

There will be plenty of speeches at your retirement party, **Name**, but let me express, here and now, my personal gratitude for all that you have taught me, and let me tell you that it has been a pleasure and privilege working with you.

Sincerely yours,

Project Completed

Dear **Name**:

You have done a marvelous job on the **name of project**. All of us at **Name of company** thank you. Your final check in the amount of **$ amount** is enclosed.

Working with you, however briefly, has been a highly rewarding experience, and we look forward to an occasion that again requires your services. Until then, I hope that you will call on me as you may require for recommendations to other potential clients.

Sincerely yours,

Dear **Name**:

Completing a project like this successfully is cause for celebration. My only regret is that it means our association is concluded—at least for the present. Your final check is enclosed.

I have greatly enjoyed working with you, and I sincerely hope we will have occasion to collaborate on another project soon.

Sincerely yours,

Chapter Twelve

Communicating with Colleagues

Step by Step . . . to What's Best for You

The "letters" in this section are internal communications—memos. Unfortunately, memos become the "junk mail" of many offices. Word processors, e-mail, and the copier all encourage the production of memos for everything. Even if they are read, they often make little impact. The effective memo, in contrast, invites attention and, where appropriate, prompts action. Think about beginning the memo with a single provocative statement, especially one aimed directly at the reader or readers.

The customary opening of the business memo, while strictly the product of convention, is quite useful:

To:

From:

Date:

Re:

Instead of "Re:," "Subj:" or "Subject:" is acceptable. Memos are not generally signed at the bottom. Add a personal touch by initialing next to your name on the "From:" line.

1. Even though the heading already announces the subject, begin the memo with a succinct announcement of the subject. Better yet, begin with a provocative statement.

2. Develop the subject or announcement in the body of the memo.

3. If appropriate, make recommendations or suggest, request, or order action.

SPREADING THE NEWS

Jump Starts . . . to Get You on Your Way

It is my pleasure to announce . . .

Beginning **date**, our general health insurance plan will be modified as follows:

The following affects us all.

After a distinguished career with **Name of company** spanning **number** years, **Name** will be retiring on **date**.

You have managed this quarter to rack up an impressive sales record— so impressive, that I'm convinced you can do even more. And I want to give you just that opportunity.

Here is something that will change your life.

This announcement concerns your livelihood and your future.

The Effective Memo: News

New Vice President Appointed

To: All

From: **Name**, President

Re: New Vice President Appointed

I am delighted to announce that the Board has approved the appointment of **Name** as our new vice president.

As many of you already know, **Name** has been with this firm for **number** years, having begun here as **job title** and having worked her way up through **job titles**. For the last **number** years, **Name** has been **job title**. During that time, sales in her division increased from **$ amount** to **$ amount**.

Before joining **Name of company**, **Name** was **job title** at **Name of previous company**. Born in **Place**, she was educated at **list schools and degrees**. **Name** is married to **Name**, a **job title** with **Name of company**, and has **number** children.

Please join me in welcoming **Name** to her new position!

Changes in Health Insurance Coverage

To: All

From: **Name**, Operations Manager

Re: Changes in Health Insurance Coverage

Beginning **date**, our general health insurance plan will be modified as follows:

item

item

item

item

item

These changes are necessary to contain the cost of the insurance so that **Name of company** can continue to offer it to employees on a non-contributory basis. If you have any questions concerning these changes, please come in and talk to me.

New Mailroom Procedures

To: All

From: **Name**, Mailroom Manager

Re: New Mailroom Procedures

Beginning **date**, the following new procedures will be in effect at the mailroom:

item

item

item

item

item

I believe these new procedures will enable us to handle mailing and shipping more efficiently. After we've all lived with them for a month or two, I hope that some of you will share your comments on them with me.

Retirement of District Manager

To: All

From: **Name**, President

Re: Retirement of **Name**, Manager of **district**

After a distinguished career with **Name of company** spanning **number** years, **Name** will be retiring on **date**.

Name was manager of **district** for **number** years, during which he created a program of tremendous growth and increased overall sales from **$ amount** to **$ amount**.

On **date**, we will all gather in **location** to give **Name** the great send-off he deserves. I hope to see you all there.

Sales Incentive Program Announced

To: All Sales Representatives

From: **Name**, Sales Manager

Re: New Incentive Program

You have managed this quarter to rack up an impressive sales record—so impressive, that I'm convinced you can do even more. And I want to give you just that opportunity.

Beginning **date** and ending on **date**, I am declaring a special incentive period. It works this way: for every **number** of sales in excess of **number** made during this period, you will earn a **percent amount** bonus on your regular commission.

The bonus will be payable at the end of the quarter, on **date**.

I know that it will require hard work to get your sales up above **number** units. But you have all proven that you thrive on hard work. Now is your chance to earn more for all that you do.

COMPANY POLICIES

Jump Starts . . . to Get You on Your Way

I've heard deep grumblings here.

Has this ever happened to any of you?

Friends, we've got a problem.

Let's help each other out.

One of the more pleasant benefits of working at **Name of company** is the discount we all enjoy as employees.

What do you do when someone from the outside asks you for financial information?

We've sprung a leak.

Things could be much better here.

Presenting Company Policies

Use of Company Car

To: All

From: **Name**, General Manager

Re: Use of Company Car

A number of people have been very unhappy around here. I have received numerous complaints from individuals who have scheduled use of the company car only to discover that someone else has taken it—without having bothered to schedule usage in advance.

Obviously, this practice cannot continue. It is rude, inefficient, and potentially destructive.

Effective immediately, all employees must schedule use of the company car at least **number** days in advance, except in cases of extreme emergency. In such cases, employees must consult the sign-up sheet and inform anyone with whom their immediate need might conflict. To avoid this situation, however, we ask that, in an emergency, employees use their own automobiles if at all possible. We have a long-standing policy of reimbursing employees for authorized use of their own vehicles.

Park in Marked Spaces Only

To: All

From: **Name**, General Manager

Re: Please Park in Marked Spaces Only

Has this ever happened to any of you?

You need to leave the office early, you got to the parking lot, you start your car, you begin to pull out of the parking lot, and you find yourself trapped. Someone has blocked the exit drive.

Please: Park in marked spaces only. It is dangerous, unlawful, and extraordinarily obnoxious to park in a way that obstructs traffic. If you arrive after the parking lot is full, you must park on the street.

We have been fortunate up to this point. Folks have been inconvenienced. But what will happen when one of us receives an urgent phone call from home and it is imperative that we get out of the lot without delay?

Let's be considerate, law-abiding, and prevent tragedy. Please park in marked spaces only.

Last Person Out Must Set Alarm

To: All

From: **Name**, Office Manager

Re: Setting Alarm

It is the responsibility of the last person who leaves at night to set the alarm.

Before you leave for the day, please ensure that you are not the last person out. If you are the last person out, follow the instructions posted in the utility closet, above the central alarm control box.

Our safety and security depend on the cooperation of all.

Employee Discounts Apply to Employees Only

To: All

From: **Name**, President

Re: Employee Discounts

One of the more pleasant benefits of working at **Name of company** is the discount we all enjoy as employees. I encourage you to make liberal use of the discount and buy as many of the products we make as you possibly can.

But, please, make sure that what you buy is for your own personal use or that of your immediate family.

It is unfair to our network of retailers for employees to act as wholesalers for friends, acquaintances, or even total strangers. You are sincerely asked not to abuse your employee discount privilege.

Treatment of Requests for Financial Information

To: All

From: **Name**, C.F.O.

Re: Handling Requests for Financial Information

From time to time, companies and individuals call us seeking information about our financial condition. We have a very open policy here at **Name of company**, which means that a great many of us have access to potentially sensitive information. We believe the benefits of this open policy far outweigh its hazards.

However, I want to caution all of you: All financial information is to be regarded as privileged. You are to refer all calls and inquiries relating to our financial status to my office for response.

ADVICE AND SUGGESTIONS

Jump Starts . . . to Get You on Your Way

We've all known each other for a good long time here.

Maybe we're *too* comfortable.

I've got some good news, followed by a little advice.

Here's an idea for you.

In reviewing our records of customer complaints from **date** to **date**, I have determined that **percent amount** of customer complaints involve **number** systems: **list**.

Name of company is joining our community in a large-scale recycling effort. You can help.

Telephone Etiquette

To: All

From: **Name**, Office Manager

Re: Telephone Etiquette

Most of us here have worked together for some time. One of the things I like most about my job is getting to know bright, friendly, interesting people like you.

The other day, I called in from outside and was greeted, not by a bright, friendly, interesting voice, but by a dull and uncommunicative grunt.

We all get tired and rushed and pressured, but when we pick up a call from the outside, the last thing we want to communicate to our customers, present and potential, is boredom, fatigue, and pressure. The best that you have to give—I know—is very good indeed. Please give your best each and every time you answer the phone. Say "Hello" and always give your name. Use phrases such as "How can I help you today?" "What can I do for you?" "May I help you?" And, at the conclusion of the call, it is always pleasant to bid your caller good day.

Thanks.

Ten Most Prevalent Recent Customer Concerns

To: All

From: **Name**, Customer Service Director

Re: Ten Most Prevalent Customer Concerns as of **date**

As I do every month **or other time period,** I have evaluated customer comments and calls to Customer Service and find the following ten items to be the most prevalent concerns our customers have. The list is arranged in order of frequency of comment:

list

I hope this assists you in dealing with your accounts.

Recent Customer Compliments

To: Sales Personnel

From: **Name**, Customer Service Director

Re: Customer Kudos

Too often, those of us in customer service communicate with those of you in sales only when we have a complaint to pass along. Necessary though such communication is, it must be annoying to receive and can't do much for morale. It also fails to reflect the true quality of our products and the quality of the attention you give your accounts.

To correct false impressions and make us feel as good as we should, I've selected to share with you some of the best customer kudos my office has received since **date**. Enjoy!

list

Recent Customer Complaints

To: Quality Control Division

From: **Name**, Customer Service Director

Re: Customer Complaints

In reviewing our records of customer complaints from **date** to **date**, I have determined that **percent amount** of customer complaints involve **number** systems:

1. item

2. item

3. item

That a pattern exists is undeniable. I leave it up to you in Quality Control to investigate the causes of failure of these systems and to make the appropriate recommendations to Manufacturing.

If you need a more detailed breakdown of customer complaints, please give me a call.

Recycling Scrap Paper

To: All

From: **Name**, Operations Manager

Re: Recycling Scrap Paper

Name of company is joining our community in a large-scale recycling effort. You can help.

Instead of discarding scrap paper in your wastebasket, please gather it in a box, which you can empty daily in the recycling bin located in the elevator corridor. The only effort this takes is changing a habit or two, but it will pay off in a better environment for all of us and for our children.

Chapter Thirteen

Communicating with Supervisors and Potential Employers

Step by Step . . . to What's Best for You

Some of the most important business letters you write are directed at prospective employers and current supervisors. Depending on your relationship with your bosses and how you feel about authority, such occasions for communication can be particularly emotion-charged. The effective letter conveys only the feelings that are productive and that are likely to evoke in your reader the "right feelings"—that is, the feelings you want her to have.

Applying for a Position

The letter that accompanies your resume or a job application is one of the most important sales letters you will ever write. As with any sales letter, there are no hard-and-fast rules concerning structure. Creativity, personality, and invention are encouraged. However, it is useful to think of the outline of the classic sales letter in composing correspondence aimed at getting a job.

1. Begin by getting your reader's attention. One effective way is turn the tables on the prospective employer. Don't come to him asking for a job. Instead, ask him to sell *you* on *his* company.

2. Develop the reader's interest in you by briefly highlighting your accomplishments, background, and so on—the qualities that make you a hot employment prospect.

3. As in the classic sales letter, work to evoke desire in your reader. You want him asking himself: Wouldn't it be great if I could get this person on my team?

4. Close the "sale" by inviting action: a phone call, a return letter, a request for an interview.

Requesting a Raise or Promotion

Requests for salary increases or promotions need to accomplish two goals. They must make the reader *feel* like complying even as they provide the *intellectual* rationale to bolster the emotional assent to your request. Accordingly, emphasize your loyalty to the firm and evoke a sense of personal regard for your reader. At the same time, marshal your arguments—based on a record of performance, length of service, industry standards and practices, and so on. Do not blatantly butter up the boss, and do not use your family ("I have a husband and three hungry little mouths to feed!") or plead poverty. Most supervisors quite rightly resent such appeals and regard them as irrelevant. Certainly, they are unprofessional.

1. If the letter is preparatory to a regular salary review, state that the review is approaching. If not, forthrightly state the business of the letter ("I'd like to talk with you about increasing my salary").

2. Establish your commitment—your special and exceptional commitment—to the firm. Your eagerness to improve it even as you develop with it.

3. Marshal the facts that support your request for a promotion or raise, including years of service, accomplishments, and the like.

4. Appeal to fairness.

5. Affirm your relationship with the reader.

6. Ask for a meeting, for serious thought prior to a scheduled salary/promotion review, or, if appropriate, a decision now.

7. Express appreciation for the reader's careful consideration.

Requests for Other Changes

Requests for changes in working conditions, hours, and so on share some of the characteristics of requests for promotions or raises. However, here the emphasis is usually more on promoting the good of the firm than it is on promoting oneself. A change, for example, in your working hours will allow you to use your time more productively *for the firm*.

1. State the request forthrightly and clearly. If possible—and appropriate—put the request in the form of remediation of a problem or undesirable situation.

2. Substantiate your request by marshaling the facts. What will your reader achieve by satisfying your request?

3. Demonstrate the feasibility of satisfying your request.

4. Close by underscoring the benefits to the company and by inviting action.

Making Suggestions

Letters and memos making suggestions present somewhat less of a challenge than requests for changes in working conditions, hours, and the like because suggestions are by their nature more obviously "disinterested"—made for the sake of the good of the firm rather than directly for one's own benefit. Accordingly, these communications should put greater emphasis on the rationale for the change and proportionately less emphasis on an appeal to the emotions.

1. State the subject of the suggestion.

2. State the problem or situation, explaining it in appropriate detail, emphasizing the impact on the firm.

3. State the suggestions and explain how they will work.

4. Invite action (usually a response or a meeting to discuss the suggestion).

Responding to a Reprimand

Responding to a reprimand usually calls for some blend of two things: an explanation, which will not be mistaken for a mere excuse or an attempt to evade responsibility; and, where appropriate, an apology, with a promise that the mistake or infraction will not be repeated. It is important to be honest and straightforward in accepting responsibility when, in fact, you are responsible for an action. It is also important *not* to accept blame if you have a legitimate explanation for the situation or if the reprimand has been made in error. Resist the temptation to respond defensively on the one hand or guiltily on the other. Indeed, your first step may be to request a clarification of the reprimand (sample requests for such clarifications are included in this chapter). In general, in responding to a reprimand, you should:

1. Acknowledge receiving the reprimand.

2. If appropriate, apologize, *then* explain the circumstances of the subject of the reprimand. If you feel that you were not at fault or that the reprimand was issued in error, say so. Do not use such emotionally provocative terms as "unfair," "off base," "wrong," or the like. It is best to avoid attacking the judgment, let alone the personality, of the person who issues the reprimand. Instead, address the facts alleged in the reprimand. If the facts are not clear to you, request a clarification. While you should avoid emotion, it is perfectly appropriate to express surprise, shock, and dismay at receiving an unwarranted reprimand, but do restrict your reaction to simple phrases such as "unpleasantly surprised" or "thoroughly shocked" or "distressed."

3. Propose action: a remedy, a promise not to repeat the error or infraction, or a call for a meeting or conference.

Resignations

Why worry about what you'll say when you resign? When you call on a friend, an acquaintance, or even someone you hardly know, you don't customarily end the visit by storming out the door or sneaking out the window or simply exiting without a word. You say goodbye. You thank the person for his hospitality. Perhaps you express regret at having to leave so soon. You comment on what a great time you had. Why? Simple human decency, for one thing. But also because you don't leave the place intending never to return, never to see the person again.

The same holds true in what I have repeatedly called the small world of business. Just because you leave a company—even under less than ideal circumstances, even involuntarily—you must not foolishly assume that you will never have contact with your supervisors and colleagues again. When you leave, don't slam the door. Keep it ajar, even if ever so slightly. In a letter of resignation, you should:

1. Announce your resignation. You may preface it with regret, if appropriate.

2. In the most positive way possible, state your reasons for resigning.

3. Give the particulars of the resignation, including date and your proposal, if any, for handling the transition to a new person. If at all possible, volunteer assistance in the transition.

4. State or restate regret, affirming the positive nature of your experience with the firm you are leaving.

APPLYING FOR A POSITION

Jump Starts . . . to Get You on Your Way

I'm in the market for an opportunity. Perhaps you have one for me.

I am responding to your announcement of a position as **job title,** which appeared in **Name of publication** on **date.**

Name, job title at **Name of company,** suggested I write to you regarding a position as **job title.**

I'd like you to sell me your company.

I don't much like the status quo, but I don't go after change for the sake of change. What I do believe in is growth.

I am delighted to respond to your request for my resume.

First Job

Dear **Name**:

I'd like you to sell me your company.

No, I don't mean that I've got the cash on hand to take it off your hands. What I'd like is to learn about your operation and the opportunities that may be available to me. I know what *I* can offer you: I am about to graduate from **Name of university** with a major in **subject**, and I just finished an internship at **Name of company**, working in the **name** department. I'm inventive, energetic, curious, and a hard worker.

I'd like to find out what your company can offer me—either now or in the future. I would be very grateful if you could set aside some time soon to talk to me about **Name of company**. I will call you within the next few days to set up an appointment.

Sincerely yours,

"Cold" Inquiry

Dear **Name**:

I'm in the market for an opportunity. Perhaps you have one for me.

You are in the business of **describe business**. As the enclosed resume indicates, I have been involved in all phases of this business since **year**. I am currently **job title** at **Name of company**, and I am looking for the opportunity to grow professionally and to provide a company like yours with the kind of expert, innovative, and enthusiastic approach it not only deserves, but needs in order to compete, excel, and prosper.

I invite you to review my resume, and I would be pleased to make myself available for an interview.

Sincerely yours,

Responding to an Ad

Dear **Name**:

This is a response to your announcement of a position as **job title**, which appeared in **Name of publication** on **date**.

I have long admired **Name of company** as an innovative and aggressive market leader, and I was excited to learn of the availability of a position in **area** and a chance to join your team.

I offer a full background in **area**, having served as **job title** with **Name of company** since **year**. Before taking the position with **Name of company**, I was **job title** at **Name of other company**. I am proud of the record I've put together at both of these firms, including such accomplishments as **list**. I invite you to read the enclosed resume for the details of my experience, responsibilities, and achievements. In addition to what you'll find there, I can tell you that I offer such important intangibles as enthusiasm, inventiveness, and a combination of self-reliance and team spirit.

I would be delighted to be given the opportunity to tell you in person more about myself and to learn more about your operation. I look forward to hearing from you.

Sincerely,

Responding to an Invitation to Apply

Dear **Name**:

I was delighted and flattered by your suggestion that I send you my application and resume for **name of position** available at **Name of company**. I greatly appreciate your confidence in me—and, false modesty aside, I can assure you that your confidence is not misplaced.

You are already familiar with my background and experience, but I would like to direct your attention to the following highlights of the accompanying resume:

item

item

item

item

I would be very pleased to come in for a talk with you and others at your convenience.

I appreciate the opportunity of applying.

Sincerely yours,

Promotion

Dear **Name**:

I don't much like the status quo, but I don't go after change for the sake of change. What I do believe in is growth. During **number** years in the **type of business** business, I have moved up from position to position, staying with each until I felt that I could no longer grow in it. Then I moved on, realizing that you only do your best—for your firm and for you—if you stretch and reach and make new demands on yourself.

I've been **job title** at **Name of company** for **number** years. As the enclosed resume demonstrates, those years have been very productive ones, during which I **list key accomplishments**.

But I have taken that position as far as it can go. I am ready to grow into **name of desired position**, and I believe that **Name of target company** has the vision that will let me grow, that will let me shape a program and run with it.

I would be delighted to make myself available for an interview at your convenience and can be reached directly at my office number.

I look forward to hearing from you.

Sincerely,

Relocation

Dear **Name**:

I have worked happily as **job title** at **Name of company** for **number** years. What I am increasingly *unhappy* about is my present location, **Name of city**, and I am looking to relocate in the **Name of target area** area.

I have researched the **type of business** firms in the area, and I am especially impressed with **Name of target firm**, because of its innovative and aggressive programs. I would welcome the opportunity to learn more about your company and to follow up on the enclosed resume in person. I am available for an interview on short notice, and I can be reached on my direct line at **telephone number**.

Sincerely yours,

REQUESTING A RAISE

Jump Starts . . . to Get You on Your Way

As you know, my annual salary review is due on **date**.

I am scheduled to review my salary status with you on **date**. I thought that it would be a good idea if I reviewed my own salary history before going into the meeting with you.

I would like to set up a salary review with you by **date**.

It has been **number months, years** since the last increase in my salary and **number months, years** since we last reviewed my salary.

Length of Employment

To:

From:

Re: Salary Review

As you know, my annual salary review is due on **date**. I have been working for **Name of company** for **number** years, and I have been delighted with my coworkers, supervisors, and general working conditions. The one area that I feel needs improvement is compensation. Since **year**, my salary has increased by only **percent amount** percent. It seems quite apparent to me that I am overdue for a more significant—more equitable—raise.

Based on the length of my service and in view of the slim increases I have been given from year to year, I would suggest that a salary increase of **$ amount** is now appropriate. Averaged over the **number** years of my employment, that would be the equivalent of having had **percent amount** annual raises—still modest, but, I believe, fair.

I look forward to speaking with you about this during my review.

Overdue

To:

From:

Re: Salary Review

I am scheduled to review my salary status with you on **date**. I thought that it would be a good idea if I reviewed my own salary history before going into the meeting with you. What I discovered is that it has been **number** years since my salary was last increased beyond a very modest cost-of-living adjustment.

I am not a person who expects an automatic raise every year. But, given my record of service to the firm, I believe that you will agree that I am now overdue for a more substantial raise.

I suggest a new salary of **$ amount**—which represents a **percent amount** percent increase over my present salary—would be appropriate.

I look forward to talking with you on **date**.

Exceptional Performance

To:

From:

Re: Request for Salary Review

I would like to set up a salary review with you within the next **number** days **or weeks**.

I feel that this is a great time for a salary review, since I recently completed **name of project** successfully and have accumulated a quarterly sales record that no one in the department can touch.

To be frank, I wanted to get to you while I'm hitting the high notes and they're fresh in your mind.

My recent performance is typical, and I would like to bring my salary to a level more appropriate to the level of my achievement.

I look forward to your response to my request for a review.

REQUESTING A PROMOTION

Jump Starts . . . to Get You on Your Way

I understand that the position of **job title** is about to become available.

I would appreciate your thinking of me when you think about **job title**.

I was very excited to learn that a **name of position** position is about to become available. I wish to be considered for promotion to it.

I'm told that Balzac said that whenever he wanted to read a good novel, he wrote one. I'd like a new job with **Name of company**, and I'm willing to invent one.

I'm ready to grow.

Seniority

To:

From:

Re: Promotion from **job title** to **job title**

With **Name** due to retire, the position of **job title** will be open. I respectfully request that you give my candidacy for that position your careful consideration, on the grounds of my record of performance and on my seniority.

I have been with **Name of company** for **number** years and have been in my current position for **number** years. I am the senior **job title** in the department, and, having worked directly with **Name** for most of those years, I am already thoroughly familiar with the position of **desired position**.

I am ready to make the move up, and I am confident that my performance will not disappoint you.

Overdue

To:

From:

Re: Promotion from **job title** to **job title**

I have been **job title** for **number** years. Twice I have been passed over for promotion to **job title**. Now that this position is about to become available again, I feel that my promotion to it is long overdue, and I respectfully request that you consider me for the position.

I have the seniority, the experience, and the skill to do the job. My years of service attest to my loyalty and commitment to the firm. I am confident that you will see this promotion as appropriate at this time.

Performance

To:

From:

Re: Promotion from **job title** to **job title**

I was very excited to learn that a **name of position** position is about to become available. I wish to be considered for promotion to it.

During the past **number** years as **job title**, I have **list major accomplishments**. It has been a rewarding post for me, but I now feel ready to move up to even greater responsibility, to bring the drive and initiative I have demonstrated in **current position** to **desired position**.

What can I do to help you make the right decision?

Create a New Position

Dear **Name**:

I am writing to you with a bold proposition because I have learned to regard you as someone unafraid of innovation, especially when innovation is clearly called for.

I have been **job title** for **number** years. During this time, it has become increasingly clear to me that what our company needs is a **new job title**, someone to manage **describe responsibilities**. Currently, these responsibilities are poorly and informally divided between the **job title** and **job title**, and, unavoidably, a great deal falls between the cracks.

The new position I propose would change this dangerous situation. The **new job title** would devote full time to a growing portion of our market, a segment we are currently slighting or even neglecting.

The person who fills this new position must have the following experience, skills, and qualities: **list**.

By now you've guessed who "the person" is. That's right, I'm proposing that you create a new job for me.

I'd like to get together with you no later than **date** to talk about it.

Best regards,

REQUESTING CHANGES IN WORKING CONDITIONS, LOCATION, HOURS

Jump Starts . . . to Get You on Your Way

I want to alert you to a condition that is having a negative impact on the productivity of our department.

This is to advise you that the following safety hazards presently exist in **name of department: list**.

As you know, I live in **Name of community/neighborhood, number** miles from this office. I understand the new facility will begin operation on **date**. It is only **number** miles from my house. You can appreciate, then, why I am requesting a transfer.

My wife **husband** and I both work full time, which has required careful management to ensure that our children are cared for properly after school. We've had things worked out for some time now, but, beginning **date**, my wife **husband** will be working a new shift, from **time** o'clock to **time** o'clock.

Conditions Unnecessarily Unpleasant

To: **Name**, Office Manager

From: **Name of department** employees

Re: Working Conditions

Those of us who work in the **name of department** department endure unpleasant working conditions that have a negative impact on our productivity. These conditions include:

item

item

item

item

item

Because we are aware that none of these conditions would be difficult or expensive to improve, we feel that our working conditions are *unnecessarily* unpleasant. Therefore, we respectfully request that management address these items in the interest of improving employee morale and, by extension, productivity.

Inefficient Workspace

To: **Name**, Office Manager

From: **Name**

Re: Inefficient Workspace

Perhaps you've wondered about something you've seen the last few days: me, walking around with a stopwatch.

I haven't gone crazy.

I've been timing how long it takes for me to walk from one part of this department to another simply doing the things I need to do to get my job done. I calculate that I spend **number** minutes each and every day—not working, but walking.

Why?

Our work area down here is poorly—inefficiently—designed. We go here for this piece of equipment, there for another, then to another place for the copying machine, and so forth. We *do* get a lot of exercise, but we also get less work done.

I recommend that we engage the services of an ergonomically oriented interior planner to study our work patterns in this department and make recommendations for rearranging the workspace. Multiply the number of minutes I am compelled to waste each and every day by the **number** employees in this department, and I believe the cost of the planner will seem trivial by comparison.

I look forward to your response.

Conditions Unsafe

To: **Name**, Office Manager

From: **Name**

Re: Unsafe Conditions in **name of department**

This is to advise you that the following safety hazards presently exist in **name of department**:

hazard

hazard

hazard

hazard

hazard

It is imperative that these hazards be remedied at once, since they represent risk of injury or even fatality.

Transfer to Another Branch

Dear **Name**:

As you know, I live in **Name of community/neighborhood**. I commute **number** miles each day. Now that we are opening a branch in **Name of community/neighborhood,** I request a transfer to the new branch.

I greatly enjoy working here, with you and the rest of the staff, but the significantly reduced commuting time the transfer would offer is just too hard to resist. I earnestly request the transfer.

Sincerely yours,

Dear **Name**:

The members of my family are getting tired of crawling on top of one another in our tiny apartment. We're moving to bigger quarters—and to a more attractive neighborhood, **Name of community/neighborhood.** That will put me pretty far—about **number** miles—from the **name of branch** branch, but I'll be only **number** miles—**number** minutes—from **name of other branch**. Therefore, I am requesting a transfer to **name of other branch**, effective **date**.

I would be grateful for all that you can do to expedite this request.

Sincerely yours,

Change in Working Hours: Coordinate with Spouse

To: **Name**, Operations Manager

From: **Name, name of department**

Re: Change in hours

As you know, my wife **husband** and I both work full time, which has required careful management to ensure that our children are cared for properly after school. We've had things worked out for some time now, but, beginning **date**, my wife **husband** will be working a new shift, from **time** o'clock to **time** o'clock. Unlike our company, hers **his** does not offer employees flex time—so it is up to me to adjust my hours in order to coordinate childcare. Here is what I propose as my new hours:

time o'clock to **time** o'clock, Monday–Wednesday

time o'clock to **time** o'clock, Thursday and Friday

I have spoken to **Names** in my department, and they are all willing to adjust their schedules to mesh with what I propose.

I would be grateful for your response no later than **date**.

Change in Working Hours: Transportation Schedule

To: **Name**, Operations Manager

From: **Name, name of department**

Re: Change in hours

As you know, I commute to work all the way from **Name of place**. I have an opportunity to join a car pool, which will not only save me money and contribute to the health of the environment, but will also ensure that my commute is not dependent on our erratic public transportation schedules.

The only problem is that everyone in the car pool is on a **time** o'clock to **time** o'clock schedule—except for me.

I request that, in order to accommodate this greatly improved transportation schedule, my work hours be changed from **time** o'clock to **time** o'clock to **time** o'clock to **time** o'clock.

I must respond to my prospective car pool partners by **date**, so I would appreciate your response before then.

Change in Working Hours: Night School Classes

To: **Name**, Operations Manager

From: **Name, name of department**

Re: Change in hours

One of the things I most like about working here is the firm's commitment to supporting staff development. In that spirit, I request a change in my working hours to allow me to accommodate a night course in **subject**, which will enhance my performance here at **Name of company**. Classes are held **day** through **day**, beginning at **time** o'clock. To ensure that I get to class on time, I need to leave work by **time** o'clock. From **day** to **day**, I propose coming in at **time** o'clock so that I can leave by **time** o'clock.

I would be very grateful for your cooperation in this matter.

MAKING SUGGESTIONS

Jump Starts . . . to Get You on Your Way

Yesterday, I saw a line of folks in the hall. I thought you were giving something away for free. No such luck. They were all waiting to use our dinosaur of a copier.

I wonder how many customers we turn away by subjecting them to a maze of voice mail and message machines because no living human being is available to answer a call?

We can do a better job.

We could make the lounge much more pleasant in a way that would invite constructive discussion.

I am putting this in the form of a letter rather than a memo because I feel that what I have to recommend is especially important.

Since **date**, my department has been receiving some disturbing calls from our customers complaining about the following problems with **Name of product**: list.

New Equipment Required

To:

From:

Re: New photocopier required

The **name of department** department has been using an outmoded and inadequate **brand and model** photocopier since **year**. Not only has the volume of our copying work far surpassed the capacity of this machine, it frequently breaks down, can accommodate paper no larger than 8 ½ × 11, can copy on one side only, and is generally temperamental. This has resulted in much wasted time and frustration, as well as significant delay in completing projects. Frequently, we send major copying projects out of house, paying a high premium to do so.

The time to purchase new equipment has come, and I respectfully urge you to authorize me to move quickly on the purchase of a machine with the following features:

item

item

item

item

item

item

Machines that offer these features include:

Name of machine, priced at **$ amount**

Name of machine, priced at **$ amount**

Name of machine, priced at **$ amount**

I have researched this equipment, and I am confident that any of these machines, all comparably priced, would serve our department adequately.

I look forward to a response at your earliest convenience.

Stagger Lunch Breaks

To:

From:

Re: Suggestion—stagger lunch breaks

I wonder how many customers we turn away by subjecting them to a maze of voice mail and message machines because no living human being is available to answer a call? Sometimes, this is unavoidable. We are tied up in meetings or on calls. But there is at least one instance in which we leave the phones unattended for no good reason. From 12:30 to 1:30, almost all of us are away at lunch.

I respectfully suggest that we make it official company policy to stagger lunch periods so that at least **number** people are available *in person* at all times.

I do not believe this would present a difficult scheduling problem, and I am confident that cooperation would be readily forthcoming.

I look forward to your response.

Introduce Flex Time

Dear **Name**:

I am putting this in the form of a letter rather than a memo because I feel that what I have to recommend is especially important.

A great many companies these days—among them, **list**—have adopted policies of flex time for their employees. Universally, such policies have been applauded by labor and management alike. Flex time accomplishes six things:

1. It empowers employees by allowing them to integrate their work time and private time more effectively.

2. It reduces traffic congestion by staggering the "rush hour."

3. It effectively extends business hours in the morning and the evening.

4. It maximizes use of the physical plant.

5. It is an essentially cost-free employee "perk."

6. It improves morale, goodwill, and commitment to the company, thereby increasing productivity and improving the quality of work produced.

I propose that you meet with me and the rest of the departmental managers within the next two weeks **or other time period** to discuss strategies for implementing flex time at **Name**.

I am convinced that we need it and will greatly benefit by it.

Sincerely yours,

Provide 401k Plan

To: **Name**, President

From: **Name**, Staff Representative

Re: Instituting a 401k plan

I doubt you will find a more committed and loyal group of employees than you have here at **Name of company**. We all enjoy working for a small company, in which we each feel that we have a personal stake. We also realize that we cannot ask too much of a company the size of ours. An elaborate retirement program, for example, is out of the question. But we are unanimous in our conclusion that a 401k plan is well within the financial capability of this company.

I would like to meet with you and **Name of controller, CFO, etc.** to discuss 401k options and to secure your agreement in principle to initiating such a plan.

I look forward to your reply.

Revise Quality Control Procedures

To: **Name**, Plant Manager

From: **Name**, Customer Service Director

Re: Revision of Quality Control

Since **date**, my department has been receiving some disturbing calls from our customers complaining about the following problems with **Name of product(s):**

problem	number of complaints
problem	number of complaints
problem	number of complaints
problem	number of complaints
problem	number of complaints
problem	number of complaints
problem	number of complaints

The nature of the complaints does not suggest a basic design problem, but the quantity of complaints does indicate that too many bad units are slipping past Quality Control. I respectfully recommend that you and your assistants review our present quality-control policies with an eye toward determining possible weak points in procedures and improving these.

I am concerned that the volume of complaints, returns, and warranty repairs will soon result in a very costly situation and will negatively affect our firm's reputation in the marketplace.

RESPONDING TO A REPRIMAND

Jump Starts . . . to Get You on Your Way

I was unpleasantly surprised to receive your memo of **date**, which reprimanded me for "**quote reprimand**."

I understand and appreciate your irritation at my reporting late on **dates**.

This is a response to your memo of **date**, in which you took exception to **action**.

This is a response to your memo of **date** regarding a report of my having been "rude" to a customer. Normally, I would just drop by your office and explain any misunderstanding. But I pride myself on courtesy, and I am so disturbed by the report you received that I feel it necessary to respond to it in writing and for the record.

I am profoundly sorry about the incident of **date**, which we discussed yesterday.

I won't sugarcoat the recent situation in Shipping. You're right: Our error rate is much too high.

I can't blame you for being angry about **issue**, but I think we need to sort the fact from the fantasy.

My supervisor, **Name**, strongly disagrees about the necessity of my having access to customer profiles.

Requesting Clarification

CONFIDENTIAL

To:

From:

Re: Your memo to me of **date**

I was stunned and dismayed to receive your memo of **date**, which reprimanded me for "**quote reprimand**."

I have always believed that the best way to handle a mistake is to come forward, admit what you did, and propose a way to fix it. In this case, however, I am at a loss. I simply do not understand the basis of your reprimand, since I am unaware of having done anything wrong.

I am eager to meet with you at your earliest convenience to get a clarification of the reprimand. I sincerely believe that one of us is mistaken in this matter.

Explanation: Lateness

To:

From:

Re: Reporting late to work on **date**

I understand and appreciate your irritation at my reporting late on **dates**. In all **number** instances, the lateness was unavoidable because of family emergencies and vehicle trouble. On **date**, my son fell on our driveway while running to catch the schoolbus. I had to render first aid, then drive him to school. On **date**, I went to start my car only to discover that the battery had died. On **date**, my son awoke with a fever, and I had to arrange last-minute childcare for him, which I thought preferable to my being absent from work.

I apologize for these late days, and I assure you that they represent unusual circumstances and a string of bad luck. Aside from these occurrences, you will find my on-time record has been excellent.

Explanation: Early Departure

To:

From:

Re: Early departure on **date**

I understand that you had tried to find me on **date**, were unable to do so, and were upset to learn that I had left early.

On that day, at **time** o'clock, I received a call from my daughter's school informing me that she had become ill after lunch. My wife **husband** was out of town, and I was the only one available to pick her up and take her home. I told **Name** what had happened and that I was leaving early. I would have told you directly, but you were in a meeting, and I did not think the incident warranted my disturbing you.

I am sorry for any inconvenience my unavoidable early departure may have caused you.

Explanation: Sick Days

CONFIDENTIAL MEMO

To:

From:

Re: Excessive sick days

This is a response to your note regarding the "excessive" number of sick days I have taken this quarter.

I agree. The number of days was "excessive."

As far as I am concerned, a single day sick is excessive. What I want to assure you of is that these were all bona-fide *sick* days. This has been an unusually bad season for me. I have had one bad cold after another. On a number of these sick days, I visited my doctor in search of a cure, and I would be happy to furnish copies of bills for your inspection.

I regret my absences, but I am even more troubled by your feeling that I may have abused the use of sick days. Please be assured that I have not.

Explanation: Apparent Rudeness to a Customer

To:

From:

Re: Report of rudeness to a customer

This is a response to your memo of **date** regarding a report of my having been "rude" to a customer. Normally, I would just drop by your office and explain any misunderstanding. But I pride myself on courtesy, and I am so disturbed by the report you received that I feel it necessary to respond to it in writing and for the record.

Except for the fact that **Name of customer** purchased and returned a **name of product**, the complaint he made to you is a complete fabrication. **Name of customer** came to me with the **name of product**, explained what had gone wrong, and asked for a refund. I responded by apologizing for the trouble he had experienced, and I asked if he was certain that he wanted his money back. I began to explain that **name of product** is generally highly reliable, and that I was sure he would have no difficulty with a replacement. He cut me short and began yelling at me, claiming that I was trying to cheat him. He was, in fact, creating such a scene on the sales floor that I considered calling security. However, I managed to calm him by assuring him that I would secure his refund in full immediately.

There was rudeness involved in this transaction—rudeness bordering on hysteria, in fact. But the rudeness was the customer's, not mine. I was relieved that the incident did not escalate into something worse—but I guess my relief was premature.

I ask that this memo be included in my permanent record, along with the customer's complaint, and your response to both.

Explanation: Apparent Rudeness to Fellow Employee

To:

From:

Re: **Date** "incident" with **Name of other employee**

I am very sorry that it has come to this. On **date, Name** and I had a dispute over **subject**. As far as I was concerned, we settled the dispute through discussion on the spot. Certainly, it was my understanding that our differences had been resolved and that the episode needed to go no further.

You may be sure that I was greatly surprised by **Name's** complaint concerning what he **she** called my "rudeness." I am sorry if anything I did or said was perceived as impolite. I never intended to offend **Name** or anyone else. Moreover, I believed the matter had been entirely settled. If this was not the case—as, apparently, it was not—it would have been far more appropriate for **Name** to discuss it further with me than to complain to you.

I respectfully suggest that we resolve this matter once and for all by meeting together in your office at your earliest convenience. I do not want to be thought of as rude, and I do not want to labor under any kind of cloud of hard feelings.

Explanation: Errors

To:

From:

Re: Recent shipping errors

I won't sugarcoat the recent situation in Shipping. You're right: Our error rate is much too high.

The reason for this is not difficult to find. We are seriously understaffed. Last week, for example, we shipped **number** units and handled **number** returns and cross-shipments. Turnaround time on shipments is only **num-**

ber days. To ship **number** units in **number** days, I have a staff of **number**. I need to put every available person into simply processing orders and getting the merchandise out the door. I cannot afford to assign anyone to quality control. Mistakes are made and are not caught until it is too late. If . I had **number** additional people, I could assign a fulltime person to quality control. We'd still make mistakes, but we would catch a far greater number of them in time to correct them.

I would like to meet with you at your earliest convenience to discuss additional staffing, which I believe is the only way we can reduce the number of shipping errors while maintaining our current volume and excellent on-time record.

Explanation: Dispute with Supervisor

CONFIDENTIAL MEMORANDUM

To: **Name**, President

From:

Re: Dispute with **Name** over access to customer profiles

My supervisor, **Name**, and I strongly disagree about the necessity of my having access to customer profiles. She argues that the profiles contain information so sensitive that strict control of access is required, which means that I must make a special request each time I need a piece of information and that **Name** dispenses that information on what she deems a "need to know" basis. While I acknowledge and respect the critical nature of these profiles, I find it very difficult to do my job effectively without free access to this information.

I have attempted repeatedly to resolve this issue with **Name**, but I have met with a brick wall on each occasion.

Obviously, we have a very basic disagreement that will require a policy decision from you to resolve. I have suggested this to **Name**, but she has declined to seek such a decision from you. Therefore, I've taken that responsibility upon myself; for I cannot be satisfied with doing a job halfway for this company.

My suggestion is that **Name** and I meet with you in your office at your earliest convenience so that we may present our arguments to you. I believe that you will be convinced of my need to have access to this material, and that you will make a policy decision that will permit **Name** to give me access to it in good conscience.

Apology: Lateness

To:

From:

Re: Late arrival on **dates**

I want to apologize for having been late **number** times recently. As I explained to you, these incidents were unavoidable; yet, I recognize, it is still my responsibility to show up at work on time.

Please be assured that I will do everything in my power to avoid late arrival in the future.

Apology: Early Departure

Dear **Name**:

This is just a note to apologize for having left work early on **dates**. In both instances, family emergencies called me away early. In the future, I will make every effort to cover such eventualities without my having to leave before the end of the day.

I greatly appreciate your understanding in this matter.

Sincerely,

Apology: Rudeness to a Customer

Dear **Name**:

Concerning the recent incident you and I discussed, I am very sorry for two things. I regret having lost my temper with **Name of customer**, and I am sorry for having put you in the awkward position of mediating what never should have become a dispute in the first place. Your reprimand to me on this occasion was perfectly fair and justified.

I apologize for the incident and for the trouble you had to take to resolve it. I promise you that nothing of the kind will ever happen again.

Sincerely yours,

Apology: Rudeness to Fellow Employee

Dear **Name**:

I have sent a note to **Name of employee**, apologizing for my rude remarks to him **her**. They were uncalled for, I now realize, and I deeply regret having made them. I only hope that **Name of employee** will see his **her** way clear to forgive me.

I owe you an apology as well. You have had to take time to resolve this dispute and to talk to me. Your reprimand was fair and fully justified. I also appreciate your understanding that tempers cannot always be controlled, but please be assured that I will not let myself lose my temper in this way again.

Sincerely,

Apology: Error

To:

From:

Re: Misdirected communication to **Name**

You were right to reprimand me for my carelessness in having sent the wrong documents to **Name**. It was an embarrassing mistake, and you can be sure that I do not cherish feeling that I made all of us look dumb.

If there is anything good that has come from this episode, it is discovering how patient and understanding you are. You had every right to blow up at me, but your note was gentle and very fair.

I promise to be more careful from now on.

Apology: Dispute with Supervisor

Dear **Name**:

I want to thank you for mediating my differences with **Name of supervisor** so sensitively. Thanks to you, I now see how I was wrong and, more important, what I can do to prevent future misunderstandings.

I apologize for any difficulty I may have caused you.

Sincerely,

Apology: Indiscretion

Dear **Name**:

I do wish I had kept my mouth shut. I had no business discussing **subject** with people outside of the department, and you were quite right to call me on it. In fact, you're entitled to be a lot more angry than you seem to be. I am grateful for your good nature and understanding.

I can assure you that I will never put our department in this situation again.

Sincerely,

Apology: Inappropriate Behavior in a Business-Related Social Situation

Dear **Name**:

There are times when you just feel like going someplace to hide. This is one of them.

I had too much to drink at your party, and I said some things I should not have said. I wish I had behaved better—behaved in a way that you and your guests deserved.

I hope you will accept my most sincere apologies and my promise that I will never embarrass you (and myself) like that again.

Abashedly yours,

RESIGNATIONS

Jump Starts . . . to Get You on Your Way

All good things, the saying goes, must come to an end, and now the time has come for me to leave **Name of company**.

I have very mixed emotions about what I must now tell you.

Effective **date**, I am resigning as **job title** here at **Name of company**.

My basic policy differences with **Name of company** have made it clear to me that the time has come to resign my position as **job title**.

I have been offered a position I cannot turn down.

For the past several months, I have been doing a great deal of thinking about my career.

As you know, I have not been well for some time.

I was thinking of telling you that I am changing jobs. Actually, I'm changing my whole life—my whole career.

With Regret

Dear **Name**:

All good things, the saying goes, must come to an end, and now the time has come for me to leave **Name of company**.

My husband **wife** has accepted a position as **job title** with **Name of company** in **City**. It is a great opportunity, and we have no choice but to relocate.

My resignation is effective as of **date**. This gives you ample time to find a replacement and, I hope, will also allow time for me to "break in" the new person. I will make myself available to do anything I possibly can to ease the transition.

I am very excited about my husband's **wife's** new opportunity, of course, but I am very sorry to leave **Name of company**, you, and the other wonderful people I have worked with so long.

Sincerely yours,

Under Unfavorable Circumstances

Dear **Name**:

My basic policy differences with **Name of company** have made it clear to me that the time has come to resign my position as **job title**.

My resignation is effective as of **date**, which should give you sufficient time to locate a replacement for me. I will do all that I can, between now and **date of departure**, to make the transition as smooth as possible.

Sincerely yours,

To Accept Advancement Elsewhere

Dear **Name**:

Name of hiring firm has offered me the position of **job title**. After much careful thought, I have decided to accept the offer, and I am, therefore, resigning as **job title** here.

My resignation will be effective on **date**.

I have found my work here at **Name of company** highly rewarding, and it has been a pleasure to work with all of you. However, my responsibility to my family and to my career make it necessary for me to move on.

Please be assured that I will do everything I can to help you find a suitable replacement and to ease the transition.

Sincerely yours,

Career Change

Dear **Name**:

For the past several months, I have been doing a great deal of thinking about my career, and it has become clear to me that it is time for a major change of direction. I have decided to return to school fulltime to study **subject**, after which I intend to begin a career as a **professional title**. For this reason, I must resign from my position as **job title** here at **Name of company**.

My resignation will be effective as of **date**.

My years here have been rewarding ones. I have greatly enjoyed working with you and with a very fine staff. Please rest easy that I am leaving my department in very good shape and that, between now and **date of departure**, I will do all that I can to make the transition as smooth as possible for my replacement.

Sincerely yours,

Reasons of Health

Dear **Name**:

As you know, I have not been well for some time. You and everyone else at **Name of company** have been very patient and understanding during my frequent absences. However, it has become clear to me that the state of my health will continue to interfere with my job here—and the demands of my position will continue to put a strain on my health.

It is, therefore, with regret that I must resign from **Name of company** effective **date**.

To the best of my ability, I will work with you to find a suitable replacement and generally to ease the transition. **Name of company** has been a great place to work, and I have made many good friends here. I truly wish that I did not have to leave.

Sincerely,

Retirement

Dear **Name**:

It has been a long, sometimes difficult, but always bright and hopeful road. On **date**, I will have reached the end of it.

Name of company, you, and the rest of the staff have made my career here extraordinarily rewarding, and I shall look back at these many years with great pleasure.

I hope and trust we will all keep in touch—and I warn you that I intend to be a frequent visitor here at the plant.

Affectionately,

INDEX